Ethics and Society in England

ETHICS AND SOCIETY IN ENGLAND

The Revolution in the Social Sciences
1870-1914

REBA N. SOFFER

UNIVERSITY OF CALIFORNIA PRESS
Berkeley   Los Angeles   London

University of California Press
Berkeley and Los Angeles, California

University of California Press, Ltd.
London, England

ISBN 0-520-03521-6
Library of Congress Catalog Card Number: 77-79239
Copyright © 1978 by The Regents of the University of California

Printed in the United States of America

To Bernard and Roger

Contents

PART IV. POLITICS, SCIENCE,
AND REFORM

PART V. REVISIONIST SOCIAL SCIENCE:
SOCIAL PSYCHOLOGY, INSTINCT,
AND ELITISM

Acknowledgments

During the research and writing of this book, many people made the way easier by their kindness. For indispensable financial support, I am greatly indebted to the Foundation at California State University, Northridge, for occasional funds; to the National Endowment for the Humanities and to the American Philosophical Society for summer grants; and, to The American Council of the Learned Societies for a semester's leave. My research was facilitated by the competence of the staff at the Bodleian Library, Oxford University; the British Museum; the Houghton Library, Harvard University; the House of Lords Library; the London School of Economics and Political Science library; the Marshall Library, Cambridge University; and the Oviatt Library, C.S.U.N. Ada Wallas, Dr. Robert Trotter, Mrs. Wilfred Trotter, and E. S. Pearson most generously shared their memories with me. For reading initial sections of the manuscript with such critical care, I want to thank Peter Stansky, John Diggins, Ronald L. F. Davis, and Gerald Meaker. I am enormously grateful to Robert K. Webb and to Sheldon Rothblatt for perceptively reading drafts of the entire manuscript. From the inception of the book, Robert Webb raised challenging and provocative difficulties and we argued about them to my great benefit. And Sheldon Rothblatt, with characteristic subtlety, made recommendations that were always to the point. Finally, my thanks to Nancy Meadows, who typed the manuscript rapidly and efficiently, aided by Lorna Hughes and Lyn Silke; to Maxine Chadwick, who did all sorts of tedious things with competence and grace; and, to Selma Feldman and Claire Bleiman, who were always ready to help.

Introduction

Modern social science developed before World War I in response to a radically transformed society, increasingly urban and industrial, and to altered perceptions of that society by theorists and reformers. The role of the English in this development has been either totally ignored or summarily dismissed.[1] But in England there was a fundamental rethinking of social concepts and practices directed toward a widespread improvement in the quality of life. This book contends that in England, from the late 1870s to 1914, an authentic, vital, and independent revolution occurred in the methodology and purposes of social science. Indeed, that revolution made important and substantive contributions to twentieth-century social thought.

Although the social and intellectual problems faced by continental and English thinkers appear to be similar, they were set in entirely different historical circumstances. The English never had to reply to the seemingly irresistible forces that overwhelmed European intellectuals. Prussian military might, virulent Austrian and French anti-Semitism, anarchistic Balkan and Italian nationalism, and a rising tolerance of violence as an antidote to frustrated reason oppressed European explanations of social, economic, political, and psychological phenomena. Thinkers such as Weber, Freud, Durkheim, and Croce succumbed to a psychological malaise that acknowledged, reluctantly, irrational forces underlying even the most rational behavior and institutions. While it can hardly be denied that the Europeans built more formidable theoretical structures than the English, their melancholy

1

revelation of irrationality resulted ineluctably in a deterministic and pessimistic social theory severed from social practice.

In England, despite a deteriorating ability to continue industrial ascendancy and the belief in progress sustained by technological success, there was confidence in the real possibility of individual and social regeneration. A complex, uniquely English, relationship between science, social theory, social problems, and ethical convictions led to the appearance of two major new traditions in social science that I call "revolutionary" and "revisionist." The new social scientists were social reformers who expected progress to occur, in the final analysis, when individuals were able to behave rationally and responsibly. Unlike the alienated, disillusioned Europeans, the English were encouraged in their optimistic expectations by consistent personal, family, and educational experiences. Combining empirical and theoretical procedures, they set out not merely to explain but to improve the individual and the society in which he lived.

The methods and purposes of the economists, psychologists, and political scientists, or "revolutionaries," were not shared by all the new social scientists. A sharp methodological disagreement separated these revolutionaries from the fourth new social science, social psychology. All four of the new disciplines were committed to the same moral purpose: the achievement of higher and more rational standards of social obligation toward those lacking the opportunities of the middle-class social scientists. And all of them found in science a surrogate religion expected to provide those standards. But the revolutionary economists, psychologists, and political scientists identified themselves as progressive liberals, while the social psychologists deliberately turned their backs on liberal ideology. The revolutionaries insisted that the direction of social events and the formation of individual character depended essentially on the rational will and conscience of the great majority of people. The "revisionists," or social psychologists, believed, on the contrary, only in the good intentions of a rational few. Just as the explicit liberalism of the "revolutionaries" encouraged them to see the individual growing more sufficient through the democratic process, the implicit conservatism of the social psychologists resulted in their revision of an older irrationalist view of human nature incompatible with a democratic vision of society.

The terms "revolutionary" and "revisionist" carry certain imprecise connotations, but they do capture the essence of the two schools of social thought that originated in prewar England. Clearly, there are other analytical categories which can be applied to late nineteenth- and early twentieth-century thought. But the concepts "revolutionary" and "revisionist" illuminate the divergent emphases within the social sciences. If an intellectual revolutionary is someone who sets out to overthrow an established tradition of thought, then the prewar economists, psychologists, and political scientists, led by Alfred Marshall, the American William James, and Graham Wallas, were unquestionably "revolutionary." For what they consciously sought were alternatives to the social, psychological, and political theories that, together, had projected so stable and reassuring an image of English society. And they did overthrow a concept of the social order — based on a passive view of the mind and a rationalist reading of political behavior — which assumed an approaching harmony between selfish and altruistic ends. The prevailing liberal wisdom on the nature of man and society was unacceptable to these revolutionaries because it implied that if social forces were already moving toward a desirable resolution, neither the individual nor society stood in need of fundamental reform. Although the "revisionists" also recognized the decline and decreasing utility of traditional nineteenth-century thinking, they sought to salvage its heart by transplanting it into a more robust body of theory. Like the revolutionaries, the revisionist social psychologists discarded positivistic social and psychological theory and an uncritical rationalism. But they found the positivists' aspirations to explain man in society completely through predictable social laws, more attractive than the new sciences' ambivalent and tentative probabilities. Although continuing an a priori social science, the social psychologists appeared to transcend positivism through their reliance upon a biological account of social evolution. Indeed, the founders of social psychology, William McDougall and Wilfred

Trotter, believed that their new discipline did not necessarily need to retain a deductive form, and they looked forward to genuinely empirical techniques that would eventually lead to new discoveries about social behavior. But the immediate goal set for social psychology by both the psychophysicist McDougall and the neurosurgeon Trotter was to show that the new irrational forces within a democratic society must be controlled by rational social scientists. The revolutionaries, viewing human nature in their own rational, voluntarist, and altruistic images, wanted to extend their own privileges and opportunities to everyone else. But the revisionists were more interested in protecting qualities that they recognized as exceptional in themselves from trespass by the great majority whom they described in genetic terms as an instinctual and incompetent crowd. Each of the founders of the new social sciences, including the social psychologists, wanted to improve the quality of individual and social life. And each saw himself as a pioneer on the brink of fundamentally new discoveries. But only the economists, psychologists, and political scientists succeeded in creating genuinely revolutionary methods and objectives for the social sciences.

While the accuracy of the designations "revolutionary" and "revisionist" is independent of any criteria of success or failure, such categories of analysis must be able to explain the actual relation between ideas and events at any given historical moment. Moreover, the effect of any form of thought depends upon whether it can command the attention of people with power. The revolutionary dream of a society able to provide social, economic, political, and psychological opportunities for rational and moral conduct prevailed until the 1930s because it was shared by those responsible people who largely controlled business, government, and education. The revisionists' bleak conviction about the fundamental mindlessness of the great majority was of little practical use to a governing group that recognized that their authority ultimately rested upon at least the tacit approval of the new democratic electorate.

During the four decades preceding World War I, accelerating social change grew increasingly difficult to comprehend, let alone direct. In England, concentrated urban growth left disease and malnutrition in its wake. It was not until Charles Booth's initial exposure of the extent of London's poverty in 1892 and Seebohm Rowntree's comparable survey of York in 1901 that debility in nearly one-third of the population was recognized as a national problem. These startling revelations were confirmed dramatically by the Boer War recruiter's discovery that more than one-third of the men examined were physically unfit for military duty.

Through the final years of the nineteenth century, thoughtful, practical men admitted the nationally debilitating effects of slum life, manifested in unemployment, semiliteracy, and apathy. That public admission encouraged the development of a professional class that was widely expected to deal with these complex social problems by expertly managing business, local government, and the civil service. The amiable amateurism of preceding generations was gradually replaced by a serious professionalism as those in power became convinced that intractable social problems would yield only to the same systematic methods that natural scientists had applied so successfully to chemistry, engineering, and especially to medicine. The generation of the 1880s, raised amid the technological triumphs of British applied science, naturally sought the solution of social problems in professional social science. To the revisionists, professional social science meant the possibility of selecting the rational few fit to govern from among the irrational many who desperately needed to be governed. The revolutionaries, in contrast, thought of their disciplines rather as open forums for the informed discussion and analysis that must precede the solution of problems. To the economists, psychologists, and political scientists, professionalism meant essentially the organization and dissemination of their reforming programs to a mass audience.

Even as the social reality of nineteenth-century England changed, the subjective interpretation of that reality was changing too. The older model of order, represented since the late seventeenth century by both positivistic science and dogmatic religion, was undermined after 1870 by the concept of randomness suggested by Darwinian science. The Darwinian emphasis upon

the role of chance in evolution disturbed potential social reformers because it threatened the promise of eventual social harmony
implicit in both progressive liberalism and organic convervatism.
Traditional assurances about a knowable universe, demonstrated
absolutely through deductive laws, were challenged further after
1870 by a new mathematics, physics, and chemistry founded
upon quantitative assessments of probability. Nearly every intellectual during these decades testified to a passionate search for
convincing grounds for ethical and social obligation among the
ruins of older faiths. None of the traditional intellectual or ethical systems fully satisfied the late nineteenth-century intellectual's
demand for standards to guide him through confusing experiences. Among the schemes of thought and conduct emerging as
replacements for the earlier formulations, only the new social sciences pledged an accurate explanation of insistent problems and,
still more important, their effective solution.

   The quest for a more satisfying interpretation of the individual-
in-society was motivated especially by the burgeoning social problems in late Victorian England. This explanation of how the
modern social sciences began does not explain further why they
assumed a particular form and content. Their form and content
was shaped, above all, by a commonly declared need for some
compelling ethic of personal social obligation that had developed
from the late 1860s within a small, closely knit, homogenous
community of energetic, thinking people centered mostly in the
universities. This community came of age convinced that it bore
the responsibility for discovering and carrying out a program of
individual and social reform. Although the development of a reformist social science necessarily required the availability of epistemological and scientific models to support reformist aspirations, the sufficient condition for such a development lay in the
intense sense of duty that the emerging reformers shared.

   First in the public schools, and then at Oxford and Cambridge,
this generation learned during the 1860s and 1870s that character and progress depended largely upon hard work and systematic
thought. Above all, they absorbed a commitment to the public
service, which was vigorously sustained throughout their adult

lives by intermarriage and interlocking careers, and by a conscious effort to continue that sense of intellectual community characteristic of serious university life. Among the families faithfully following this pattern, the Balfours, Sidgwicks, Haldanes, James Wards, Keynes, Marshalls, and Toynbees, were typical. This relatively small group, unique in the scope and vigor of its activity, altered the whole direction of science, education, letters, and government. Its members, remorselessly intent upon improving themselves and everyone else, were an intensely idealistic generation that left the shelter of public schools and universities to take their place in the most vulnerable areas of public life. In addition to the more traditional careers of politics, the civil service, and literature, they pioneered completely new vocations in slums, county councils, and public lecture halls. Wherever they worked, they succeeded in disseminating their convictions with remarkable effect. Confident of the authority and ethical strength of "scientific" reform, they succeeded in achieving the influence necessary to transform undergraduate enthusiasm into mature practical policy.

These middle-class idealists were filtered through an educational system designed to supply the personnel that governed English institutions. But neither their privileged position in society nor their largely classical education had prepared them to contend with the unprecedented crises that overtook their world in the 1870s. Trained in the 1860s both at home and school to trust the efficacy of reason and goodwill, this generation came to maturity in a decade disrupted by economic depression, by the birth pains of a mass democracy and, most seriously, by the loss of spiritual, emotional, and intellectual certainties. Every generation, since at least the 1760s, suffered its own corrosive encounter with new and unsettling events. Beginning in the second half of the eighteenth century, population grew enormously in cities ill equipped to house or feed it. Industry bordered periodically on chaos in an unpredictable rhythm of glut, unemployment, and revival; and the specter of political revolution hovered over the country. After the middle of the nineteenth century, the real standard of living rose appreciably for some working-class groups, the railroads brought a measure of stability to industrial production, distribution, and consumption, and political quiescence replaced the threat of revolution. To those who watched nervously as England emerged successfully from the recurrent crises of the 1840s, the events after mid-century were encouraging. Influential figures as disparate as John Stuart Mill, Matthew Arnold, George Eliot, Walter Bagehot, Herbert Spencer, and Alfred Tennyson overcame their inner doubts about the reliability of both their knowledge and their experience by believing that they lived in a fundamentally rational world.

But for the generation that guided thought and practice from the 1870s to 1914 it was more difficult to sustain any epistemological confidence. Unlike their immediate predecessors, they were bereft of the traditional certainties. Instead of facing only one kind of unsatisfactory experience, as for example Anglicans did in their religious thinking in the 1860s, nearly all their most cherished beliefs and feelings were exposed to attack from every side. Ever since the late seventeenth century, most Englishmen had believed that God, man, nature, and society could be understood through the kind of rational demonstration characteristic of mathematics. Beginning in the 1870s, however, traditionally comfortable epistemological and ontological theories were eroded fatally by the new sciences. In particular, the concept of chance, inherent especially in Darwinian biology, subverted the ascendant rationalist reliance upon a determinate physical, social, and psychic order regulated by discernible natural laws.

As a corollary of the weakening of traditional faiths, a religious, philosophical, and psychological vacuum was left in ethical accounting. Both the earlier model of pervasive social order as well as the structure of religion had carried within them ethical sanctions to promote what was accepted as socially desirable and to combat the unacceptable. But in the 1870s, deprived of such well-defined sanctions, the individual was torn between a desire to decide rationally upon the right course of action and his fear that there were no compelling grounds for moral discrimination, let alone for ethical conduct. Until the Great War, the generation of the 1870s behaved as though they were under an obligation to labor toward improvement of the quality of life, but they were unable to find any foundation for the moral imperatives to which they clung.

In addition to religious and positivist principles, nineteenth-century ethics had rested most confidently upon the assumption that rational individuals had moral free will. But as early as the 1840s the ethical doctrine of personal responsbility began to be undermined by increasingly deterministic interpretations of mind and behavior. By the 1870s there was little theoretical assurance from any source that goodwill would result in good ends. When reformers turned to traditional psychology to explain thinking and conduct, they discovered a considerable gap between associationist theory and actual behavior. Without any promise of the eventual efficacy of their reformist intentions, they could not confidently approach the urgent social, economic, and political problems they felt called upon to solve.

The crises of confidence that began in the 1870s produced only momentary confusion and dismay within the reforming community. They would not admit despair and instead optimistically launched a long-range search for more durable foundations for the activist values they could not relinquish. That search was impeded, however, by the inadequacy of traditional models of explanation, predicated on an assumption of universal and static order, actually to explain their novel experience. It was not until the new social sciences emerged in the 1880s that the reforming community was offered analyses of thought and conduct to encourage their idealistic activism. This was hardly a coincidence since the new social scientists addressed themselves precisely to those problems of individual incapacity and social inequity so disturbing to that community to which they themselves belonged.

The liberating discovery of the new social scientists was that in the new genetic and physical sciences an acceptance of the tentativeness of all knowledge was replacing positivistic aspirations to certainty. If nature, man, and society were in an endlessly evolving flux, then efforts to discover a complete system of natural psychological and social laws were clearly impractical. Instead, the new social scientists adopted an empirical and piecemeal arrangement of problems in a hierarchy of importance governed by the state of knowledge and the amount of data available. Emphasizing dynamic change, individuation, and probability, the new social sciences, and especially the revolutionary fields, provided reformers with working theories and practicable techniques. The tentative suggestions of economists, psychologists, and political scientists were translated into effective social remedies in the hands of educators, county councillors, civil servants, and businessmen.

But even the most effective reforms risked rejection by the reforming community unless it met their ethical criteria. Convinced of the need to be theoretically consistent and empirically objective, it never occurred to anyone within that community that a "scientist" should also be morally neutral. Moreover, no one in the reforming community, not even the social psychologists, suspected either the fallibility of science or the depths of irrationality and violence latent in everyone. Indeed, neither the revisionists nor the revolutionaries could have lived in a world where human nature excluded any possibility of meliorative reform.

Both the revisionists and the revolutionaries were well intentioned in their desire to create intellectually honest and professionally rigorous modes of inquiry and practice. But there is something especially appealing in the revolutionaries' conviction that their disciplines ought to contribute to the qualitative improvement of individual life. They were the last group of thinkers to act out the enlightenment ideal by behaving as if they were entirely reasonable people able to cultivate higher standards, not only in themselves but in everyone else. Although neither innocent nor uninformed, their driving, optimistic energy shielded them from the doubts and disappointments revealed later in the work of the revisionist social psycholgists.

On both sides of the Atlantic, from the 1880s to the 1930s, the revolutionary social scientists' liberal emphasis upon the necessity for environmental change triumphed over the revisionists' genetic determinism. The revolutionaries' victory was not due to the greater reliability, coherence, or persuasiveness of their writing. Nor were their theories necessarily more logical or convincing in their conformity to external evidence. Both groups were selective in their choice of data, although each was sure that it was using that data scrupulously. But even if the revolutionaries were more correct in their analysis of contemporary problems and in their prescriptions — and a case can be made for this position — it does not account sufficiently for their dominance. After all, much of history is cluttered with the debris of solutions accepted and actions taken confidently on the basis of an inaccurate understanding of events. A better explanation for the success of the revolutionaries' optimistic social science lies in the intellectual and psychological requirements of a society that depended upon science to create a better world. The revolutionaries' social science reflected the commitments of the wider community directing English thought and institutions. When that community asked for proof of the practicability of their programs, the revolutionary social scientists mustered a powerful case in support of cultural and environmental reform. Before the war, few people were willing to listen to the social psychologists' troubling analyses of instinctual and anonymous crowds acting mindlessly against their own interest.

Even after World War I, despite differences developing within the proliferating social studies, the unifying theme of social science continued to be the expectation of measurable qualitative progress. Until the depression and the rise of fascism in the 1930s, the hopeful revolutionary tradition was irresistible to those people who administered education, government, and business in England and the United States because they believed that social science would discover and implement means for overcoming the sources of social conflict and disorder. Even William McDougall, the most influential of the prewar social psychologists, converted in the 1920s to a psychology concentrating upon the individual purposefully controlling himself and his environment. For nearly half a century the revolutionary tradition persuaded Englishmen and Americans that only a genuinely scientific study of society would provide the rational analysis and moral direction upon which policy must depend.

PART I
Science and Social Theory

1.

Deductive Science and Positivist Social Theory
in the Nineteenth Century

Nineteenth-century social theorists were convinced that explanations of social phenomena must be scientific in order to be adequate. And they agreed further that any proper science was, like physics, a set of absolute and inflexible rules discovered by scientists and of an order higher than mere empirical generalizations.[1] The physical model was especially attractive to social thinkers because it appeared to offer a logically satisfying, successful approach to the disturbing and puzzling events occurring within an expanding industrial and urban society. Social theorists set out to discover fundamental principles that would render their experience intelligible, predictable, stable. A compelling, largely unconscious desire to discover an ordered reality led writers as diverse as John Stuart Mill, Walter Bagehot, Henry Thomas Buckle, Herbert Spencer, and T. H. Huxley to seek basic regularities in human nature and society from which a descriptive social science could be deduced.

Behind this quest there lay a communal psychological aversion to ignorance and all its ramifications. As William Stanley Jevons observed of his contemporaries, a truly philosophical mind could not tolerate doubt because doubt was a "confession of ignorance" and involved a "painful feeling of incapacity."[2] The structure of nineteenth-century social science had been determined by a question intended to avoid precisely such "incapacity": "What are the discernible laws that govern private and public life?" Instead of approaching society as an indeterminate and malleable entity, theorists attempted rather to abstract uniformities and "laws" from the flux of changing attributes. There was heated debate on the nature and rigor of such laws, but theorists and activists alike agreed that society was governed by fundamental and invariable principles of uniformity.

It was not until the late 1870s that an authentic revolution in the method, substance, and purposes of social thought successfully attacked the traditional search for laws by developing an inductive and behavioral social science concerned with immediate social reform. To the revolutionaries, a "law" meant merely a regularity of human behavior under a specific set of circumstances, a regularity that could be observed directly or whose existence could be surmised through the process of inductive reasoning. A law implied no more than that individuals were likely to react in certain ways to particular situations. Since each case occurred in special and varying circumstances, there were no absolutely reliable methods of verification, let alone of prediction. In place of the certainty promised by positivistic social science, the revolutionary social scientists adopted a concept of verification based only upon inductive probabilities. The practical implication of their epistemology was that individuals were not bound by those supposedly inherent forces represented by social laws. If instead people created and controlled their own social existence, then inductive "laws" or principles could have no coercive or deterministic content and a social activist was limited only by his own ignorance or ineptitude.

To understand the nature and scope of the prewar revolution in social thought and practice, the assumptions of the orthodox traditions of Victorian science, and their corollary social science, must be made transparent. First of all, nineteenth-century science was an absolute, missionary religion. Whenever scientists philosophized about their subject to wider audiences, they reinforced the lesson that there was an immutable and regulative order behind the flux of experience. A striking, though by no means atypical, instance of the way in which eminent scientists preached the faith was the public lectures delivered at the Royal Institution in 1854 to plead the cause of "Scientific Education."[3] In the lectures, the prevailing scientific dogma was unmistakable.

None of the speakers made the slightest effort to relate science either to ordinary affairs or to practical problems. On the contrary, they obviously valued science as predominantly an intellectual pleasure arising from a revelation of the complex, hidden mechanisms of the physical world by means of elegant mathematical models and clever demonstrative reasoning.[4] The central purpose of science was the discovery of the existing structure of reality, rather than the imposition of subjective constructs. Even the mathematician George Boole, almost unique in his awareness that the laws of nature were merely *"probable* conclusions," nevertheless insisted that the business of science was "not to create laws but to discover them."[5] Although a dichotomy between theoretical and applied science did not really exist in the nineteenth century, physicists concentrated upon theoretical "correlation" in which phenomena which had seemed to be "capricious and isolated" were brought into a "consistent and comprehensive order."[6] Science was not recognized as an inherently manipulative instrument until the twentieth-century revolution in physics. No nineteenth-century scientists could have spoken legitimately of "inventing the future."[7]

To the nineteenth century, the order of reality was not merely immanent but permanent; it could not be compelled through science to be other than it was. John Tyndall, the important popularizer of science spoke for his contemporaries when he observed that scientific inquiry was nothing more than the procedure for understanding the "visual record of the Creator's logic."[8] Only Michael Faraday, the self-educated Fullerian professor of chemistry at the Royal Institution and brilliantly successful experimental physicist, warned against the illusion of absolute and complete knowledge: "In drawing a conclusion it is very difficult, but not the less necessary, to make it *proportionate* to the evidence: except where certainty exists (a case of rare occurrence) we should consider our decisions as probable only."[9] It is true that Faraday's ignorance of mathematics compelled him to represent reality through physical models rather than by means of abstract mathematical formulas. But his skepticism about deductive theory came mainly from his belief in laboratory experiment as the means for testing conclusions, from his conviction that natural laws were simply summaries of existing levels of knowledge, and from the Sandemanian text that absolute truth was possible only for God.[10] His caveats were ignored by the scientific establishment until the end of the century. Far more acceptable was William Hodgson's definition of science as the "order which binds the parts into a whole" or, more simply, as the "pursuit of *Law*,"[11] that rational description of the fixed and uniform qualities of a static universe. As late as 1870, even so transitional an economist as Jevons could still insist that the social sciences would develop fruitfully only as the "necessary complement" to the physical sciences.[12] Physics supplied social theory with a convenient epistemology and a reassuring method for reducing the contradictions within experience to something resembling coherence. But the tension between changing empirical experience and a static causal science remained taut throughout the century.

The dichotomy between explanatory theory and ordinary experience had been established by the authority of John Stuart Mill's *Logic* (1843).[13] Mill had been torn between his faith in the eventual discovery of a social science based upon causal laws, on the one hand, and his commitment to individual moral responsibility, on the other. He admitted that the scientific process began and ended with experience, but at the same time he understood social laws as immutable and determined. Proceeding deductively, Mill tried to reduce problems of both individual behavior and social process to principles as closely analogous to demonstrative physical laws as possible. Once the basic social postulates were understood, social and individual tendencies could be predicted, he believed, with substantial accuracy. Although Mill tried to modify the causal qualities of his social "tendencies" by imputing moral responsibility to individuals for their own actions,[14] he never succeeded in reconciling a determined social process with free individual choice and conduct.

Despite the fact that he was a sincere moralist and a liberal advocate of social change, Mill unwittingly contributed to a tradition of social science suspicious of reform. Indeed, a belief in a regular social mechanics did not interfere with actual reform

efforts: if the direction of social processes could be grasped sufficiently, then an individual reformer could devote himself to promoting the most desirable elements within that process. But a
view of inevitable social development, while not restricting individual reformist activity, certainly did not encourage individuals
to throw themselves into novel and unprecedented projects for
radical change. In Mill's 1851 revision of the *Logic* he moved
closer to voluntarism by arguing that instinct, too, was susceptible to willed "mental influences" and education;[15] and as rector
of Saint Andrews University in 1867, he simultaneously emphasized the determined conditions of existence and the need for
individual initiative in the battle between good and evil, a battle
that changed as human nature and society changed.[16] But despite
such gestures toward freedom of the will, as long as the "fundamental problem" of social science was understood as the search
for laws of progress on the basis of which society necessarily
evolved, the role of individual morality was problematic.

When Victorian social theorists took ordering models from
physics, they satisfied aesthetic and intellectual cravings for an
internally consistent system derived logically from deductive postulates, but at the expense of their ability to control and improve
rapidly changing social conditions. The discovery of social laws
turned out to be the discovery of evidence that social progress was
occurring. Even social scientists who declared themselves free of
all "systems of opinion or doctrine" were witnesses for the inevitable march of progress.[17] Throughout the century, the developments of methods of social inquiry testified to recurrent, though
variously motivated, efforts to reduce complex social phenomena
to more manageable, often quantitative, form. What these
efforts lacked, especially after mid-century, was a satisfying theoretical explanation to provide meaning beyond the specific
project investigated. Until the end of the century some "social
scientists" abandoned theory altogether to flounder in mere facts,
while others, who gathered facts in confirmation of a priori
assumptions, moved increasingly away from social reality. Creation of an empirical social science was retarded before the 1870s
by the lack of empirical social theory. The deductive models that

had dominated social theory were unable to predict, explain, or influence events. And by the end of the century, industrialization, social dislocation, chronic unemployment, agricultural decline, and steadily mounting discontent had persistently corroded traditional social theory. Clearly, there was no evidence, in any aspect of social life, of the order idealized in theory, and an insistence upon finding such order in experience only led nineteenth-century social theorists deep into blind alleys.

The nineteenth-century physicist's assertion of the increasing unity of knowledge was especially reassuring to those who, for whatever reason, wanted to believe that the overwhelming disunity of experience was subject to a coercive order that existed behind events. The desire to discover order filled even such apparently militant opponents of theory as the statisticians. Explicitly disavowing questions of cause and effect as legitimate concerns for social inquiry, they continued to believe implicitly in rigorous social causality.[18] It was often precisely those social activists concerned with specific social problems, as much as the theorists, who made such a priori assumptions about underlying order. This is evident in another activist group, that typically Victorian organization, the National Association for the Promotion of the Social Sciences, founded in 1856 to discover the best measures for reforming individual character and for eliminating the social diseases that pervert character. Its major conviction—that a society is a rational consensus of interests willing and able to agree upon and implement social remedies—assumed an underlying order that would be discovered by the investigatory techniques of social science.[19] Burdened by their increasingly untenable assumption, the N.A.P.S.S. was as ill equipped as the deductive theorists to explain the growing economic and social discontent of the 1890s.

At the end of the century, some discarded theory completely to concentrate upon quantitative and experimental techniques. But the effect of their work was a narrative miscellany characterized initially by Charles Booth's statistical inquiries into the life and labor of London's poor and then by Seebohm Rowntree's survey of poverty in York. Booth was convinced, correctly, that existing theory had failed from a "want of reality" because it was based upon a "series of assumptions very imperfectly connected with the observed facts of modern life."[20] And although his work lacked systematic and critical analysis, it did contribute to the eventual growth of a sociology of poverty. Inspired by Booth, the Quaker industrialist Rowntree studied poverty in York through more direct and perceptive sampling techniques that led to specific wage and social-security recommendations. But his work too was without an adequate conceptual form.[21] The tradition begun by Booth and Rowntree produced a torrent of Blue Books and government reports, which buried reformers from 1900 to 1914 under masses of unevaluated information.

Another reaction against the inadequacy of nineteenth-century social theory came in the form of specific critiques of institutional abuses as exemplified by the Webbs and the Fabian movement. Beatrice and Sidney Webb, together with the other Fabians, devised conspicuously successful techniques of investigation, research, and influence, but their impatience with theory, their indifference to problems of methodology, and their retention of utilitarian psychology and ethics left them outside of the revolutionary developments occurring in the social sciences. For the Webbs, method meant that particular procedure, generally a manipulation of institutions and their personnel, that would accomplish specific goals of reform most efficiently: the Webbs were concerned essentially with performance. Neither the Booth-Rowntree census of the condition of England nor the Webb's prescriptive remedies were able to substitute for the social and economic theory they had discarded. Many late-nineteenth-century social reformers were too preoccupied with practice to inquire into theory; and they were content to employ a wide variety of eclectic methods meant only to achieve particular results. To reach their immediate goals, they adopted convenient social science tools without pausing to question their own implicit assumptions about social cause and effect.

Victorian social theorists in common with Victorian reformers had accepted the concept of causality, but they were uneasy, as

Mill had been, about its deterministic implications. If the individual and society were governed by immutable laws, then existing practices, thought, and conduct could harden into institutions and habits independent of their inherent merit. But no Victorian social observer was willing to take either success or survival as a criterion of worth, especially since the gap between their ideals and social reality showed few significant signs of narrowing. They were all deeply interested in questions of value, and few were willing to allow the structure of the past to determine either the present or the future.[22] Despite the restrictions that deterministic theory imposed upon reforming activity, theorists and reformers behaved as if they could indeed change the environment so as to produce better lives for everyone. Throughout the century, a persistent belief in an underlying, demonstrable order coexisted incompatibly with a tradition of social revolutionary thought and practice, as evident most remarkably in Bentham's disciples.

To understand the dilemmas in which social theory became enmeshed in the nineteenth century, we must remember that since the late 1600s, British social theorists began with either a normative or a psychological assumption. They discussed human nature as they wanted it to be or as they thought it actually was. But neither normative theory, derived from rationalist biases, nor psychological precepts, rooted in the intuitionists' "common sense," was sufficient to explain actual behavior.[23] Both schools were consistently critical of prevailing ethics, but neither could find any ethical imperative inherent in its views of social process. Eventually, every social critic was compelled, by default, to appeal to the individual's ethical conscience, although with serious qualms about the efficacy of such an appeal. A functioning ethical conscience depended upon an assumption of freedom of the will — an assumption increasingly difficult to maintain. At the beginning of the nineteenth century, the dilemma of determinism versus voluntarism was cast in biblical terms, and after mid-century, it was recast in the still more formidable rhetoric of science. In early nineteenth-century England, the theological paradox was resolved, at least in practice, by evangelicalism which empowered the individual to carry out God's plan through his own energetic devices. Even the N.A.P.S.S., in their *Melioria: A Quarterly Review of Social Science,* understood social science as applied Christianity.[24] It was more difficult to find a working solution for the scientific formulation of the ancient problem of the justification of human behavior.

By emphasizing a mechanistic causality, many of the most dramatic results in Victorian science had implicitly undermined voluntarism. Hermann von Helmhotz's theory of the conservation of energy as applied to living systems excluded individual free will entirely because the course of events is already accounted for in the universe. The study of reflex action in frogs indicated further that behavior might in fact be completely automatic.[25] The most damaging evidence against individual freedom was marshaled in the "moral statistics" of the Belgian, Adolphe Quételet. In *Sur l'Homme* (1835) he argued that figures showed that the constancy of crime seemed "quite independent of human foresight."[26] Although Quételet was never quite convinced that free will was impossible, many of his readers, like the Cambridge logician-mathematician George Boole, were carried away by his startling statistics to conclude that where large numbers of men were involved there was a "very remarkable degree of regularity in their behavior."[27] Ever since the Marquis Pierre Simon de Laplace's *Théorie Analytique des Probabilités* in 1812, statistics had been used as a graphic demonstration of causality. Quételet followed this conventional usage as did James Clerk Maxwell three decades later, when he studied the technical subject of the thermal behavior of molecules. But when Maxwell thought about the broader implications of his statistical model he was disturbed by its limiting effect. In 1873 he urged scientists to study the "singularities and instabilities" rather than the "continuities and stabilities" of things to dispel that "prejudice in favour of determinism which seems to arise from assuming that the physical science of the future is a mere magnified image of the past."[28] And he saw that if "averages" or "general laws" or "predetermined tendencies" were to be applied to social phenomena, then the qualities distinguishing individuals from one another would be ignored.

Among those qualities, the one that most interested social theorists was moral responsibility.

Throughout the nineteenth century, assurances of increasingly moral behavior had been provided by a progressive reading of individual and social growth. The idea of progress enabled nineteenth-century social theorists to treat the ideal and the real as if they were indeed complementary parts of knowledge and experience. When, in the last half of the century, the notion of beneficent forces began to be challenged by Darwinian biology, by reflex studies in physiology, by a reinforced mechanism in physics, and by the erosion of religious conviction, faith in progress yielded, for many people, to suspicion of process. Clearly there were causal tendencies at work in history, but it was by no means certain that they necessarily worked in man's best interest. A progressive and secular view of history, developed in the late eighteenth century, had the great advantage of appearing to reconcile individual activism with a belief in causality. Individduals, responding to religious, humanitarian, and psychological imperatives, were resolved to take some action against conditions they found deplorable. And it was precisely to provide evidence for the efficacy of their activist ethic that they moved toward a reassuringly progressive view of history. If an individual concentrated upon achieving "progressive" goals, then his efforts could result in accelerating the undetermined rate of progress. This functional rationalization had the practical effect of minimizing any potential conflict between social causality and individual reformism. Moreover, it permitted the reformer to find psychological consolation for his temporary defeats by reflecting that because his purposes were progressive, they would irresistibly triumph in the long run.

There was enormous, if specious, comfort in this line of reasoning, but it had two consequences that reformers could not entirely accept. First, it depended completely on the belief that progressive forces did in fact move history. Second, it created a moral dilemma by implying that ultimately progressive, and therefore "good," ends justified means that were not necessarily desirable in themselves: a factory worker's output might eventually contribute to growth of British industrial production and a better life for everyone even though the immediate conditions of his own life were totally unsatisfactory.

During the second half of the century, when the processes of history came to be viewed as intrinsically neutral, it appeared to reformers as if prevailing but undesirable tendencies might become dominant. For those unwilling to accept this variant of determinism, there was the option of making moral voluntarism and historical processes consistent by assigning them different levels of influence: Charles Kingsley's inaugural address as regius professor of history at Cambridge in 1860 admitted broad patterns in history, but he made progress depend entirely on individuals acting according to conscience. But Kingsley was no more successful than J. S. Mill. The innate direction reflected in causal laws could not be reconciled with an assumption of genuinely free will at any level. None of the nineteenth-century theories of ethics and society ever explained why actual human behavior deviated so widely from the norm postulated by social theorists.

At the end of the century, the ethical dilemma of social theory was reformulated in a secular version of the religious conflict between a higher and lower self. The evangelical struggle between spirit and flesh was translated by T. H. Green into a neo-Hegelian social conflict between individual rights and political obligations. The most ambitious reconciliation of both positive social laws and individualist morality had been attempted by Herbert Spencer, who thought that he could devise a physical science of ethics. Green pointed out that the effect of Spencer's reconciliation would be an acceptance of current behavior as if it were the only behavior possible.[29] What Green offered in place of naturalistic ethics was an index for measuring the quality of existing behavior against superior standards that ought to exist.[30] Oxford Idealism, influenced by Green, asserted that ethical value, like social structure, was imposed by mind.[31] And at Cambridge, G. E. Moore persuaded a brilliant generation of undergraduates that ethics were neither predetermined nor governed by natural laws, but arose, rather, from the intrinsic "goodness" of certain states of consciousness.[32] Although the ethical and social theories developed at Oxford and Cambridge at the turn of the century differed in content and purpose, their point of congruence lay in their rejection of both evolution and conventional values, perpetuated through history, as a sufficient source of judgment.

In the last two decades of the century, social reformers in search of supportive social theory found little inspiration in the unresolved contradictions between positivistic explanations of a progressive social order and their own experience. Nor could they persuade themselves, as many of the antitheoretical reformers of the N.A.P.S.S. and the various statistical societies had done, that social and moral progress would be demonstrated if sufficient statistics were accumulated. After 1880 reformist social theorists rejected a progressive reading of history, but they were divided by their views of human nature and their presuppositions about the nature of society. Their lines of division were drawn along the old philosophical borders that separated rationalism from empiricism. Rationalism, or deduction, and empiricism, or induction, had never been sharply antithetical or incompatible attitudes, but they implied different emphases and methods. Induction emphasized the importance of experience by beginning the process of explanation with sensory data, while deduction began with logical, rational axioms whose abstractness went beyond any information contained in experience. The rationalistic model invariably attracted theorists who valued social stability more than the freedom of individual will, while empiricism appealed more to advocates of social change and individual choice.

Rationalism had been bolstered throughout the nineteenth century by the typological and ideal physical sciences. Although challenged by a growing interest in experimental science at the end of the century, rationalistic physics reemerged in 1905 in the newer and grander structure of relativity.[33] Empiricism never enjoyed the prestige of rationalism during the nineteenth century, but it became more respectable as a result of the "quantitative" procedures of Darwinian science, the success of statistical methods in practical policy questions, especially in public health, and the rising pressure of social problems whose solutions could not be postponed indefinitely.

Rationalism and empiricism coalesced at the end of the century when intellectuals agreed that "facts" were a function of mind. No one was any longer willing to believe that facts were "merely *recognized* by a mind, not *made* by it."[34] This unwillingness to accept any reality independent of mind was affirmed by the new sciences of biology, psychology, anthropology, and much of sociology in their concentration upon origins rather than essences. It was one thing to agree that facts were constructs, but the bases for accepting such facts as valid presented an entirely different kind of problem. While physical and social scientists concurred during the last decade of the century that whatever was found to be "true" would be compelling for everyone who knew all the relevant data, there was fundamental controversy about the nature of truth. Rationalists understood truth as that which cohered with the established body of knowledge, while empiricists required truth to correspond to given facts from the ordinary world.

The rationalist's quest for unvarying regularities was virtually unchallenged until Darwinian biology insisted upon the importance of historical origins and the process of development. Natural selection gave social scientists a very different kind of scientific model based upon a clinical interest in comparing individual phenomena. The biologist inducing general propositions from observation learned, as Huxley pointed out as early as 1854, "the utterly conditional nature of all our knowledge." Huxley himself, of course, continued to expect that such conditionality would be overcome since it was not an essential attribute of knowledge itself.[35] But biological procedures, essentially quantitative in methods and assumptions, could hardly yield anything more than tentative conclusions.[36] By the close of the century, William James could point to the entirely new "quantitative imagination" that had "swept" over his generation. Evolutionary theory had produced a far vaster scale of time, space, and numbers than ever imagined, and the interpretation of these varying quantities implied the fluctuating character of what could be known.[37]

The example of physics so dominated social thought that the potentialities of biological models were largely neglected until the late 1870s. Nor did Victorian social thinkers turn to the alternative concepts of knowledge and method developed throughout the century by mathematics and medicine. Mathematics had been singled out, especially at Cambridge, as the discipline most appropriate for intellectual training. Medicine, on the other hand, was taught and practiced outside the educational establishment. Unlike mathematics, with its abstract postulates and its aloofness from human problems, nineteenth-century medicine concentrated upon the treatment of immediate human misery. Yet neither mathematics, with its lofty intellectual status, nor medicine, with its impressive victories over threats to public health, ever rivaled the effect first of physics and then of biology upon the form and method of social thought. Social theorists were relatively indifferent to developments in mathematical thought and they deliberately rejected medical practice as a viable model for social analysis.

Although mathematics never directly provided either a method or an epistemology, it did serve social thought indirectly in a special way: as a paradigm of rational explanation, mathematics was the highest form of physics and the purest form of thought. In 1854 Boole equated the laws of thought with the laws of mathematics, explaining that deductive generalizations were given validity by the "ability in our nature to appreciate Order, and the concurrent presumption, however founded, that the phenomena of Nature are connected by a principle of Order." Unlike the collected facts of experience, the general propositions of mathematics and thought were "necessary" truths.[38] Boole's equation of the subjective tool of mathematics and thought with an objective natural order meant that when mathematics was used to explain natural phenomena, a mechanistic and deterministic world must be revealed. Two decades later, Boole's formula for explanation still held true; for example, in James Clerk Maxwell's and Ludwig Boltzmann's laws of statistical mechanics, an a priori deductive imposition of mathematical order upon the physical quantities of heat and entropy.[39]

Statistics belonged to probability theory that, since the early nineteenth century, had developed as a form of deductive thought that subjected chance phenomena to predictable laws. Quételet's statistics led Boole in the 1850s to devise a deductive general theory of probability that would permit a social scientist to make successful predictions. Then, in the early 1870s, the political economist W. Stanley Jevons was influenced by Boole to interpret probability to mean that there are no necessary or sufficient causes. This interpretation implied that natural laws were the result of fortuitous and random events. A similar conclusion was to be reached by Darwinian and Mendelian biology and by atomic physics. All these sciences relied, in common, upon mind to impose order upon randomness through the essentially deductive method of mathematical probability.

One of the most enterprising applications of deductive probability theory to random social phenomena was carried out in Francis Galton's *Hereditary Genius* (1869). In an attempt to demonstrate that intellectual achievement was a direct function of heredity, Galton adopted Quételet's normal law of error to measure ability. But he never questioned whether this technique actually could explain circumstances in the observable world. Then, in 1889, Galton proclaimed Quételet's bell curve as a "wonderful form of cosmic order." The "huger the mob, the greater the apparent anarchy, the more perfect is its sway...." Not realizing that he confused the pattern imposed by his theoretical tool with the actual conditions he set out to investigate, Galton marveled how, in large samples of chaotic elements, an "unsuspected and most beautiful form of regularity proves to have been latent all along." Lost in admiration, Galton saw the tops of the "marshalled rows" forming a "flowing curve of invariable proportions" and "each element, as it is sorted into place, finds, as it were, a preordained niche accurately adopted to fit it."[40]

Galton's disciple Karl Pearson, a first-rate mathematician, went beyond Galton's simple use of causation to develop the statistical concept of "correlation" as a tool for explaining social science through the same mathematical formulations characteristic of physical science.[41] Pearson's sophisticated reaffirmation of the deductive use of statistics, though successfully challenged by the new social scientists, would continue to have its adherents. Surprisingly, a biologist like Raphael Meldola was able to assure his Oxford audience, in the Herbert Spencer Lecture of 1910, that even where there were enough observed facts to permit their quantitative expression, the important conclusions in science were arrived at "deductively by men who have never carried out an experiment or made an observation—through the most powerful and potent of all weapons—mathematics."[42]

By contrast to the persistent, although unsolicited, influence of mathematics upon social thought, medicine had no effect at all. Until it became concerned with primary causality, medicine could not provide models readily acceptable to those searching for a fundamental analysis of the origin and nature of social problems. Nineteenth-century medicine had been diverted from more basic research by the nearly overwhelming problems of public health and their imperative demand for immediate solution. The fatal consequences of urban congestion led investigating and reforming doctors, like Southwood Smith, to abandon the time-consuming study of primary causes of disease in favor of the identification and removal of more obvious secondary causes. An emphasis upon preventive measures produced the "sanitary idea," surely the most effective invention of early nineteenth-century medicine. But the effect of such emphasis was the treatment of conspicuous symptoms rather than of the underlying pathology. On rare occasions, very general causal relations were identified, such as William Farr's isolation of a London water company as the source of the cholera epidemic of 1866; but discovery of the specific cause of cholera had to await the development of bacteriology.[43] Nineteenth-century medical study and practice, particularly when faced with epidemic disease, normally sought restorative palliatives. Their organic emphasis upon restoration and stability was hardly congenial to social theorists committed to the discovery of either fundamental social laws or methods of progressive development. William James rejected his medical training and turned to a revolutionary psychology because he found medicine to be a superficial mode of soothing suffering through remedies based largely upon ignorance;[44] and the founders of British social psychology, William McDougall and Wilfred Trotter, ignored their medical backgrounds to root social theory in a priori assumptions and a deductive methodology.[45] In the end, the medical profession taught only one important lesson to a new generation of social scientists already impressed by biological procedures, a lesson implicit in all the new genetic sciences: the value of quantification as an instrument of social observation.[46]

At the end of the century, the availability of biological models spurred the revolution in the social sciences and also permitted a refurbishing of the older tradition of positivistic social science in the work of the anthropologist Edward Burnett Tylor and the sociologist, Edward Westermarck, corecipient with Leonard Trelawney Hobhouse of the first chair of sociology at the University of London in 1907.[47] Both men used empirical research to verify their conclusions, but the masses of data they gathered was little more than window dressing for a familiar stock of a priori social concepts. Selective research supported their original conviction that the past, present, and future were necessary and continuing stages in the fundamentally beneficent development of man and his institutions.[48] The comparative sociology and anthropology influenced by Westermarck and Tylor saw history as a revelation of conditions necessary for social progress and sufficient for individual action. In practice, their "empirical" methodology simply used evolutionary concepts to create a reassuring history of moral progress which claimed the discovery of new evidence for the familiar nineteenth-century belief in the growth of the individual from irresponsible irrationality to mature reason.[49] It was not until the 1920s that the influential "British school" of anthropology emerged as an innovative discipline.[50] But before the war, the traditionally positivistic conclusions of both a "new" anthropology and a traditional sociology failed to satisfy early-twentieth-century social critics who found the ordinary man's irresponsibly irrational behavior so frightening.

2.

Revision, Revolution, and the New Sciences

By the end of the century, positivism was a dying tradition in the social sciences. It was replaced by an immediately more influential and ultimately more enduring attempt to develop genuinely professional disciplines in which theory and practice supplemented and corrected each other. For the sake of analysis, those involved in the creation of the new disciplines may be divided into two distinct categories: revisionists and revolutionaries. Economics, psychology, and political science were the revolutionary fields, social psychology was revisionist; and sociology, sundered into conflicting fragments, vacillated between traditional positivism, revisionism, and revolutionary social science until after World War I.

Throughout the second half of the nineteenth century, sociologists quarreled about the nature of the oldest of the social sciences. While G. J. Shaw-LeFevre, in his presidential address to the London Statistical Society in 1877, reminded his colleagues that the "science of Sociology" was "essentially a deductive" one concerned with causality, the following year, John Kells Ingram, president of the Economic Science and Statistics Section of the British Association, urged that the section be converted into a Sociology Section based upon an inductive methodology. Then when Henry Sidgwick was president of that section in 1885, he discarded traditional positivism and sociology entirely to argue that it was "our business" to "carry on more limited and empirical studies of society...."[1] After the founding of the Sociological Society in 1904, debates upon method and purpose grew still more vehement. Sides were drawn between practical social administrators addressing particular social problems and theoreticians like L. T. Hobhouse, editor of the *Sociological Review,* who urged that the most immediate concern for sociologists was the development of theory. These differences culminated in a schism in 1911 that has still not healed.[2]

Revisionist social psychologists began, as the revolutionaries did, with a rejection of rationalist psychology and teleology, but their "science" continued to be deductive. Although they wanted moral conduct to improve, they could find no evidence of the growth of social morality, nor were they willing to trust individuals to conceive and carry out meliorative processes. On the contrary, they were alarmed by the values and conduct perpetrated from the past and by the manipulative forces to which individuals so readily succumbed. Starting from an irrationalist view of human nature and beguiled by the image of an organic society, they emphatically rejected a rationalist and voluntarist view of human nature and the possibility of a rational democratic society. The effect of revisionist social science was conservative social theory which attempted, unsuccessfully, to reconcile an understanding of morality as the individual's obligation to be reasonable, equitable, and altruistic, with a pessimistic view of human nature.

Inevitably, their distrust of ordinary people drove them toward revision of the positivist social theory that they had set out to repudiate. Because they could not overcome their profound fear of individual irrationality, they opted in the end for a managed society and the security of universal laws. Social psychology found morality, reason, choice, and experiment in evolutionary tendencies largely independent of individuals. William McDougall, the most influential of the social psychologists, used deductive and axiomatic principles to disclose an increasingly ordered process of evolution. In this process individualism was a temporary and regrettable stage: the unpredictable and irrational impulses moving individuals were to be absorbed eventually in the more reliable reason of a supracollective mind.[3]

The revolutionary social sciences began in the late 1870s with the moralistic idealism and progressive assumptions of their positivistic predecessors, but by means of a new methodology they transformed these assumptions into a theoretical and practical social science aimed at immediate reform. Their moral conviction that individual and social life should be more rational and more humane came into conflict with their observation that neither reason nor altruism showed any sign of increasing. To escape from this dilemma, they reinterpreted progress as the deliberate, calculated activity of informed individuals guided by evolving sciences derived from experience. None of the revolutionary social scientists were willing to question the dependence of their moral principles upon progressivist assumptions. Unless people and institutions did progress, unless they were in fact capable of changing for the better, the desirable, ethical characteristics of altruism, goodwill, and social responsibility would never be widely diffused throughout society. Individual choice was the moral fulcrum of the revolutionaries. But choices made in ignorance were hardly real alternatives. The economist Alfred Marshall, the American psychologist in England, William James, and the political scientist Graham Wallas adopted inductive methods to extract from a comprehensive range of information those factors genuinely vital to individual needs.

The immediate thrust of the revolution in English social thought changed the problems considered appropriate to social science. Revolutionary social scientists relinquished fruitless quests for a comprehensive scheme of social laws. Instead, they extended the narrow concern of earlier reformers with individuals or small groups, and they limited theoretical analysis to the specific social anomalies that demanded immediate critical attention. These thinkers recognized that neither the social theories nor the institutions inherited from the past were sufficient to deal with the multiplication of social, economic, and political conflicts between various social interests. When intellectuals in the last three decades of the century considered the potential power of barely literate democratic masses, they remembered their responsibility as reflective people. Both the revisionist and the revolutionary social scientists transmuted this common sense of guilt and unease into an effort to provide direction and leadership through "science" rather than charisma. But only revolutionary social science was, to use T. H. Kuhn's suggestive hypothesis about the structure of scientific revolutions, the "tradition-shattering" complement to the "tradition-bound activity" of "normal" or prevailing views of human nature in society.[4]

The revolution had been heralded by a number of works that rejected the methodology and epistemology popular in traditional theoretical and applied social science. In the economics of the 1870s, the transitional economist Jevons as well as Alfred Marshall, had arrived independently at an analysis of "utility" that broke decisively with the classical system;[5] and in 1874 Jevons argued that economic and social problems should be treated through "sophisticated" probability theory.[6] In psychology, William James's startling discussion of consciousness, separating the study of mind and behavior from conventional epistemology, appeared in the English journal *Mind* in 1879. Although these new concepts were debated strenuously in the 1870s and 1880s, they did not have a significant impact upon the wider intellectual community until 1890.

The American James, as a result of frequent, always stimulating, excursions to Oxford, Cambridge, and London, became a welcome and influential participant in English intellectual life for three decades. There, he found provocative discussion, excitement about his new ideas, and a sphere of influence greater than in America.[7] At least part of that influence was due, as was Marshall's, to an insistence upon behavioral tests. Both systematic expositions immediately became classics in their fields, virtually unchallenged in England for a generation. In addition, Marshall and James each inspired critical disciples who applied the new faith in a reforming social science to problems that had eluded solution in the nineteenth century.[8] Then, in 1908, Graham Wallas created a revolution in political thought by applying Marshall's quantitative method and James's pragmatic psychology to the study of politics in his *Human Nature in Politics*.[9]

The emphasis upon technical analysis, quantitative and comparative methodology, and a tentative theoretical structure were all revolutionary, but not as revolutionary, perhaps, as the ends toward which the new social sciences were directed. Modern economics, psychology, and political science were intended by their founders to be potent methods for reforming individual character and public institutions. Marshall, James, and Wallas all had in common the desire to make social science a transforming instrument to impose rational and moral imperatives upon the anarchy of psychological and social conflict. Even though no reassuring faith in moral or rational progress could be extrapolated from the events of the late nineteenth century, all the new social scientists were determined to retain rational and moral criteria for progressive change. An insistence that science serve ethical ends prevailed among late nineteenth- and early twentieth-century reformers, despite the diversity of their ends; but the revolutionary social scientists could not rely ultimately upon any beneficent movers like evolution, progress, reason, or God.[10] On the contrary, they intended their science to be a prolegomenon to change, defeating actively regressive forces including the determinism of chance. William James's pluralism, the heart of his psychology and philosophy, developed in opposition to the idea that an individual is forced to act, or to believe, in any special way because of given circumstances. James's psychology challenged not only the older epistemological analysis of consciousness but the newer mechanism of behaviorism. All the various forms of mechanistic psychology adopted a robot model to explain behavior as essentially reactive, responding innately or through learning, to imposed stimuli.[11] James would not accept "automaton-theory" with its "*a priori* and *quasi* metaphysical grounds" because he viewed behavior as a consequence of consciousness, at all times "primarily a *selecting* agency."[12] Free will was "true" in James's evaluative judgment of truth, because of its meliorative content as a "general cosmological theory of *promise*" with the same fruitful function as any other "doctrine of relief" that promised individuals a better future.[13] Marshall's synthesis of history and analysis in his *Principles* tried to delineate those economic conditions requisite to successful meliorative change, while Wallas's synthesis of psychology and politics exposed the forces obstructing such change. When James wrote in his *Principles* that the most probing question we are ever asked is: "Will you or won't you have it so?"[14] he spoke for the revolutionaries. As an economist, Marshall's question was: "How far is it possible to remedy the evils of the present day?"[15] while Wallas queried individual vulnerability to manipulation and its practical defenses.[16]

All the new social scientists, whether revolutionary or revisionist, were very clear about what they considered to be their ethical obligation: they were less certain about the methods best suited to carry out that obligation. Part of their problem arose from their role as pioneers. There were as yet no professional social sciences able to train members to use specific methods to analyze social problems, to synthesize disparate information, and to check theory against experience. Still less was there any agreement about the priorities of problems to be studied. Although able to isolate the questions they wanted to answer, they had great difficulty in selecting and verifying the data required to answer these questions.

When the new social scientists tried to build their "sciences," they were confronted by divergent and conflicting view of scientific method which included mathematical demonstration, experimental empiricism, impressionistic intuition, and individual perception as well as the dialectical process of comparing similar and dissimilar events. In all these views, the only common assumption was that scientific thought, properly understood, was the means by which human progress was best accomplished.[17] The turning point came when the revolutionary social scientists pioneered a scientific method using both experience and theory to resolve crises through an understanding of their causes and consequences.

Every variety of social thought at the close of the century was concerned fundamentally with the theoretical refinement of a genuinely objective scientific method. And social theorists could turn to new philosophers of science, like Karl Pearson, who defined method probabilistically as an "orderly classification of facts followed by the recognition of relationship and recurring sequence."[18] Or they could accept William James's still broader description of science itself as a "certain dispassionate method." Pearson was a great innovator in method, but his use of the novel technique of biometrics was no more than a methodological prelude to the eugenic changes he considered essential to the preservation of a strong society. James, on the other hand, knew that if science and its methods were degraded to a particular set of results that one should "pin one's faith upon and hug forever," it would serve only sectarian purposes.[19] In common with James, the other revolutionary social scientists came to understand method as a flexible and expanding set of procedures that would observe and test theory and experience.

In order to confirm their own directions and to indicate possible pitfalls, the revolutionary social scientists were keenly interested in the methodological changes fermenting in other disciplines. While they chose inductive procedures and experimentation, they found no ready use for a mathematics increasingly indifferent to experience. The trend of nineteenth-century mathematics in England, from Boole through William Kingdon Clifford, John Venn, and Bertrand Russell, was toward the question of mathematics and logic, careful analysis of internal consistencies as opposed to the discovery of new truths, and an emphasis upon knowing simply "what can be deduced from what."[20] Although at the end of the century even the most traditionally deterministic sciences were taking account of experiment as a proof of a priori principles, or as an inductive process leading to the formulation of new principles, the new mathematics was cut away completely from the empirical world. The new algebra no longer dealt with quantities; geometry in its non-Euclidean form was not concerned with spatial relationships and figures in nature; and even arithmetic now studied "trans-finite" numbers that could not be counted.[21] Moreover, traditional physics, demonstrated through a mathematics understood as the most concise and truest expression of physical reality, was challenged in the last quarter of the nineteenth century by the indifference of the new mathematics to reality and by the extension of experimental facilities, beginning with the foundation of the Cavendish Laboratory at Cambridge in 1871.[22] While the growing emphasis upon experiment in the physical sciences indirectly sustained the revolutionary social scientists' reliance upon concrete experience, the new mathematics was largely irrelevant to their methodological needs.

Only the development in mathematics of statistics and probability theory directly interested the revolutionaries as methods facilitating the investigation, collection, and comparison of large quantities of psychological, social, economic, and political data. One of the earliest applications of the new statistics to social problems was the eugenicists' development of probability theory in the early twentieth century to prove their absolute belief in the dominance of heredity over environment. The revolutionary social scientists were wholly opposed to the eugenicists Francis Galton, Karl Pearson, and their disciples at the Galton Laboratory and the Biometric Institute in the University of London, for subordinating their method to a priori socially conservative ends.[23] Although the revolutionaries rightly attacked the reliability of the statistics gathered by Pearson and his coworkers, and although they repudiated any tool imposing deductive order upon the rich diversity of experience, their real concern was for purpose more than for method. Just as tenaciously as the eugenecists believed in the force of nature, the revolutionaries held to the formative effect of nurture.

Retaining from their predecessors a psychological and moral view of science as necessarily the source of objective methods for distinguishing truth from error, they broke sharply with the past in their treatment of truth as a human value. James insisted that our convictions about the "truth" of scientific laws were much more like a "religious faith" than like an "assent to a demonstration." He was considerably impressed by that aspect of Karl Pearson's philosophy of science which found science "true" only in the sense of yielding a "conceptual shorthand, economic for our descriptions."[24] Pearson thought of science as a "mental shorthand" for the "sequences of our perceptions," a means of classification and reasoning, but not an "explanation." All that we could ever know about "laws" was that as a matter of experience, a certain sequence had occurred and recurred in the past. We call that "causation," and our belief that it will recur in the future we call "probability." Pearson influenced James's view of the tentative nature of scientific knowledge, but he never succeeded in carrying James to the conclusion that science was a unified, progressive enterprise in which the observed relationships and sequences would fall eventually into increasingly comprehensive formulas.[25] Pearson's skepticism about scientific "truth," derived from his understanding of probability theory, was contradicted by his faith in an inexorable idea of progress.[26] James found no such reassurance. Instead, evolutionary doctrines taught him to accept a "plastic world" in which almost all our "functions, even intellectual, are seen as 'adaptions' and possibly transient adaptions" to practical human needs.[27]

All the revolutionaries treated thought, experience, method, and judgments about them as ephemeral expressions of particular needs in concrete historical circumstances. Moreover, "truth" was, as James put it, simply a collective name for "verification processes."[28] It may be that James and the others confused the definition of truth with the criterion for testing it. But the effect of their emphasis upon the continuous testing of every proposition, and of its outcome by every conceivable test, made the old methodological antitheses irrelevant to social science. Induction and deduction were understood rather as compatible and complementary procedures in verification. Every method, whether relying upon rationalism, empiricism, experiment, quantification, or assessments of probability, was accepted as valid in the Edwardian preoccupation with measurement.

Measurement was not a new concept in social science, but it was used in a novel way at the end of the century. In his provacative analysis of revolutions in science, Thomas S. Kuhn suggests that the function of measurement is either to precipitate a crisis by exposing anomalies in prevailing theory or to aid in the choice between competing theories.[29] While this analysis does not explain developments within recent social science, it can be applied fruitfully to the positivistic social science ascendant until the 1880s.[30] Measurement, whether of wage and price indexes or of voting patterns, did precipitate a crisis by disclosing the inability of traditional economic and psychological and political theory to analyze accurately problems of behavior and organization. The precise detail supplied by systematic measurements enabled the emerging social sciences to choose those epistemologies and methods most appropriate to the explanation of a particular problem. But the turn-of-the-century controversy over measurement as the essential method of social science often became a discussion of the validity of technique to the exclusion of more essential problems of purpose. This reflected a growing intellectual concern for defining problems more precisely. In 1903 G. E. Moore complained that disagreement in philosophy arose because attempts to answer questions were made without first discovering "what it is which you desire to answer."[31] The new social sciences suffered from a similar confusion about their appropriate functions.

Although the revolutionary social scientists tried to restrict their analysis to measurement, their reforming ambitions spilled over the limits of the methodology they had adopted, because they never thought of themselves as objective and disinterested students of academic problems. They were passionate partisans of individual well-being — moral, mental, and material — to be achieved within a liberal, democratic society. Service to ethical ends motivated Marshall's economics, James's psychology, and Wallas's political science, just as it did Rowntree's sociology of poverty and Hobhouse's social philosophy. When James argued, in 1879, that the individual could not remain neutral or skeptical in moral questions, he was voicing the pervasive reforming ethic of his time.[32] A commitment to a muscular progressivism, a disciplined exercise of will and reason, characterized every variety of reforming thought and conduct at the turn of the century. For this reason, the revolutionary social scientists were bound to gain ascendancy over revisionist social sciences devoted essentially to an exposé of the naïve expectations of reformers trusting futilely in the force of individual reason and goodness. This ascendancy was sustained through the late 1920s as social science was expected, increasingly, to provide guidance for ethical progress, to suggest "what might be" and "what ought to be."[33]

To best serve their reforming purposes, the revolutionaries attempted to make their disciplines rigorously professional. But they were restricted initially by the stubbornly persistent and widespread admiration for amateurism in educational and supposedly "professional" institutions. Paradoxically, this uniquely British prejudice may have facilitated the revolution in the social sciences by encouraging social scientists to develop independent standards for determining competence and for evaluating purpose. The proliferation of amateur science throughout the nineteenth century, exemplified by T. H. Huxley's remarkably successful effort to be equally proficient in a staggering variety of subjects, had encouraged men without formal preparation to pursue a wide range of scientific problems, often quite effectively. Increasingly, however, the revolutionary social scientists saw that the intensive development of their disciplines had to rely upon consistent professional training and practice; amateurism could be as much a liability as a liberating force.

But even by the end of the century, and with few exceptions, professional standards were neither precisely defined nor enforced by professional bodies.[34] Educational administrators, too, were unwilling to regard specialized studies as essential elements in their curricula.[35] The effect of this absence of compelling professional traditions was that the revolutionary social scientists were able to resist the positivist canons so deeply rooted in the public schools, universities, and "scientific" associations. The limited objectives of these institutions, their isolated and aristocratic values, were, in any case, simply too narrow for social scientists who wanted to reach the greatest number of people.[36] If progress depended upon values, as the revolutionary social scientists believed, then the problem was to discover what those values should be and how to diffuse them throughout society. Through systematic inquiry into the origins and nature of individual behavior in different circumstances, all the new social scientists developed professional and highly specialized disciplines with distinct methodologies, plans of study, and apprenticeship requirements. But the revolutionaries went still farther by insisting that through social science the conflicts between individual desires and social needs would be reconciled so that a democratic society could also be a moral one.

Despite the sweeping optimism supporting the reformist temper of the prewar decades, on the eve of the war Graham Wallas found thought, literature, and politics permeated by a "pervasive fear, conscious or half-conscious, that the civilization which we have adopted so rapidly and with so little forethought may prove unable to secure either a harmonious life for its members or even its own stability."[37] Wallas had played a significant part in creating such fear, although it was certainly far from his intention. In the enormously influential *Human Nature in Politics* he had revealed the fallibility of reason as the first step toward strengthening thinking and purpose. An effect of his work that he had not foreseen was to discourage intellectuals from actively pursuing social and political goals. Wallas's own experience in politics, and his careful study of actual political behavior led his further than either Marshall or James in his repudiation of the intellectualist fallacies perpetuated in deductive social and political theory. But he only meant his iconoclasm to clear away the remaining debris of defunct theory, so that human nature and society could be understood more accurately. While both Marshall and James denied the reality of compelling social laws, neither had been willing to consider that individual reason and will might not be strong enough to overcome internal compulsions and social pressures. James's exploration of the nature of belief should have made him more sensitive than Marshall to instinctual influences upon thought and behavior. Although he understood the evolutionary relation between instinct and habit, the educational role of imitative instincts, and the important instinctual role of "sociability and shyness," James would not conclude that instinct determined either social, economic, or political behavior.[38] James recognized that mind was, like nature, a "real jungle, where all things are provisional, half-fitted to each other, and untidy,"[39] but he wanted to believe that reason could convert jungles into tidy Cambridge gardens.

Unlike either James or Marshall, Wallas never confused his reformist ideals with actual conditions; his faith was as deep, except that it began in great skepticism. Through a devastating critique of the ethical and rationalist psychology sufficient for Marshall, and even James, Wallas initiated a behavioral political science concerned as much with human nature as with political institutions. Accepting T. H. Green's moral axioms, he tried to find criteria for converting those axioms into orindary canons of behavior. He understood, as the other revolutionaries did not, that even the best-intentioned sense of obligation had little opportunity for effectiveness unless armed with psychological knowledge of the motives and conditions influencing actual conduct. James had described psychology as the "most powerful ally of hortatory ethics,"[40] but he had never suggested any practical application of this principle. Marshall, too, believed that psychology and ethics were inseparable and essential approaches to any attempt at reform. As a young man, he was torn between the study of psychology and the study of economics. When he chose, it was because of the "increasing urgency of economic studies as a means towards human well-being."[41]

In common, the revolutionary social scientists relied upon individual commitment as a spur to reform. But they admitted that individuals live in complex groups that restrict their activity. A study of history led Marshall and Wallas to argue that it was not individual selfishness or apathy that created basic social problems, but rather an anarchy of forces and purposes working against each other. James came to a similar conclusion by analyzing the psychological origins of consciousness and behavior. History and psychology revealed to the revolutionaries a gratuitous complex of random processes within society and within the individual. To defeat the irrationality and inhumanity often produced by such processes, the revolutionary social scientists turned to "scientific" planning. While quarreling about immediate priorities, they agreed completely that no part of society could be left to develop haphazardly. Their emphasis upon organization occasionally obscured the more fundamental problems of the structure of a specific organization and of the immediate program it ought to serve. Clearly, increased rationality and morality are desirable ends, but it is not as clear that there is any necessary relation between efficient organization and either constructive thinking or selfless conduct.

What the revolutionaries did understand very well was that means and ends were not to be confused. Organization, whatever form it took, was simply a means of achieving carefully designed ends. No matter what the specific content of a particular reform, it had to conform to an overriding purpose. Most broadly put, that purpose, agreed upon by all the revolutionaries, was to enhance the quality of life experienced by every individual. This meant that everyone must have the opportunity for comprehensive education; for leisure; for productive, remunerative, and satisfying employment; for political participation; for self-knowledge; for recreation; and, above all, for responsible conduct. Each of the revolutionary social scientists chose careers that would enable them to extend and enrich the quality of individual life. Since all opportunities for improvement depended on an economic base, traditional economics was the earliest target of the revolution in the social sciences.

PART II
Economics and the Quality of Life

3.

Political Economy and Economics until the 1870s

By the late 1860s there had been a general agreement that "whatever is in accord with the laws of political economy is necessarily right and expedient and vice versa."[1] While the reality of such laws would not be seriously questioned until the last quarter of the nineteenth century, from the 1820s there were strenuous debates about how they should be defined, interpreted, publicized, and applied. The most distinguished and long-lived arena for these debates was the Political Economy Club founded in 1821 by Thomas Tooke for the purpose of "Mutual Instruction, and the diffusion of the just principles of Political Economy."[2] The Political Economy Club, as the economic historian W. J. Ashley described it in 1907, was "the assembly of the elders of the new Church" filled with the "spirit of ecclesiastical fervour."[3] Starting in 1821 with a group that included Malthus, Ricardo, James Mill, and Robert Torrens, the Political Economy Club continued into the twentieth century to elect an extraordinary and eminent membership of economic writers, university dons, statesmen, bankers, businessmen, merchants, journalists, and civil servants. When John McDonall said in 1905 that the Political Economy Club's history "may be said to be the history of Political Economy" he was not exaggerating.[4] On the evening of May 31, 1876, a glittering assembly met at the club to celebrate the centenary of Adam Smith's *Wealth of Nations* and to inventory the accomplishments and future prospects of their science. When all the speakers had finished it was evident that substantially everyone agreed: the demonstrative laws of political economy had proven

in experience to be so accurate that the science was "closed" because its inquiries were to all intents and purposes accomplished.[5]
Although there were a few economic heretics in the mid-1870s,
their influence was negligible in comparison to the self-satisfied
orthodoxy perpetuated by the Political Economy Club and by
academic economists in the universities.

When J. A. Hobson arrived as a student at Oxford in the late
1870s, no serious opportunity existed for economic studies there.
He had tried to learn economics even earlier, but the only course
of studies he could find was given by the Cambridge University
Extension Movement at Derby in 1875. And even the Derby
course ignored Jevons's *Political Economy* which had appeared in
1871, and used J. S. Mill, Henry Fawcett, and a few chapters
from Adam Smith to teach that the natural laws of economics
"established the justice, necessity, and finality of the existing economic system."[6] Hobson's experience was hardly unique. As long
as the dead hand of classical economics continued to determine
the content of university economics, the revisionist efforts of such
professors as J. Thorold Rogers and Francis Ysidro Edgeworth at
Oxford, John Kells Ingram at Dublin, and W. J. Ashley at Birmingham met with little success. Even when the universities introduced a broader range of economic subjects few students benefited since these subjects were generally classed as optional.[7] The
effectiveness of any new economics taught within the universities
was limited further by the examination system which continued
to require a knowledge only of classical economics.

In the early 1890s a Committee on Economic Training in Britain was set up by the British Association for the Advancement of
Science to make a detailed study of the curricula and examinations in Britain, the United States, and the Continent. The committee reported in 1894 that on the basis of its investigation economics was still an entirely unsatisfactory subject of study in Britain. Moreover, they found a lack of public support for economic
studies which they attributed to the "legacy of distrust and misunderstanding" from the preceding generation's view of the economist as a "compound of text-book theory and ignorance of
fact."[8] Only at Cambridge, owing initially to the influence of the

political economist Henry Fawcett from 1863 to 1884, and then after 1885 to Marshall, were there efforts to include a comprehensive range of economic questions in the older degree courses.[9]

There was only one dissenting voice raised against the orthodoxy celebrated at Adam Smith's centenary. It was Sir George Campbell who, in his inaugural address to the Economics and Statistics Section of the British Association [Section F], maintained that as "economic action is affected by moral causes which cannot be exactly measured, it becomes more and more evident that we cannot safely trust to a chain of deduction; we must test every step by an accurate observation of facts and induction from them."[10] Campbell's sound advice was drowned out by the resounding echoes of applause at the Political Economy Club banquet, echoes that continued for more than a decade.

If the satisfied participants at the banquet had been more perceptive, they might have understood that what characterized the nineteenth-century economics and the physical sciences they had emulated was not exhaustiveness but exhaustion; mechanical and static metaphors could no longer explain satisfactorily the dynamic and relativist character of actual experience. Henry Sidgwick's complaint in 1887 that the theory of political economy, along with its most important practical applications, was considered as "finally settled by the great majority of educated persons in England,"[11] was not an accurate assessment of the years following the centenary. Instead of consensus, there were growing signs of dissension, especially evident in the annual meetings of Section F. Beginning with John Kells Ingram's presidential address on "The Present Position and Prospects of Political Economy" in 1878, and continuing through the Reverend Philip H. Wicksteed's "Scope and Method of Political Economy..." in 1913, there were three decades of continuous debate about the proper nature, contents, methods, and purposes of economics. Even Sidgwick took part in these often acrimonious discussions through his writings on political economy and as president of Section F in 1885. After 1890, Marshall set the new house rules that would guide debates well into the 1920s.

In the course of this debate, Ingram, a political economist, philosopher, poet, and regius professor of Greek at Dublin since 1866, attempted to persuade Section F that economics should be part of a larger Comtean scheme of scientific sociology based upon historical, inductive methods intended to aid in the formulation of economic laws and tentative practical prescriptions.[12] Ingram was clearly a transitional figure and not a reforming social scientist. For one essential characteristic set the reformers apart from other social and economic critics: an insistence upon the development of separate, specialized, professional, and expert disciplines, capable of explaining a set of problems, isolated temporarily, for purposes of analysis, from the larger social context in which they actually occurred. The same year Ingram urged that political economy become more of a "science," Bonamy Price, supposedly the orthodox professor of political economy at Oxford, rejected deductive economics by arguing that political economy was no science at all but a practical, commonsense study dealing with tendencies rather than with absolute and uniform laws.[13]

The debate was carried a step farther in 1885 when Henry Sidgwick delivered his presidential address. Two major quarrels were current among political economists at this time. First, there was the methodological dispute among exponents of induction and deduction or the historical and analytical approaches; second, there was the policy dispute between those who insisted that private and public ends would be reconciled eventually in a free economy and those who proposed instead greater state interference in the economy in the interest of immediate social justice. Sidgwick straddled both these debates, but he failed to satisfy even himself, let alone his audience. He found that his belief in the virtues of the rational, economic individual, no matter how idealized, was often incompatible with the solution of pressing social problems.[14] In his address on "The Scope and Method of Political Economy," Sidgwick made an effort to defend classical political economy against the social and ethical criticism of such historicists as Thorold Rogers and against Ingram's Comtian or sociological appeal for the unity of all social sciences. Sidgwick continued to insist upon self-interest as the moving force in economics, and he accepted the importance of facts and induction, but only within a larger explanatory scheme regulated by deductive methods of analysis. At the same time he disavowed an "orthodox" political economy that assumed the "universally beneficent and harmonious operation of self-interest well let alone," but held tenaciously to a general rule of noninterference which allowed political economists to discover cases, such as drugs or child labor, that might be exceptions to that rule.[15]

The unresolved tensions inherent in Sidgwick's economics reflected the divisions among economists generally from the late 1870s and 1880s. But though these controversies gradually eroded the certainties of classical political economy, the old dogmas still continued to influence public attitudes and activities until Sidgwick's close friend, Alfred Marshall, brilliantly synthesized ethics, analysis, and experience in a comprehensive economics that reconciled the outstanding quarrels. Between 1876 and the publication of Marshall's *Principles* in 1890, the road for a new economics was cleared by the growing discrepancy between economic theory and economic realities; by the failure of Jevons in his attempt to revise classical political economy; and, by the new emphasis upon experiment, measurement, and hypothesis in the physical as well as the natural sciences.

While traditional political economists presumed the harmonious and beneficent operation of a rational market, the actual economy drew growing criticism at the end of the century on moral as well as social grounds for entrepreneurial myopia, mismanagement, and irresponsibility; for the multiplication of unresolved conflicts among economic interests; for technological obsolescence; and for the slums and human waste that developed around industry. The revelations of widespread poverty by William Booth and by Charles Booth and the creation of a more militant trade unionism among the great unskilled bulk of the working classes, dramatized in the dock strike of 1889, led to growing public dismay over the distributive inefficiencies of a reputedly progressive economy in which, as Charles Booth maintained, one-third of the population lived below a subsistence level. Clearly, the teachings of the old school had been "contrasted with the exigencies of society and the current of events" and found wanting.

By the 1880s, as the Cambridge economist H. S. Foxwell recognized rightly, a new economics was emerging from a convergence of theoretical criticism, historical method, and "humanistic feeling" represented in the work of W. Stanley Jevons and Alfred Marshall. Foxwell was too generous to Jevons. For unlike Marshall, Jevons held fast to the impersonal, deductive, mechanistic economics that Foxwell found repugnant because of its indifference to "injustice" and extensive "social wreckage." But apart from his misunderstanding of Jevons's assumptions, Foxwell was a keen and perceptive student of economic theory. Condemning the political economy of the 1840s and 1850s for its "unmoral" pretensions that economic action was subject to mechanical laws independent of morality, he saw in the 1880s that "public opinion" was becoming "increasingly sensitive to social suffering and to social needs." He attributed this change in economic attitudes in part to the growing democratic and socialistic feelings within the churches.[16]

Indeed, among all religious denominations a heightened sense of social obligation had culminated in the creation of active reform groups like the Anglican Christian Social Union. Established in 1889 to approach economic problems from a religious and ethical base, the C.S.U. gave effective organization to a radical Christian socialism that had fermented in the universities from the late 1870s in such groups as the "Holy Party" of 1875 and PESEC (politics, economics, socialism, ethics, and Christianity), created in 1879 by Henry Scott Holland and Wilfrid Richmond. When the C.S.U. founded the *Economic Review* at Oxford in 1890, edited by L. R. Phelps of Oriel, John Carter of Exeter, and W. H. J. Campion of Keble, an organ was available to promote Richmond's promise that political economy shall be a "branch of morals" to "enforce the principle that economic conduct is a matter of duty," while providing a forum for all varieties of economic criticism.[17]

Another attack against orthodox political economy in the universities came from the historical school. Historical economics, rooted in Ricardo, was developed in the 1830s by Richard Jones's discussion of economic laws as nothing more than the historical expressions of economic events occurring in different times. Jones was neglected until his works were collected and published with an introduction by the formidable Cambridge mathematician, philosopher, and political economist William Whewell in 1859. A hiatus occurred in the development of the historical study of economics until the 1870s. Then, Sir Henry Maine's legal and historical emphases led T. E. Cliff Leslie to a historical attack upon political economy. At the same time, Comte's influence persuaded both John Kells Ingram and the economic historian William Cunningham that economic history "is the best propaedeutic to political economy."[18] But even when native historical tendencies were bolstered by the newer work of the German historical economists in the late nineteenth century, the essential effect was to provide British economists with "support of their existing predilections."[19] Despite its limited effect, the historical school did contribute an important critique of classical economic theory. As Foxwell saw correctly, they eroded classical political economy by their attempt to replace "speculative wordplay" and static deductive assumptions by "statistical inquiry and historical research."[20]

The most distinguished spokesman of the British historical school was James Thorold Rogers, Drummond professor of political economy at Oxford, from 1862 to 1867 and from 1888 to 1890. Rogers, as Foxwell observed, maintained "almost single-handed, and with world-wide reputation, the historical repute of English economists," and yet no school was founded around his work.[21] During the early phase of his work in 1868, Rogers wrote a thoroughly orthodox *Political Economy,* in which he accepted government interference in the economy only for an ill-defined protection of the weak against the strong or for an equally vague "promotion" of national resources.[22] But over the next ten years, Thorold Rogers's intensive study of labor and working conditions converted him from a classical political economist into a perceptive critic of economic dogma and an energetic proponent of social reform. In his *Six Centuries of Work and Wages* (1884), a masterful popular summary of the first four volumes of his *History of Agriculture and Prices*, Thorold Rogers argued that the opulent or at least easy circumstances of most writers in political economy had made them oblivious of the harsh realities of the "industrial war" that went on around them. The role of the social scientist, he argued, was to discover how such warfare might be mitigated by a close, inductive study of economic conditions. When the "researches of the economist tell us the truth, his laws are beneficent, just as the physical laws, which connect disease with its causes, and show us thereby the means of prevention, are also beneficent. It is only when the economist becomes arrogant, and avows that he is a guide to all social actions, instead of being an interpreter of certain definite results," that he becomes useless.[23]

From the late 1870s, Thorold Rogers consistently represented a minority position among political economists, not only because he rejected classical political economy but because of his growing advocacy of trade unionism. While he retained the classical economist's simplistic psychological assumption that the individual always pursued his own best interest, he dismissed the sociological conclusion that such pursuit invariably contributed to the public good. Instead, he pointed to what seemed to him an obvious economic truth that it was in the employer's best interest to exploit his labor as much as possible, while it was in the employee's interest to sell his labor as high as he could. The effect of trade unions upon the economy would hardly be disastrous, he thought, because working men were not about to "ruin themselves" and were as "acute as their employers in discerning what price the market would bear."[24]

Unlike the crowd psychologists who, a generation later, were to find mindless instinct dominant in groups, Thorold Rogers was a rationalist who believed firmly that reason, superior judgment, and incorruptibility were exemplified in collective activity. Despite Thorold Rogers's strictures upon political economy, his colleague and biographer W. J. Ashley concluded in 1889 that throughout his career he had remained "orthodox" and "conservative," especially in his dismissal of the claims of evolutionary socialism.[25] Still, it was Thorold Rogers who wrote the obituary for the old orthodoxy that Marshall's powerful *Principles* would later effectively inter. In the preface to his *Economic Interpretation of History,* Thorold Rogers testified that his studies had taught him that "much which political economy believes to be natural is highly artificial"; the vaunted "laws" of economics were "hasty, inconsiderate and inaccurate," and instead of being "demonstrably irrefutable" were often "demonstrably false." The authority of classical political economy, which seemed so securely entrenched at the centenary of 1876, was now, he felt, "repudiated"; its conclusions were being assailed and its arguments and recommendations were increasingly irrelevant because of its "traditional disregard for facts" and persistent preoccupation with definitions. In place of the crumbling orthodoxy, Thorold Rogers called for a political economy that would analyze social conditions, rather than defend abuses. Not only was laissez-faire on trial but in "some quarters the verdict has already been given."[26] In this judgment he reflected quite clearly the revolution in economic thought that would culminate three years later in the publication of Marshall's *Principles.*

University economists like Rogers and Foxwell were not alone in their interest in reviving economics so that it would apply directly to the solution of economic and social inequities. From the late 1870s, university economists, businessmen, individualists, and collectivists joined together in an attempt to understand contemporary economic problems. Marshall organized the Economic Club in 1899 out of such a nucleus group, the "Economic Circle," that had met at the home of a stockbroker named Henry Raime Beeton. This same group led, ultimately, to the founding of the Fabian Society, and it was at Beeton's that one of the founders of Fabianism, Graham Wallas, developed his earliest interest in a science of politics.[27]

In 1890, Foxwell's students at University College, London, formed an association of postgraduate students in London with a membership consisting largely of practical civil servants but including Marshall and other academic economists and reformers as well. This Economic Club met at University College from 1890 to 1920 and then moved to the London School of Economics under the presidency of William Beveridge.[28] Another important group was the London Ethical Society, which drew together Oxford Idealists, members of the Charity Organisation Society, Fabians, civil servants, economists, businessmen, and university and schoolteachers. Influenced especially by T. H. Green's rationalist theology, the Society, led by J. H. Muirhead and Bernard Bosanquet, was formed in 1886 by Green's students working out of Toynbee Hall. In 1897 the society became a School of Ethics and Social Philosophy directed by E. J. Urwick and it was absorbed eventually by the London School of Economics, with Urwick as the first professor of Social Philosophy.[29] All these reform groups began as voluntary, essentially ethical, organizations that relied upon individuals to transform society, and eventually became effective forces in the development of early twentieth-century social policy.

No critique of existing economic theory, practices, and institutions was as incisive as J. A. Hobson's attack upon markets, whether monopolistic or "free," as intrinsically unfair modes of distribution. His discovery of cyclical unemployment, the maldistribution of incomes, and the imbalance between capital and consumer goods,[30] provided a more fundamental and perceptive analysis of the economy than any contemporary, including Marshall; but Hobson's conviction that consumers behaved irrationally because economic institutions were irrational narrowly restricted his appeal. For although the intellectual community was always divided in its assessment of social and economic priorities and appropriate methods, it was bound together by rationalist assumptions that prefigured the kinds of analyses they would consider as competent. And they denied, with considerable success, the theories of radicals and conservatives alike. Though Hobson had little in common with the social psychologists, he shared their exclusion during the prewar years.

F. Y. Edgeworth, the Drummond professor of political economy at Oxford, found Hobson's *Physiology of Industry* (1889) incompetent because it violated accepted principles of psychology and sociology. From the inner circle that he represented, Edgeworth denied Hobson the credentials that identified legitimate economists to a wider intellectual community. After 1889 Hobson could no longer find extension lectureships in economics in London, Oxford, and Birmingham, although he had done such work for many years successfully, and invitations to talk to such nonacademic groups as the Charity Organisation Society disappeared.[31] Toward the end of his life, Hobson complained justly that his economics had never been taken seriously enough for anyone to dispute them. Instead of being refuted, he had been ignored.[32] Although Hobson had some success as a journalist writing for the *Contemporary Review* and for the *Manchester Guardian* between 1899 and 1902, he never received recognition as an economist. No university in England, not even the London School of Economics whose founders were his friends, ever asked him to join its staff. His name was put forward for membership in the Political Economy Club, but he was not elected. Hobson did become a member of the Royal Economic Society, possibly because its bylaws made it extremely difficult to exclude anyone, but he never wrote for the *Economic Journal*.

The humanistic and moral goals of Hobson's economics were very similar to those proposed by Marshall, but while Marshall remained tied to the nineteenth century, Hobson belonged to the future. Marshall's idea of the "Noble Life" and his insistence upon both private and public cooperation in the solution of social problems coincided, as Joseph Schumpeter observed, with those of the "average intellectual Englishman in 1890."[33] But Hobson, in his movement toward a more socialistic state dependent on planning "the whole of economic life,"[34] and in his insistence upon the necessary dependence of economics upon politics, stood outside the consensus that governed intellectual life at the turn of the century. At the heart of that consensus lay a belief in the success of reasoned free will in creating precise social sciences committed to specific reforms. Hobson's valuable insights were neglected, not only because of his unorthodox views of economic conduct and organization and his advocacy of economic determinism in *Imperialism* (1902) but also because he rejected the quantitative methods being developed by economists anxious to turn their subject into a more exact instrument.[35]

While Hobson vigorously attacked the inadequacy of classical economics to describe and resolve economic problems, Jevons, the most important economist after Ricardo and before Marshall, tried to construct new barriers against any attack. Jevons's definition of the contents, methods, and limits of economics was regarded as authoritative until it was superseded by Marshall's *Principles* in 1890. The simplest and most popular of Jevons's books, *Political Economy* (1878), went through five editions in nine years to sell 99,000 copies.[36] Beginning his career in 1866 with a Malthusian analysis of England's diminishing coal reserves,[37] Jevons strove, during the next two decades, to patch the holes in political economy by making economics a comprehensive and ruthlessly logical system. Jevons was a conservative at heart, and his reluctance to abandon cherished assumptions and the conclusions derived from them even when the latter were inconsistent with one another or with experience, led him to prodigious and ultimately unsuccessful efforts at renovation. Although Jevons's advocacy of mathematical methods, his concept of marginal utility as the source of value, and his repudiation of the labor and cost-of-production theories did provide a bridge between the defunct classical tradition and the new economics, his hedonist psychology, laissez-faire social philosophy, and positivistic quest for economic laws "as binding and irrevocable as physical laws"[38] trapped him in the camp of the classical political economists.

Jevons's economics was flawed by the same psychological and sociological inconsistencies that had undermined classical economics: he encouraged active individual efforts for private and public improvement while simultaneously denying the possibility of progress. In his essay on coal reserves, for example, Jevons continued the classical economist's gloomy projection of a future based upon increasing scarcity. The 1820s had been a decade that hardly encouraged progressivist assumptions, and Malthus's grim predictions of an ever-burgeoning population and dwindling resources, reenforced by Ricardo's quantity theories of labor and value, recognized no possible alternatives, either willed or accidental, to eventual economic disaster. In Jevons's dismal science, a meager vision of the past continued to color the future, even though industrial and technological development and growing social stability made the idea of progress more tenable in the 1860s than it had been during the chronically hard times of Malthus and Ricardo. When Jevons predicted England's decline because of diminishing coal reserves, he assumed, as did the earlier prophets of exhaustion, that the shape of the future was already determined. His bleak view of economic regression did not, however, deter Jevons from urging individuals to improve themselves and to choose "*between brief but fine greatness and a longer continued mediocrity.*"[39] Yet, little genuine choice remained in a world where the laws of economics, modeled upon the "science of Statistical Mechanics," were thought of as describing a permanent and predictable structure behind apparently transient events.[40]

Jevons's attempts to make political economy a true or deductive science reflected the prevailing belief in an ordered reality that would be revealed systematically through universal laws whose validity increased in proportion to their distance from the confusing data of immediate experience. It was only in the 1870s, when some members of Section F began to apply statistics to practical problems like drainage and sanitation, that intellectuals first rejected, in effect, the view of science as a higher function of mind elaborated through deductive methods. Jevons's presidential address to Section F in 1870 deplored any treatment of "the word *statistical* as if it were synonymous with *numerical.*" We must not, he warned, "suppose that the occurrence of numerical statements is the mark of statistical information."[41] Jevons did not persuade all the members of Section F to abandon inductive projects and, in the 1870s, a movement developed within the British Association to jettison the Section, on the grounds that it was no longer genuinely "scientific."[42] Francis Galton found in 1877 that Section F was not devoted sufficiently to the discovery of a natural order revealed by "precise measurements and definite laws, which lead by such exact processes of reasoning to their results, that all minds are obliged to accept them as true."[43] Those, like Dr. William Farr, who argued against Galton that Section F should be maintained nevertheless agreed with him and with Jevons that essentially deductive methods were most appropriate for the science of economics and for statistics. Farr and the secretaries of the Statistical Society found that Galton's criticism of Section F was simply mistaken. They argued that the Section was in fact encouraging a "scientific method"[44] still derived from the same static, mechanical physics and mathematics that appealed to both Jevons and Galton as the most appropriate source for those a priori forms necessary to the ordering of experience. Few defended as "scientific" the inductive activities associated with inquiries into sewers and garbage collection.

Deterministic science was especially attractive to Jevons, but unlike most of his contemporaries, he anticipated what was to become the overwhelming burden of twentieth-century thinkers: the trauma of doubt. From the turn of the century, the most common experience for thoughtful men was the daily confounding of rationalist expectations by irrational and unexpected events moving toward ends difficult to foresee, let alone predict. The inadequacies of national life exposed by the Boer War and underlined by the alarming political behavior of the new democracy led to the growing anxiety that those responsible for solving social problems would become helpless when their values and concepts were challenged by increasingly perplexing experiences. As early as 1873, Jevons discerned that when any individual, and especially a "scientist," was forced by anomalous or inexplicable phenomena either to fundamentally question the prevalent view of social order or to admit ignorance, he became paralyzed by a "painful feeling of incapacity."[45] The predicament identified by Jevons was recognized repeatedly through the next two generations without anyone devising a reassuring psychological or conceptual escape. Quite independently A. J. Balfour, the Conservative party leader and philosopher, and Wilfred Trotter, the prominent surgeon and pioneer of crowd psychology, later acknowledged that reality was neither ordered, systematic, or even reasonable. To avoid the unbearable insecurity caused by unrelieved doubt, Balfour eventually recommended an irrational leap into faith, while Trotter warned that to be effective an individual must learn to bear the pain of suspended judgment.[46] Jevons, on the other hand, had tried to resolve the dilemma by defining mind as a tool for comprehending the inherent order within the world and by further defining science as the objective description of that order.

From the 1870s, the debate between proponents of orthodox political economy and their critics turned increasingly on their definition of science. Jevons dismissed the Comtean search for social laws with the contention that in human affairs cause and effect were rarely proportional; and yet he persisted in treating the social sciences as the "necessary complement to the physical sciences."[47] The only practical difference between physical and social science, he argued, lay in the degree of precision, a methodological problem he hoped to resolve by means of mathematics. Through methodology, Jevons intended to enclose economics in a comprehensive and consistent system. His case for the reality of the laws of political economy depended upon proof that such laws were scientific; this meant that the analysis of the structure and method of science was logically prior to an understanding of political economy. If political economy was analogous to the static science of physics, then the laws it discovered were indeed predictive descriptions of a synthetic unity underlying transient events. If, on the other hand, political economy was an inductive science comparable to biology, then its "laws" were simply tentative hypotheses or convenient summaries of observation which accepted the identity of experience and reality. Proof, in either case, rested upon the validity of a particular methodology. This meant that Jevons could not resolve differences among political economists until he had settled the dispute on method.

In his *Principles of Science* (1873), Jevons made deduction and induction complementary and essential attributes of reasoning, comparable to the process of adding and subtracting.[48] Induction, "simply an inverse employment of deduction," arranged complex and heterogeneous facts under uniformly acting laws that ordered knowledge systematically.[49] When the "Newtonian method of deductive reasoning" was "combined with elaborate experimental verification," science triumphed.[50] But the "true method of inductive investigation" relied on the fact that theory was primary, and confirmation, in fact, only secondary.[51] There was really "no such thing as a distinct process of induction"[52] since only general laws derived from hypothetical generalizations made prediction possible. Rejecting J. S. Mill's associationist contention that reason proceeds from one particular to another, Jevons argued that the "fundamental process of reasoning" lay "in inferring of a thing what we know of similar objects." And it was on this principle, he insisted, that "the whole of deductive reasoning, whether simply logical or mathematico-logical is founded." All inductive reasoning rested "on the same principle" of generalization.[53] Induction merely took deductive steps "backwards from any observed combinations of events to the logical conditions" behind those events.[54]

For Jevons generalization was not only the essential method of reasoning and science, it was also the test for the limits of knowledge. Scientific discovery became the "innate power of insight" into the "one in the many," independent of observation and trial and error experience.[55] Jevons ruled that no theory that had a "number of striking coincidences with fact," should be discarded "until at least one *conclusive discordance* is proved, regard being had to possible error in establishing that concordance."[56] Classification, a crucial technique for the genetic sciences, was absorbed easily by Jevons into his view of the deductive character of science: arranging phenomena did not necessarily imply either observation or measurement. Jevons made classification mean the discovery of the general among the particular. An adequate knowledge of particulars was impossible until they were regarded as "cases of the general."[57] The "limits of classification" or generalization were identical with the "limits of exact knowledge."[58]

When Jevons wrote in his major work on economics, *The Theory of Political Economy* (1871), that "Political Economy if it is to be a science at all must be a mathematical science,"[59] he meant the demonstrative mathematics of traditional physics modified only by the probability theory which Pierre Simon de Laplace, L. A. J. Quételet, and George Boole had developed from a priori postulates. It was only in the twentieth century that assessments of probability were based upon numerical samples and quantitative techniques, and even then the statistics of John Maynard Keynes and L. B. Stebbing remained tied to deductive systems.[60] The probability by which Jevons tested laws did not require the production of numerical data as a necessary part of the test,[61] but he did warn that one could never be certain that the future would be either like the present or the "outcome of the past." Since the laws of nature were reflected in generalized correlations demonstrable through past experience, then a probable future certainly could be anticipated by extrapolation from those laws.[62] But when he actually applied deductive laws of probability, as he did in repeated efforts to prove that economic fluctuations were caused by sunspots, the results hardly vindicated the method. In "Solar Period and the Price of Corn," (1875) and again in a more detailed paper, "The Periodicity of Commercial Crises and its Physical Explanations" (1878), Jevons confused correlation and causality. When he found that both commercial crises and sunspots occurred at average intervals of 10.444 years, he used probability theory to reach the questionable conclusion that "it becomes highly probable that the two periodic phenomena, varying so nearly in the same mean period, are connected as cause and effect."[63]

The year before his death, Jevons still chose to emphasize from the corpus of his work those attempts to substitute "exact numerical inquiries, exact numerical calculations, for guess-work and groundless argument...to investigate inductively the intricate phenomena of trade and industry."[64] But, as his editor H. S. Foxwell observed uncomfortably, Jevons left no "distinct indication of the particular inductive methods he regarded as most appropriate for the purposes of the economist."[65] It was not Jevons's untimely death that led him to ignore genuinely inductive procedures but rather his view that facts "alone without theory" were nothing but "mere disconnected records."[66] In Jevons's most explicitly empirical forays into "exact" economics, the figures he borrowed and the indexes he based upon them were never more than imprecise numerical values serving a priori social and ethical assumptions.

Jevons's characteristic manipulation of empirical data is apparent in an early and important paper, "A Serious Fall in the Value of Gold Ascertained, and Its Social Effects set Forth" (1862), which tied prices to the quantity of gold in Britain to predict, incorrectly, an imminent fall in the value of gold. Jevons invented the index number to compare the prices of 118 commodities listed in the *Economist* from 1845 to 1850 and from 1860 to 1862. Through this comparison he hoped to prove that a depreciation of gold and a permanent rise in prices were occurring. Against an index price based upon the average of fluctuations in the rate of interest from 1844 to 1850, he measured an "average price" arrived at by taking the mean of the highest and lowest prices from the mid-month number of the *Economist*. Indeed Jevons's analysis of the relation between prices and the quantity of gold could have been a valid theory of prices, or of the existing money supply, if he had compiled his index less arbitrarily. When he studied the rise in the curve of general prices since 1853, however, he simply ignored the role of speculation, credit inflation, and currency in the determination of prices. Arbitrarily, he set aside these phenomena with the unwarranted assumption that their economic effect was a constant: since they always lead to falling prices, they do not have to be considered when prices rise. The only remaining explanation for a yearly average price rise since 1852 was, then, to suppose "a very considerable permanent depreciation in gold."[67] Jevons's explanation was weakened further by the criteria that governed his selection of figures. Excluding from his table all commodities that showed "exceptional" price changes, he ignored variable conditions of supply and demand for each commodity, and assumed further that in an average of 118 articles "all individual discrepancies will be neutralised."[68] Contrary to Jevons's predictions, by 1884 the price of gold had risen.

Although Jevons's a priori assumptions and methodological inconsistencies prevented him from achieving a truly empirical economics, he did refine his own comparative methods, especially by the use of logarithms to take geometric mean ratios of yearly changes in prices. These figures were expressed in a series of graphic tables, diagrams, and curves that could be used to show proportional variations.[69] Jevons's comparative methods were used effectively by other economists, especially Marshall, when applied to reliable, accurate, and comprehensive data. The "apparent contradictions" that Marshall found in Jevons's figures were due to Jevons's persistent subordination of mathematical and empirical tools to the individualistic laissez-faire social philosophy that had become an essential part of economic analysis in the early nineteenth century.[70]

Jevons's application of economic principles was consistent with both the pessimistic and the optimistic elements in the Ricardian tradition. In "A Serious Fall in the Value of Gold," Jevons dismissed the adverse social effects of his predicted depreciation of gold by arguing that a reduction of 10 to 30 percent in the real income of ordinary people would be compensated for by the "general increase of industry, profit and general prosperity which is taking place," even though he had no figures to substantiate any general increase in wealth or in mercantile and industrial profits. Jevons's belief in individual incentive and his ignorance of the realities of poverty led him to accept the view that adversity had the "most powerfully beneficial effect" of stimulating individuals to greater efforts. Moreover he believed that "natural fluctuations" would always inflict "hundreds of hardships" that would simply have to be endured by individuals. In the classical manner, Jevons warned the government that interference in such natural calamities would mistakenly undermine "all individual forethought, and liability to disaster."[71]

The kind of limited progress that Jevons and the earlier classical economists had admitted as compatible with their anticipations of a larger regressive future, depended upon the economic man's increasing independence and self-reliance and upon a corollary decline in social services. The trade unions offended Jevons, as they had his classical precursors, because they impinged upon the "prices and rates at which men find it possible to exchange with each other."[72] Friendly societies were acceptable because they did not interfere with either the natural regulatory economic forces or with the thrift and self-reformation upon

which individual progress depended. The economically imma-
ture were to be protected legislatively, as women and children
had been in factory and mine acts after 1803, because they were
incapable of the free economic choices of the adult male striding
through the marketplace.[73]

Ironically, what was original in Jevons's economic thought
stemmed precisely from his anachronistic social philosophy. In
conformity with the utilitarian tradition, Jevons treated economic
conduct as a consequence of individual desire for pleasure and
aversion to pain, but at the same time he severed the concept of
value from the Ricardian cost and quantity of labor theories;
instead of approaching value from the classical perspective of
supply, Jevons began with the psychological nature of demand.
Demand was based upon the individual's assessment of whether
or not he should exert himself either to produce or consume a
particular commodity. The subjective measure beyond which
such exertion no longer seemed worthwhile was called "final," or
"marginal," utility. Utility was Jevons's name for the pain and
pleasure that moved men. While such motives could not be measured directly, their effect upon prices could. As for Bentham,
and later Marshall, money became Jevons's index of an individual's desires. Marginal utility depended not only upon an individual's judgment about the economic effort he was willing to
expend but also upon supply. When labor changed the supply of
goods, it also changed the marginal utility of the last item mar-
keted. Supply, in turn, was determined by the cost of production.
This meant that supply was responsible for that final degree of
utility which gave a commodity its particular value.[74] For Jevons,
the laws of the market rested on an "ultimate" theory of value
derived from the marginal utility of goods, services, money, and
labor.

Undeniably, Jevons's introduction of the marginal utility of
value in 1862,[75] and his repudiation of the labor and cost of production theories in 1871 marked the way for a departure from
classical economics. But it was not until Alfred Marshall defined
economics as the science of well-being that a tradition dominant
for seventy years was finally eclipsed.

4.

Alfred Marshall and the Revolution in Economics

Only occasionally has the gradual evolution and continuity of the social sciences been broken by intellectual events that may truly be described as revolutionary. In economics, such an event occurred with the publication in 1890 of Alfred Marshall's *Principles of Economics*. With his combination of dazzling analytical technique and an ethical plea for improving the quality of life, Marshall created a new economics concerned with individual well-being. Although radicals and collectivists, like J. A. Hobson and R. H. Tawney, criticized Marshall for impeding social reform by continuing classical assumptions about individual efficacy and social harmony, until after the war these critics were kept outside the sphere of economic influence created by Marshall and defended vigorously by his effective disciples. Even before publication of his epochal *Principles,* Marshall's students were in "half the chairs in the United Kingdom . . ." and their role in the teaching of economics in England was even greater.[1] From 1890 and until the late 1920s, the development of theoretical and applied economics was dominated overwhelmingly by the ideas of Alfred Marshall. Marshall stood at the beginning of the larger revolution in social thought which attempted, from the 1880s to 1914, to establish empirical social sciences that would reform human nature and society. By changing economics from a presumably objective science of wealth to an explicitly subjective science of welfare, Marshall provided the generous reforming impulses of his intellectual community with new models, new methods, and precise goals.

In economics, beginning with his modest *Economics of Industry* in 1879, Marshall gradually gained unique and pervasive authority as a "great father figure."[2] Through his influence, British and American undergraduates were transformed in the early twentieth century into reforming economists, civil servants, educators, statesmen, and writers. Marshall amply fulfilled his pledge that the "dominant aim of economics in the present generation" must be to contribute to a solution of social problems.[3] He did this by developing flexible tools of economic analysis that served the rational and moral progress of human nature in society, and by setting the professional standards of social responsibility that would later characterize the economics of A. C. Pigou, John Maynard Keynes, and Joan Robinson. When Roy Harrod writes that the "subject matter of economics is the welfare of human beings,"[4] he is identifying himself with the tradition begun by Marshall in 1885 when he became the professor of political economy at Cambridge.

Marshall's authority rested upon his ethical and empirical interpretation of the methods and purposes of economics and upon his revision of the political economists' central analytical concepts of hedonism, utility, value, and static time. Through a reconciliation of the outstanding conflicts in classical economics, Marshall was able to create at Cambridge the only cohesive "school" of economics in England. His conception of the nature and ends of economics, his paternalistic personality and his authoritative position, the traditions at Cambridge receptive to "scientific" innovation, and the failure of Oxford and the new London School of Economics to develop significant rival schools, left to Marshall the crucial role in establishing and perpetuating a consensus of economic opinion which would determine the theory and practice of economics in the Anglo-American community. As A. W. Coats concedes in his perceptive analysis of the sociology of British economic thought, there really was no "coherent, theoretically systematic alternative to the Marshallian approach" until the 1930s.[5] By 1890 economists had already accepted Marshall's rule that each particular economic event always occurred in unique and variable circumstances that could not be explained in terms of general economic events. Both the classical political economist's positivist desire for a deductive and "complete" economic theory and the naïve historicist's belief in autonomous facts succumbed to Marshall's synthetic insistence that the accumulation and analysis of data were complementary processes in the solution of economic problems.

Although recent scholars have lamented the lack of sufficient theoretical guidance for social action during the last two decades of the century,[6] new principles to guide theory and practice had in fact been generally accepted by the late 1880s in the universities and among a wider and very influential group of activists who shared a desire for systematic change. But it is true that the translation of these new principles into effective social application was delayed by intellectual rather than practical difficulties.

Men imbued with reformist principles had increasingly gained control of legislation and administration since the turn of the century. The result was that bureaucratic and parliamentary channels were opened for the implementation of new theory. When Marshall transcended the scholastic dichotomies in political economy between analysis and history, theory and fact, induction and deduction, generalization and statistics, he removed the theoretical obstacles to the program of social change which the Liberal government would legislate from 1906 to 1911.

Alfred Marshall tried to make his revolutionary economics appear consistent with the classical tradition, calling it only a "modern version of old doctrines" supplemented by "the new work."[7] While Jevons aggressively sought controversy because of his faith in the originality and correctness of his economics, Marshall learned from his friend Benjamin Jowett to detest controversy as a waste of energies better directed toward the progress of economic theory and practice.[8] In part, Marshall's moderation also followed from a desire to heal the epistemological and methodological rifts that increasingly divided economists after 1876. He tried to resolve all the debates outstanding in economics at the end of the nineteenth century by dialectically treating the opposing elements as complementary aspects of larger processes. Only on three occasions did Marshall break his rule about avoiding controversy. In 1892 he responded to his former student the economic historian William Cunningham who had misrepresented him as the formulator of absolute laws of economic causality and behavior.[9] Then, in 1903, he was drawn reluctantly into the public debate over free trade by signing the university economists' manifesto rejecting Chamberlain's proposed tariffs. Finally, when the Galton Laboratory published an especially sensational memoir in 1910 alleging that its accurate statistical procedures proved biological determinism, Marshall refuted this conclusion by exposing its procedural inadequacies. Throughout his long career Marshall continued to believe that "it is more important to establish truth than to confute error." The need for conciliation among economists was essential for the growth of economics, and it was more important for Marshall to put "one brick . . . in the slowly rising economic edifice than plant a hundred brickbats exactly between the eyes" of anyone who, like Henry George, was wrong in his understanding of economic issues.[10] Whenever Marshall's economics was criticized, he incorporated the criticism into new editions of the *Principles*.

Marshall's intellectual background reflected the influences that turned undergraduates from the late 1860s increasingly toward careers that promised the greatest opportunity for public service. As students stayed on longer to complete degree courses, enrollments multiplied, matriculations tripled, and an increasing number of graduates needed suitable employment. Public service was an obvious career for university-trained people. In Marshall's case, he had intended to enter the Anglican clergy, but instead he came via mathematics and physics to metaphysics and ethics. Psychology attracted him, too, but by 1867, two years after graduating from Cambridge as second wrangler in mathematics, he had decided to concentrate upon economics. Marshall explained: "I had come into economics out of ethics, intending to stay there only a short while; and to go back as soon as I was in a position to speak . . . with those men of affairs who dashed cold water on my youthful schemes for regenerating the world by saying, 'Ah! You would not talk in that way if you knew anything about business or even Political Economy.'"[11] Marshall never really left ethics;

instead, he found in economics the kind of knowledge necessary and sufficient for controlling the material conditions that restricted the moral progress of human nature in society. For the rest of his long life, Marshall read exhaustively and critically; he spent his vacations touring factories, workshops, potteries, mines, fishing villages, and farms; he visited the homes, markets, churches, and recreational places of workingmen; and, from the mid-1870s, he compiled cumulative tables of figures on money, prices, wages, rent, taxes, exports, imports, and demographic and technological changes.[12] His study of business and political economy from 1867 taught him that economic life could not be described entirely by a set of assumptions derived from Adam Smith, David Ricardo, and the Reverend T. R. Malthus, assumptions transmuted since the 1820s into analytical and predictive natural laws.

Although he created a revolution, Marshall was no revolutionary. For at the core of his new economics there lay four conventional presuppositions, characteristic of the intellectual community to which he belonged: the rationalist conviction that every man seeks what is best either for himself or his children; the idealization of "work" as a therapeutic determinant of character; faith in moral and material progress based upon satisfactory opportunities for the individual's physical and mental development; and, acceptance of the potential value of competitive, but equitable, free enterprise.

Marshall's assumptions were almost universally shared. It would be impossible to find an influential thinker in the late nineteenth century who did not believe that the responsibility for social welfare depended ultimately upon strengthening individual character. Clearly this conviction was in John Stuart Mill's mind when, in the late 1860s, he urged the universities to train more effective fighters in the incessant war raging "between Good and Evil."[13] As late as 1914 social reformers still believed that the war could be won only by individuals fighting with determination against inequalities that prevented the development of character. When social and economic problems grew more insistent in the

1880s, the locus and strategies changed considerably, but the reliance upon individual responsibility persisted. The revelation of London's poverty in Charles Booth's "arithmetic of woe" relied upon a morally outraged "intensity of feeling" to move the world toward good.[14] Rowntree, too, was certain that the good path of social progress would open before "patient and penetrating thought if inspired by true human sympathy."[15]

Both Booth and Rowntree wanted problems to be understood more accurately and precisely, but they continued to rely vaguely, as Marshall did, upon dedicated, altruistic individuals for the remedy of social injustice. Socialist and individualist reformers alike clung to a moral code that expected every individual to "undertake labour of *social value* . . . which is really useful to the community."[16] It was entirely consistent with contemporary faith in the efficacy of a moral person that socialism should be described as an attempt to teach the wealthy a new morality, rather than as a doctrine of class war or social revolution.[17] Every other program of social reform developed in the late nineteenth and early twentieth centuries began with a similar statement of faith.

Marshall was very much a man of this time. While understanding that his economics rested on rationalist "assumptions as to the moral character and motives of ordinary men," he continued obstinately to insist upon the psychological correctness of those assumptions until his death.[18] These preconceptions led Marshall to ignore the development of radical, anti-intellectual, and collectivist critiques of social, economic, and political forms made by some of his contemporaries, but they did not limit his own attack upon existing social and economic ideas and institutions. From the 1870s until World War I, what was vitally new in Marshall's economics transcended what he had inherited, and he was able to challenge successfully the prevailing economic theories and the social policies such theories justified. In the 1920s Marshall was still a late-Victorian reformer, an intellectual relic whose rhetoric was inspired by a set of values increasingly incompatible with the complex realities of the new century and, ironically enough, with the newer forms of criticism that he himself had stimulated.[19]

Marshall's economics idealized rational, ethical, and altruistic individuals as the principal source of social and economic welfare. Even though people were moved by complex impulses and motives, individuals were generally rational enough to select those occupations for themselves and their children that seemed to them "on the whole the most advantageous."[20] Marshall focused on people as consumers rather than as producers and he persisted in the belief that their actions were necessarily rationally directed toward the satisfaction of wants. His protection for the consumer lay essentially in the warning that individuals must be wary of any economic deception, coercion, or exploitation. Force and fraud would be controlled partly by competition and partly by laws that established equitable rules and penalized their infractions. In this context, if employers provided wages and conditions of labor which created a satisfactory standard of living, the efficiency of labor would increase. This did not mean that an immediate or even eventual "natural" harmony of interests would result. On the contrary, Marshall advocated legislation to protect the weak from the powerful and to alter social attitudes so as to promote increased individual responsibility for general social welfare. But though Marshall spoke out insistently for mandated economic reforms, he believed, in the end, that a just society depended ultimately upon the social conscience of those with economic power.

Marshall's economics is, in effect, a theory of the way in which individual character actively progresses in relation to economic wants and their satisfaction.[21] The purpose of every reform, as of economic studies themselves, was not simply material change but the "progress of man's nature."[22] As an expert witness before the Royal Commission on the Aged Poor in 1893, Marshall disavowed the humiliating workhouse tests and the family disruption resulting from Poor Law administration to insist that the purpose of state aid must be to "raise a man."[23] Just how self-respect was to be dispensed along with welfare funds Marshall never said and, in any case, he agreed to the testing of recipients by criteria similar to those used by the Charity Organisation Society. Only those willing to help themselves, he felt, would benefit from the aid given them. Merit tests for relief were especially popular among second- or third-generation heirs of self-made men considerably higher on the greasy poles than their abilities necessarily warranted. Unlike these men, Marshall knew that his own position was due to ability and effort, and this knowledge prevented him from confusing accidents of birth or wealth with worth. Rich and poor were equally tested by Marshall, and he was convinced that failure by the poor was due, in considerable part, to the callousness of the rich.

In place of the calculating "economic man" invented by nineteenth-century political economists, Marshall imagined a reasoning ethical man whose idealized attributes were drawn from the intellectual interests and economic standards of himself and his comfortable university friends. Thus, Marshall's earliest and most persistent remedy for poverty was the promotion among the less fortunate classes of education, opportunities, and skills that would enable them to emulate the middle classes and compete with them successfully. The middle-class model proposed by Marshall required later marriages, thrift, and a general submission to employers. Prefiguring Pareto's circulation of elites, Marshall saw in the lower classes the latent force that would enable a periodic rejuvenation of the economy by means of the displacement of those dissipated third-generation businessmen who had lost the work ethic that had so successfully inspired their grandfathers.[24] Marshall greatly admired the ordinary man who could live with the constant insecurity of his uncertain economic situation and he envied those who rose above such limiting circumstances. But he wanted, in essence, to convert them all into cultured and respectable "gentlemen."[25] Only a generation later, in the writings of romantic anarchists like Stephen Reynolds, would the alleged purity and nobility of lower-class culture and values be contrasted with the corrupt values of a materialistic middle class, incapable of spontaneity and joy.[26] The successful people Marshall knew best were driven to succeed by their "desire to master difficulties" wherever they found them. Since social problems raised far greater difficulties than personal ones, the successful man was bound to assume responsibility for the public good.[27] But what would be the criteria of success for these men? Marshall's test was a basic "standard of comfort" well beyond the simple abolition of poverty and ignorance, a standard that would promote human abilities and the capacity to live as reasonable and moral beings rather than as mere "producing machine(s)."[28] Clearly such a "standard" was no disinterested precept induced from economic experience, but rather an a priori ethical ideal.

Marshall's early interest in ethical philosophy, his subsequent experience with social work, and his reformist conception of economics gave him his own "categorical imperative," which inextricably linked "true happiness," with self-respect and the performance of social obligations.[29] While Marshall recognized that the economist has "seldom any special authority" on matters of moral obligation, he believed that he could strip away false arguments and reveal the real economic questions "which must be decided by the common sense and the moral judgment of the community at large."[30] It is not surprising that Marshall's "categorical imperative" turned out to be more imperative for idealistic university students than for business leaders. His expectation that ordinary people would become increasingly reasonable and altruistic as the conditions of their existence improved was to prove equally illusory.

Marshall's optimism about the future rested upon his Victorian eulogy of "work" as a therapeutic experience essential for the progressive education of character and the rational faculties. The Nonconformist tradition, which made work a testimony to godliness, along with Marshall's own pride in overcoming his natural aversion to work, prepared him to believe that rational character developed only when challenged by continuous obstacles that must be met and overcome. Like William James, Marshall was always torn between a reluctance to work and compulsive feelings of responsibility. Both men resolved their predicament in the same ways: by escape into neurotic ill health on the one hand and on the other by compulsive work based on the rationalization that it was absolutely necessary to the maturation of reason. The son of the cashier at the Bank of England, Marshall made himself preeminent in economics by enormous labor and by successive challenges overcome. At the age of eighty he continued to believe that work was "not a punishment for fault; it is a necessity for the formation of character and therefore for progress."[31] All his life he believed that work "in its best sense, the healthy energetic exercise of faculties," was not simply the purpose of life, but was "life itself."[32] He tried to reconcile the hedonism of classical economics and his own notion of a work-oriented categorical imperative by arguing that social "good lies mainly in that healthful exercise and development of faculties which yields happiness without pall."[33] Labor was the primary means for achieving dignity and self-respect. Unless individuals were actively occupied in improving their lives, they degenerated. Progress occurred when individuals vigorously fostered the moral strength, resolution, energy, and self-discipline that allowed them to take advantage of proffered opportunities.[34]

In common with the other reforming critics of the late nineteenth century, Marshall's energetic rationalism culminated in a voluntaristic idea of progress. In place of an unavoidable future of increasing scarcity that the earlier political economists had projected, Marshall made progress depend upon the individual's "higher social nature," the altruism latent in everyone which recognized and responded to the demands of common good.[35] Not implacable objective forces but the subjective effort of reasoning men, provided with realistic opportunities, moved society. Through social justice and a broad cultural, social, and intellectual education, ordinary people could be surrounded from "birth upwards by almost all the influences" characteristic of the life of "gentlemen." The state was responsible for this kind of educational system because every individual whose thought, tastes, feelings, interests, and purposes were "low and limited" would not only restrict himself and his family, but would "regressively affect the community around him."[36] The evolution of representative government, communications, and collective associations for mutual benefit had, so Marshall believed, produced a level of knowledge and self-reliance that would make it possible for individuals to exercise "true self-controlling freedom."[37]

Marshall's voluntaristic altruism was hedged by his discovery of progressive tendencies in the actual development of nineteenth-century industry. While rejecting any deterministic interpretation of a future forged by blind forces, he found evidence of growing efficiency in the organization and use of capital and labor, efficiency that more than offset the erosion of natural resources which had perturbed the classical economists. Marshall's careful studies of nineteenth-century economic history led him to conclude that the growth of middle- and upper-class prosperity had not led to an increase in lower-class poverty, though he did recognize that the rapid increase of wealth in Britain had not resulted in a corresponding "diminution of want."[38] In part he attributed the persistence of poverty to the absence of a genuinely competitive economy that would provide the poor with real opportunities to improve their condition. Marshall did not believe that competition was motivated fundamentally by greed. Not only was fair competition "absolutely essential for progress" but the act of competing was a pleasurable, satisfying process independent of the eventual win or loss that might follow.[39] He admitted that economic competition could, and often did, result in dishonesty and adulteration, but the state could "repress such evils" and employers should be "persuaded" to act in the consumer's interest by labeling goods precisely.[40] To increase the real ability of the lower classes to compete in the economic market, Marshall urged extensive and rigorous training in skills so that the unskilled, who would be more in demand because of their reduced numbers, would receive better wages. Such increase in the efficiency of labor meant to Marshall a corollary increase in production and in the amount of money available for raising the wages of ordinary workers. If employers and employees were willing to transcend limited personal ends for higher social priorities, and if raw materials and capital investment were not threatened by military spending, then the future promised marked improvement over the past.

When an economic balance was established between the availability of natural resources and the increasing efficiency of labor and capital, Marshall's "law of constant returns" prevailed. In effect, the "law of constant returns" was a promise of steady eco-

nomic progress that depended upon the individual's willingness
to increase his labor and his self-denial. England's relative decline
in competition with the United States, Central Europe, and the
East was attributed by Marshall to businessmen and trade union-
ists who sacrificed the benefits of industrial organization and
technological innovation to narrowly defined self-interest.[41]
While Marshall's ethical-rationalist psychology may have misled
him about the force of altruism in economic choice, he perceptively anticipated that disputes over wages between employers
and employees would become more important than the definition
of efficiency and profit-sharing. What Marshall did not foresee is
that the conflict would occur increasingly between two monolithic entities, trade unions and corporations, each bureaucratic,
oligarchical, irresponsible, and primarily concerned with the
expansion and perpetuation of power.

Until World War I, Marshall accepted the validity of capitalism provided it were renovated so as to distribute wealth and
opportunity more justly. Collectivists, especially the Fabians,
were impatient with Marshall's reliance upon a reformed capitalism to remedy economic inequities, but they too accepted the
rationalist-voluntarist psychology upon which capitalism rested.
The major difference between Marshall and the collectivists was
that Marshall's analysis of a quasi-static marketplace projected a
future that continued, if more humanely, existing property and
business arrangements. Marshall's ideal of desirable change was
drawn from the dominant economic institutions and practices
characteristic of the late nineteenth century, but his economics
asked a more modern question: How were available resources to
be allocated so as to provide the practical conditions necessary for
a qualitatively fuller life for everyone? At the same time as Marshall, the American economist John Bates Clark had developed
marginal analysis, but Clark's confusion of the real and the ideal,
in his famous *The Distribution of Wealth* (1899), justified the
status quo. For Marshall, on the contrary, distribution was an
ethical problem. Elimination of crippling social and economic
disabilities depended upon a more equitable distribution of
money, goods, services, and opportunities throughout the com-

munity. The first lectures that he gave as professor of political economy at Cambridge dealt precisely with the "Distribution of Wealth."

For the nineteenth century's eulogy of success as the fitting reward for effort, Marshall substituted the standard of mutual benefit. In the long run, he argued, the economic organizations that benefited society most would prevail.[42] An unshakable faith in moral commitment as a necessary corollary of reason and effort led him to an unrealisitc reliance upon philanthropy and led him, toward the end of his long life, to assure himself that social progress had occurred even though economic conditions remained essentially what they had been when he attacked them in the 1870s. Although he well understood the immediate profitability of economic selfishness as opposed to the long-range and less tangible benefits of social altruism, Marshall never gave up hope that the wealthy would correct the deficiencies of private enterprise by sharing their own access to nature, culture, and recreation with ordinary people. Marshall was convinced that the aggressive qualities that promoted success in business were part of a flow of surplus energy, not unlike surplus capital, which could be turned toward social melioration as an investment that would yield the businessman psychological satisfactions greater than making money.[43] As long as there were businessmen like Charles Booth and Seebohm Rowntree, who did assume such social responsibilities, Marshall's expectations were not entirely fanciful.

While Marshall expected the wealthy to engage in meliorative activities, the universities were to train reforming economists who would attack social and economic problems scientifically. Rational goodwill remained the major virtue in Marshall's hierarchy of social values, but he saw that without specialized skills, good intentions were insufficient. The newest thrust in social reform in the early 1880s involved idealistic young people, perhaps best exemplified by the undergraduates living in settlement houses, who attempted to treat poverty symptomatically. Marshall warned them that reform efforts would be futile without an understanding of the larger causes. In 1885 he concluded his inaugural address by promising to increase the number of Cambridge men concerned with social suffering and with making available "to all the material means of a refined and noble life."[44]

Beyond the teaching of economists, Marshall wanted the universities to teach economics to future businessmen. Marshall's campaign in 1902 to introduce a separate Cambridge tripos in economics and political science was successful because he solicited and won support from the industrial and commercial communities. Cambridge had suffered a decline in collegiate income and was seeking an increased endowment base for the university in order, *inter alia,* to promote new studies. And, it is interesting that Marshall's campaign was not directed to the businessman's altruism, but to his self-interest in improving his future prospects.[45]

While Jevons and earlier political economists had emulated the deterministic physical sciences, thereby strengthening the social status quo, beginning in the 1870s economists who wanted a rigorous methodology consistent with reformist purposes turned to the dynamic and evolutionary epistemology inherent in the inductive techniques of the genetic sciences. It was not until the 1890s that similar models became available in the new physics to encourage rather than inhibit the reforming and voluntarist interests of the new social scientists.[46] At the turn of the century, the static image of the world suggested by mechanics gave way to an evolutionary view, first in astronomy and then in the fundamental analysis of atoms. Although in the early 1870s Clerk Maxwell had rejected the notion that future physical science would be a "mere magnified image of the past," he expected simply increased knowledge of an essentially static physical world.[47] But by the century's end, instead of viewing reality as an ordered structure requiring revelation through the reflecting order of mind, many physicists had come to believe with W. C. D. Whetham, a Cavendish Fellow and historian-philosopher of science, that the function of physics was "merely" to construct mental models of phenomena, testable by their internal consistency and their "concordance with the results of further experiment."[48] The question of whether such models corresponded to the "ultimate reality behind phenomena," and whether "indeed there be any ultimate reality," was relegated to metaphysics outside the province of natural science.[49] As Whetham described it, and as most physicists have come to believe subsequently, the real purpose of science is not to penetrate an "ultimate reality" but rather to find connections that would make it possible to correlate phenomena. "Explanation," then, would be no more than a restatement of a particular "phenomenon in terms of other phenomena which previously are familiar to the mind, and therefore appear to be better understood." The use of a model, therefore, introduced order into what would otherwise be intellectual confusion by allowing for a "systematic and progressive use of natural resources."[50]

The new scientific models helped the new social scientists' efforts to bring theory and practice together by allowing them to impose rational direction on the randomness of reality and to ignore the deterministic fatalism implicit in earlier scientific assumptions. Disciplines committed to discovering how social and economic processes might be made more efficient and more humane were now liberated from a view of science that had treated what existed as if it ought to exist. After all, Marshall had become an economist precisely to achieve such a liberation by putting "mankind in the saddle" over the "things" that dominated them.[51] He had been disturbed in the late 1860s by the trend in psychology toward a mechanistic epistemology that denied self-consciousness. In two unpublished papers written before 1870, Marshall spoke on behalf of free will and for an evolutionary methodology that would make possible more accurate phenomena of mind.[52] Biology, he felt, provided precise methods for the comprehensive and comparative measurement of changing data, and Marshall saw the future of economics foreshadowed in the biologist's treatment of problems genetically, in their own time and place.

Evolution gave Marshall a social and ethical theory in which individual attempts at self-sufficiency yielded increasingly to the greater rewards of mutual responsibility. He adopted the biological concepts of complex, interdependent, and evolutionary forces, and rejected the physical metaphors that tried to explain economic tendencies crudely as pressures toward a "mechanical equilibrium."[53] A holistic concept of society, a study of economic history, and a psychology appreciative of the subtlety, complexity, and unpredictability of human nature despite its rational potential, precluded for Marshall an economic science as accurate and precise as nineteenth-century physics. Any attempt to reduce disparate social and economic phenomena to absolute laws imposed rigid and inappropriate models upon constantly changing economic processes. While in America John Bates Clark used marginal analysis to describe a static market controlled by determined and predictable forces, Marshall's marginal and quasi-static analysis, unlike Clark's, never confused a simplified segment of economic experience, artificially isolated for analytical convenience, with an entire evolving economy.[54]

Marshall made economics into the kind of developmental science that collected, arranged, and reasoned about particular classes of facts before summarizing their uniformities in inferential statements of economic tendencies. Absolute "a priori reasoning" was rejected in favor of detailed, statistical, verifiable evidence collected and examined through sophisticated graphic and comparative techniques. Theory was simply a useful tool to aid in reasoning about those motives that were measurable, but Marshall dismissed the positivists' quests for a deductive social science.[55] Economic problems had no exact precedents; they had to be solved by studying the correlations of multiple events at many different levels. The effectiveness of economics in dispatching problems depended on "access to a vast mass of facts" that would check one another as part of a cumulative store of current data.[56]

When the economist disentangled "the interwoven effects of complex causes" through a "wide and thorough study of facts" and through general reasoning, that alone was "economics proper."[57] Marshall invented graphic statistics to display the mass of information necessary for generalization and for forestalling any simplistic assignment of causality to limited and partially understood events. As Marshall anticipated, this technique became especially useful in showing percentages of increase or decline in one sector of the economy as compared to others.[58] Through short steps of inductive and deductive reasoning, Marshall arrived at "laws" applicable only to unique problems. These lawlike statements, analogous to the descriptions of tides rather than to the exact laws of gravitation, were no more than selected phenomena in a very narrow "range of circumstances" existing together temporarily in a given location and moment. Every "change in social conditions," Marshall insisted, required a "new development of economic doctrines."[59]

The publication of Marshall's *Principles of Economics* in 1890 electrified theorists and activists. Every major newspaper applauded the birth of a "new" and "revolutionary" economics, and *The Times,* overcoming its tradition of understatement, predicted that Marshall's book would become the authoritative work for the next generation.[60] When L. L. Price reviewed the *Principles* in the *Economic Journal* (March 1892), he reflected the consensus of contemporary economists that the work effectively ended a period of controversy and instituted a period of construction in that it resolved all major methodological disputes and provided a theoretical context in which the processes of production, distribution, and consumption could be studied together for the first time in their simultaneous operation.[61] All the great economists of the next generation, including Keynes, Schumpeter, and Knight, were to agree that the *Principles* was the critical turning point in the development of their discipline.[62] As late as 1931, Paul Homan, the American economist at Cornell, could conclude that "so far as there is today any generally accepted body of economic doctrine it is largely what Marshall made it. For a generation . . . economists have been engaged in modifying, interpreting, extending, and in general, embroidering Marshall's economics." Homan accurately described Marshall's extraordinary influence upon the profession he had done so much to create by observing that "one can hardly differ radically with Marshall and still be regarded as thoroughly intelligent." Subsequently, "for the dissenters and nonconformists, Marshall had been very generally the point of departure."[63] Even Marshall's severest critics have admitted that in 1890 his work was unquestionably original and the extent of his influence over the next three decades astonishing. Joan Robinson, Keynes's brilliant and formidable student, complained that the "search for Marshall's hidden assumptions has occupied a whole generation, and almost threatened at one time to turn the English economists into a school of higher-critical theologians." And though she rejected the Victorian certitudes about reason and character to which Marshall clung, her stipulation that an economist had to have "a strong interest in human welfare" has a distinctly Marshallian ring.[64]

Marshall shared the dominant view, which was largely correct until World War I, that what occurred at the universities would shape public and private life. He was himself the product of the tradition launched at Cambridge by the teaching revolution of the 1860s, which stressed the training of leaders rather than scholars, and his many friends at Oxford had been taught "citizenship" there.[65] In 1903 Marshall was pleased to report to the Royal Commission on the Aged Poor that the "best educated and most intelligent minds in England, the students at Oxford and Cambridge," were becoming informed social reformers.[66] Marshall's ambitions for university students were fulfilled to remarkable degrees. Unprecedented numbers of economists, statesmen, civil servants, educators, and writers went forth from the universities to attack social problems vigorously and successfully. University-trained specialists replaced their amateur predecessors in finance, government, and journalism with an authority that was rarely challenged. When, in the 1930s, Keynes succeeded in persuading governments that economic fluctuations must be controlled in the interest of public welfare, he was carrying out the lessons he had learned when he was Marshall's most precocious student at Cambridge.[67] Through his ascendant influence in the universities and in the new professional societies over a period of three decades, Marshall not only posed the problems that absorbed economists but offered the techniques for solving them as well.

Next to the university itself, the Royal Economic Society, founded by Marshall in 1890 as the British Economic Association, provided a forum and an organ, *The Economic Journal,* for the continued association and mutual cooperation of reformers interested in translating economic principles into effective social innovation.[68] The movement to form an economic association for the

"advancement of theory, . . . consolidation of economic opinion,
. . . encouragement of historical research, and . . . criticism and
direction of industrial and financial policy" began in 1887,[69] although the association was not founded until Marshall convened
a meeting of some two hundred influential people at University
College, London, on November 21, 1890. Marshall made it clear
that he desired no "standard of orthodoxy" since "economics was
a science, and an 'orthodox science' was a contradiction in
terms." He proposed that the new association start "from an absolutely catholic basis," including every school of economics and
promoting economic knowledge by frank discussion, free from
the kind of controversy that had so long impeded progress.[70]
While a reserve power to reject applicants was given to the council, it is testimony to Marshall's influence that this power was
never used. The Royal Economic Society remained a genuinely
open body attracting not only professional economists but a variety of lay persons seriously concerned with economic problems.[71]

If we accept Geoffrey Millerson's reasonable definition of a
profession as a "type of higher grade, nonmanual occupation,
with both subjectively and objectively recognized occupation
status, possessing a well-defined area of study or concern and
providing a definite service, after advanced training and education," then economics was not a profession until Marshall made it
one.[72] The move toward professionalization was accelerated in
1894 when the British Association for the Advancement of Science was informed by its committee on economic training that in
the previous two years there had been a marked increase in the
popular and academic demand for lectures on economics and
allied subjects.[73] In 1901 the Bachelor of Science (Economics)
degree was introduced at the University of London and the first
finals exam was given in 1904.[74] By 1907, W. J. Ashley was explaining the definite revival in economic studies as a result of
growing interest in social questions and the need for more systematic training for municipal and political administration. Although a chair of political economy had been established at
Owens College, Manchester, in the 1860s and at Edinburgh in
1871, it was not until Marshall became professor of political economy at Cambridge in 1885 that any of the major universities

"secured in its chair of economics an effective head of a living department of university study."[75] Chairs were then established at Toronto in 1888, Liverpool in 1891, Glasgow in 1896, followed by Birmingham, Leeds, and Bristol. In 1903, after lobbying among influential figures in every area of life, Marshall established at Cambridge an independent school and a separate tripos in economics and political science.[76]

As "the most distinguished economist in England," Marshall actively influenced policy through his role in Parliamentary Commissions of Inquiry in the 1880s and 1890s.[77] As a member of the Royal Commission on Labour from 1891 to 1894, he drafted those sections of the final report dealing with trade unions, minimum wages, and the irregularity of employments. The Gold and Silver Commission in 1887, the Royal Commission on the Aged Poor in 1893, and the Indian Currency Committee in 1899 heard Marshall as an expert witness. He also prepared Memoranda on Taxation for the Royal Commission on Local Taxation in 1899; and in 1903 he wrote a free-trade Memorandum for the Treasury which was published by Lloyd George in November 1908 as "The Fiscal Policy on International Trade."[78] Marshall also signed the free-trade *Manifesto* drafted by J. S. Nicholson, professor of political economy at Edinburgh; F. Y. Edgeworth, editor of the *Economic Journal;* and Charles Francis Bastable, professor of political economy at Dublin, and published in *The Times* on August 15, 1903. It is hardly surprising that politicians resented the economists's intrusion into policy matters. Marshall anticipated criticism of the *Manifesto* on the grounds that economists ought not to presume to speak on matters largely political, but his response, characteristically, was that economists must always "speak decidedly" about those issues in which they were specially competent.[79] He was adamantly opposed to the prime minister's contention that economists endangered their scientific authority in economics by participating in political quarrels.[80] On the contrary, Marshall, driven by a strong sense of public service, continued before the war to study industry, distribution, money, and value in unprecedented and objective detail so that he might "speak decidedly" on behalf of economics as a reforming instrument.

5.

Economic Analysis: Means and Ends

All social scientists in the late nineteenth and early twentieth century, whether revolutionary or revisionist, wanted to develop objective disciplines to remedy the unprecedented problems thrown up by changing social conditions. Marshall's requirement that theory be a means of acquiring "power to order and arrange knowledge, especially with reference to the eternal opposition of forces impelling people to do, and forces holding them back," was accepted by his contemporaries because they agreed that social forces were clearly out of control.[1] Differences among the various social scientists came from their divergent identifications of critical "forces"; from their assignments of social priorities; and from their selections of the purposes that the ordering "power" should serve.

Quarrels about policy generally centered on methodological disputes. The reason for this lay in the pervasive conviction that social science could be protected by a logical and empirical methodology from external pressures and ideological pleading. Although the substantive issues were reducible to irreconcilable psychological and sociological assumptions, the substance was often obscured by the form. This dispute over ends and means became a raging quarrel that culminated in 1910-1911 as a national issue. On one side were the reforming, liberal social scientists Marshall, John Maynard Keynes, A. C. Pigou, and L. T. Hobhouse and, on the other, the revisionist, conservative disciples of the eugenicist, Francis Galton. Although centered upon method, the real issue was nature versus nurture. Both camps of social scientists drew their evidence from the new biology, but the eugenicists' data upheld biological determinism, while the reformers' data demonstrated that a superior social and economic environment would improve human nature and behavior.

The eugenicists' case for nature, rooted in Darwinian theories of natural selection, was proven, so they contended, by applying statistical order to the laws of chance characteristic of heredity. Beginning with Galton, the eugenicists treated the various natural and social sciences as if they differed only in the degree to which they correlated cause and effect statistically. Galton, a half-cousin and close friend of Charles Darwin, founded a school late in his career when, at 67, he published his *Natural Inheritance* (1889) proposing correlation as a precise tool of biological and social analysis. In common with the later social psychologists, Galton moved from a medical training to an understanding of progress as the control of undesirable biological tendencies.[2]

Since the founding of the Statistical Society of London in 1834, statistics had been used as a means of reducing random phenomena to a regular and predictable order, aesthetically and psychologically satisfying. Quételet's "l'homme moyen" was actually considered to be a "type of beauty."[3] Galton adopted Quételet's normal law of error in his *Hereditary Genius* (1869) to measure genius and ability on the a priori assumption that such a law applied to "nature's magnitudes,"[4] even though George Boole, the eminent Cambridge mathematician, had described that law more accurately in 1854 as the law of "the equal distribution of ignorance."[5] At first, recognizing that chance played a major role in hereditary transmission of qualities, Galton wanted "the laws of chance" and the "statistical methods that are based upon them" to disclose the conditions under which heredity acts.[6] By 1907, in his Herbert Spencer Lecture at Oxford, Galton had moved from statistical description to an argument for "interference with the pitiless courses of Nature" to improve the racial qualities of mankind.[7] Galton's faith in the determining force of heredity meant that natural random selection had to be directed to socially desirable ends through a scheme by which only nationally desirable physical and mental qualities would be reproduced in future generations. To Galton and the eugenicists, physical, economic, social, and educational opportunities were essentially irrelevant to the improvement of man's hereditary stock.

Galton's proof that nature was stronger than nurture began in 1876 with his invention of psychometric instruments for measuring and correlating physical sensations and mental, physical, and behavioral qualities. The first anthropometric laboratory was set up by Galton in 1884 at the International Health Exhibition in London to measure "Human Form and Faculty."[8] Galton's correlations used mathematical laws to arrive at the "Jewish" and other "types" presented through composite photographs first published in *Photographic News,* April 17, 1885.[9] Galton became convinced that these portraits were like Quételet's "l'homme moyen." Much more than averages, they were "pictorial equivalents of those elaborate statistical tables out of which averages are deduced."[10]

It is hardly surprising that Marshall and other liberal social scientists reacted angrily against a method that reduced complex, unique, individual qualities to social and ethnic caricatures. Galton's credit as a scientist was reduced further for the reforming social scientists when, at the turn of the century, he launched his "science" of eugenics for treating selective mating, birth and death rates, and heredity as mass problems with statistical solutions. Their opposition increased when the Eugenics Laboratory, created by Galton and directed by his leading disciple, Karl Pearson, published work that concluded that their data showed "little sensible effect of nurture, environment, and physique on intelligence."[11]

All the Eugenics Laboratory publications before the war contributed to the argument that mental deficiency was inherited. Since the feebleminded were sexually more prolific than other people, they were contributing to national degeneracy and should be prevented from reproducing. Of the many corollaries of this argument, one of the most distasteful for reforming social scientists was the view that medical progress mistakenly prolonged the lives of those who weakened the average quality of the race stock

to society's detriment.[12] It was even argued by the eugenicists that
social problems in the lower classes could only be alleviated by selective breeding since those problems were due to inferior biological stock.[13] As Galton emphasized in his Herbert Spencer Lecture, the good of the species had eminent priority over any individual goods; the "consciousness" of society would act for its own
advantage and it would be difficult to "overrate its power over the
individual in regard to any particular on which it emphatically
insists."[14] The most famous and most controversial study published by the Eugenics Laboratory was the memoir by Karl Pearson and Ethel M. Elderton in 1910 denying that children of alco-
holic parents were adversely affected by their parents' drinking.[15]
When *The Times* carried a summary of the memoir on May 21,
1910, Marshall rushed into an attack upon the accuracy of any
methods purporting to disprove environmental forces.

Two years earlier Marshall had appealed to William Bateson's
Mendelian biology to argue that "if it is true that good wheat
sown year after year on barren soil degenerates, why should it not
be true that the social life of many generations of parents—quite
independent of selection—affects the nerves, and the quality and
the character of later generations." Pearson's and Galton's methods had already been rejected by Bateson, the leading geneticist
of the early twentieth century. While Pearson and Galton dealt
with "averages," Bateson's work systematically analyzed individuals through breeding experiments with flora, fauna, rabbits,
and poultry.[16] When the Royal Society created an Evolution
Committee at the turn of the century, Bateson undertook precise
experiments in heredity and variation. His Report to the Committee concluded that the "properties of each character in each
organism have, as regards heredity and variation, to be separately
investigated, and for the present, generalisation in reference to
those properties must be foregone." There was simply insufficient
data to make any pronouncements on variation in heredity.[17]
Consistently, Bateson insisted that biology must be an "exact
science." But "exactness" was "not always attainable by numerical precision: there have been students of Nature, untrained in
statistical nicety, whose instinct for truth save them. . . ."

Bateson never denied that studies of heredity and variation "*must* be built of statistical data," but he wanted the ground to be prepared by "specific experiment" which answers "specific questions." Galton and Pearson's false methodological assumptions came, Bateson charged, from their lack of training as naturalists.[18] From seeds in the same pod, he argued, "may come sweet peas climbing five feet high while their own brothers lie prone upon the ground. The stick will not make the dwarf peas climb, though without it the tall can never rise." When applied to social problems the biologist's knowledge meant that "education, sanitation and the rest" were opportunities that must be given.[19]

The recognition that the quality of the parents' physical and mental life must affect the qualities of their children, was all, Marshall claimed, that "we 'social people' want."[20] In *The Times,* the *Journal of the Royal Statistical Society,* the *Cambridge Review,* and the *British Medical Journal,* Marshall, Keynes, Pigou, and the physiologist and surgeon Victor Horsely, attempted to repudiate the eugenicists' conclusions by questioning the precision of their statistical analysis, frequency curves, correlative coefficients, sampling, data, classification, and mathematics. From May 1910 until January 1911, the controversy continued furiously in popular and scholarly publications and in L. T. Hobhouse's critical discussion of the "Value and Limit of Eugenics" in his *Social Evolution and Political Theory* (1911).

The revelation of appalling conditions of national health among Boer War recruits, dramatized further by Booth's and by Rowntree's discoveries that approximately one-third of the population lived below what middle-class observers thought of as "subsistence," meant that any discussion of efficient remedies was bound to attract national attention. The eugenicists, just like the reforming and revisionist social scientists, believed that they were serving a higher social morality, and they certainly never intended to provide a convenient justification for the status quo. But eugenics, with its promise of a higher level of national efficiency at no cost to the old social order, may have been particularly attractive to those people with essentially conservative inclinations. When the eugenicists asked for a planned reduction of the biologically bereft, easily identified as the poor, they struck a responsive chord within the comfortable classes whose customary social and economic arrangements had been threatened by discontent since the 1890s.

From 1880 Karl Pearson had been a socialist with a reform ethic and a view of work and individual dignity very similar to Marshall's. The Boer War was for Pearson, as for many other Englishmen, a turning point in his life. Beginning with his *National Life from the Standpoint of Science* (1900), Pearson jettisoned his belief in continued social progress toward a humane society and adopted instead a form of natural selection that saw civilization as the result of race rivalry in which the physically and mentally fitter survived.[21] Assuming that such a struggle was inevitable, if not desirable, Pearson became devoted to eugenics as the method of improving Britain's racial stock in the future. From 1900 Pearson abandoned two interests that had consumed his attention for twenty years: fundamental social reform and the methodological foundations of science. He set out, instead, to discover statistical methods that would persuade public opinion of the urgent need to adopt eugenic population controls.

The introspective concern with methodology for the first decade and a half of the twentieth century—the great debate about which tools and methods were most appropriate to the differentiating social sciences—centered not only upon the limits that were to be measured but upon the meaning of measurement. Until the pressures of World War I created social and economic policies that temporarily outran existing theory, the discussion about method in the social sciences was, in a larger sense, a debate about whether the sacrifice of individuals, groups, ideas, or institutions was really necessary for the control of the present and the future. Bertrand Russell called attention to the political uses of the new sciences in his "Politics of a Biologist," a discussion of George Chatterton-Hill's *Heredity and Selection in Sociology* (1907). Although agreeing with eugenicists like Chatterton-Hill that the birthrate had become the main factor in selection, Russell opposed their social Darwinism by suggesting that population growth was controlled, in effect, by economic motives. Society,

then, had to be organized so as to provide education and opportunities necessary for distinguishing desirable from undesirable
parents.[22] Like Marshall, Russell was unwilling to find "desirability" in an accident of social position.

The statistical method was generally understood in the nineteenth century to be an ordering device that demonstrated the
uniformities believed to exist in nature. Statistics were used to discover the nature and extent of a particular set of conditions only
when pressing problems required precise information as a necessary condition for their solution. This was especially true in medicine and public health. To William Farr, in 1871 president of the
Statistical Society and commissioner of the census, statistics were
an instrument of observation which revealed the incidence of disease and mortality so that they might be controlled. William
Ogle, the physician whose specialty was nervous diseases, used
quantitative data to relate health to occupation in the 1880s.

In the social sciences, the assumption that society moved
according to progressive laws of regular development led, especially in the various statistical societies, to a use of figures as proof
of that progress.[23] Statistical theorists uncritically accepted the
prevailing epistemology which confused what was known with
what actually existed. This epistemological confusion had been
supported by the fulfilled ambitions of nineteenth-century mathematicians. William Whewell, who dominated mathematical
studies at Cambridge from the 1820s to the 1860s, had found perfect agreement between the order of the mind and the physical
order of nature, while his eminent contemporary George Boole
had equated the laws of thought with the laws of mathematics
and the laws of nature.[24] The knowing subject and the objective
world he attempted to know were united in what John Tyndall
observed with admiration as the "visual record of the creator's
logic."[25]

The new physics, biology, and mathematics, however, urged
separation of epistemology and ontology. Darwin, Mendel, the
atomic physicists, and the non-Euclidean mathematicians envisioned a realm in which apparent order was due to blind chance,

and the universe was but a fortuitous collection of random, irrational, and unpredictable events. The new sciences, emulated by the emerging social sciences, were saved from a frustrating encounter with disorder by probability theory that permitted the imposition of sufficient symmetry upon randomness so that future processes could be anticipated within set limits. Certain knowledge was no longer possible, but this did not mean that reality was an unstructured miscellany or that knowledge could not be verified objectively. The statistical character of knowledge assumed by probability theory denied positivist laws and adopted, instead, limited generalizations, but probability theory was entirely consistent with determinism. When James Clerk Maxwell, Ludwig Boltzmann, and Willard Gibbs introduced probability into the description of aggregate matter, they denied the possibility of absolute knowledge, but, at the same time, they reenforced the nineteenth-century mechanistic model of nature. In particular, their reduction of the physical quantities of heat and entropy to statistical mechanics made it appear as if other unsolved physical problems might be treated similarly.[26]

The recurrent patterns that nineteenth-century statisticians believed they found were incompatible with freewill assumptions. Quételet's data on rates of crime, marriage, and suicide troubled him because he could never decide whether his statistics really proved the absence of human freedom.[27] Boole's study of Quételet's social statistics led him to wonder if there might be a general theory of probability by which the social scientist could predict events successfully. Boole tried to resolve the dilemma by granting individuals free will, while considering the effect of their behavior in terms of repeatable sequences that implied a larger deterministic scheme. To do this Boole resorted to the standard device by which nineteenth-century deterministic theories allowed for individual activism: he made individual voluntarism compatible with "regularity in the motions of the system of which he forms a component unit," and reserved the necessitarian rules of probability theory for the behavior of large masses of men which, he felt, "actually exhibit(s) a very remarkable degree of regularity." Social science, then, could use statistics to find general lawlike truths without denying a sphere of individual autonomy.[28] This tradition was also followed by Francis Galton. Although Galton never claimed precision for biological or social statistics, his binomial symmetrical distribution of frequencies, later extended by Karl Pearson to any value of probability, in effect imposed determinism upon the process of heredity.[29] For Galton and Pearson as for Whewell and Boole half a century earlier, probability continued to be a deductive mathematical mechanism for clarifying repetitive patterns, rather than an empirical technique for amassing data from experience.

Marshall's inductive use of statistics broke sharply with the a priori tradition of late nineteenth-century physicists and eugenicists. Especially in the field of chemistry, Marshall found that scientists were no longer interested in formulating general laws or in precisely describing generalized processes, but rather in using quantitative techniques to classify, identify, and characterize substances.[30] Marshall borrowed the distinction between "quantitative" and "qualitative" analysis from chemistry in order to resolve the inductive-deductive quarrel by finding both processes essential without giving precedence to one over the other. By 1890 Marshall succeeded in imposing upon economists a general agreement about methodology: theoretical analysis and the search for facts were "like the left and right foot in walking," useless alone and strong in combination. In Marshall's judgment, "qualitative" analysis had already resulted in substantial agreement about the nature and consequences of various economic forces, but less progress had been made in discovering the "quantitative determination" of their relative strength. The result was that economics suffered from imprecise and incomplete data, a deficiency that could be remedied by the "slow growth" of thoroughly "realistic statistics."[31] Although Jevons had been the first economist to call for a statistical economics in trying to relate the periodicity of commercial crises to sunspots and in contending that a permanent rise in prices was due to the depreciation of gold, he had arbitrarily selected figures to support deductive assumptions.[32] In place of this nineteenth-century kind of statistical analysis, which merely speculated about the distributive functions in economic phenomena, Marshall wanted those phenomena separated, counted, indexed, and compared. To Marshall, statistics were either a test of what the economist hoped to find or an attempt to explore the complex relation between causes and effects by weighing economic factors in comparison with each other and through time.[33] Graham Wallas found Marshall's case for quantitative analysis so persuasive that he founded political science upon the growing store of comparable data about political behavior.[34]

The growth of quantitative economics that began in the 1890s was owing to many factors, including the resolution of methodological disputes and the clarification of concepts. Statistical techniques were improved; the number of those trained to use statistics in mathematical and economic analysis increased; the number of periodicals publishing studies using mathematical economics grew; and, the ranks of competent economists excited about using quantitative techniques for empirical purposes steadily expanded.[35] While the work of economists such as F. Y. Edgeworth, Gustav Cassell, and Knut Wicksell was important in many of these developments, Marshall was crucially involved in the active promotion of all of them. But above all the most distinctive feature of all Marshall's work, as Joseph Schumpeter correctly maintained, was his "vision of a theoretical apparatus" for effectively gripping "statistical fact" through an essentially "temporary structure" of tentative conclusions.[36]

It was in mathematics that Marshall found his theoretical tool for describing the relations between economic phenomena. Despite his training in the deductive mathematics ascendant at Cambridge in the 1860s, Marshall never used mathematics, as Jevons did, to mirror the structure of knowledge and the configuration of reality. Like the econometricians of today, he felt that the use of mathematical models as systems of measurement or observations had actually to be tested against empirical results before such models could be accepted as scientific quantification.[37]

The existing gap that persists among different schools of economics today, and between economists and the public, may well be proportional to the abuse of Marshall's succinct criteria for applying mathematics to economics: "(1) Use mathematics as a shorthand language, rather than as an engine of inquiry. (2) Keep to them till you have done. (3) Translate into English. (4) Then illustrate by examples that are important in real life. (5) Burn the math. (6) If you can't succeed in 4, burn 3."[38] To encourage the greatest number of people to read economics, Marshall relegated his sophisticated mathematical apparatus to appendixes in the *Principles*.

In 1884, Jowett, who had encouraged the study of economics at Oxford, warned Marshall that mathematical forms and symbols should be kept to a minimum in the *Principles* because they were not "real instruments of discovery" but simply "a mode of expressing a few truths or facts." Marshall apparently never forgot Jowett's dictum that "Political Economy is human and concrete and should always be set forth in its best literary form."[39] Half his professional life was dissipated in laborious efforts to clarify the *Principles* through seven further editions. Early in his career as the first principal of University College, Bristol, a successful adult education experiment launched in 1877, Marshall conceived the mission of making economics intelligible to ordinary people whose minds, bodies, and pockets he hoped to enrich through his new social science. It was ironic that as soon as economists accepted Marshall's mathematical and graphic tools, they began to elaborate the specialized mathematics and argot that separated them increasingly from the wider public Marshall saw as the economist's only legitimate audience.

Unlike Marshall, nineteenth-century economists spoke to a much narrower audience. Instead of devising theory for explicit policy, they worked to construct an analytical system independent of any external influences or purposes. Walter Bagehot argued typically that economics must concern itself logically with analysis as the precondition for eventual understanding and activity. In 1876 he justified economists who avoided ethics, since they were properly describing only that part of human nature in which man was "the money-making animal."[40] But despite such disclaimers, classical political economists in fact adopted an ethical system that reduced motivation and behavior to a universal calculus of pleasure and pain; they confused their mechanistic psychology and utilitarian ethics with objective criteria of utility and value. An emphasis upon individual interests over social problems was readily adapted to an economic philosophy that often exaggerated individual opportunity by underestimating the vicious effects of poverty, ignorance, ill health, and futility upon individual judgment and will. Marshall, on the contrary, did not believe that objective analysis required moral neutrality and, in making his economics an ally of social ethics, he set the tone for the new social sciences. In 1885, Marshall unequivocally pledged his professorship at Cambridge to the duty of alleviating "lives dragged on through squalor and misery" and "haggard faces and stunted minds."[41] Five years later, Macmillan advertised Marshall's *Principles* as a work that gave unique attention to the "ethical" motives that influenced the ends people chose and the methods by which they pursued them.[42]

Until the 1880s most social scientists deceived themselves, as Bagehot had done, into believing that their premises and conclusions were rigorously objective and scientifically disinterested. But after 1880, with the exception only of traditionally positivistic sociology and anthropology, the social sciences committed themselves to ethical purposes and to the study of policies most likely to fulfill those purposes. This was true of Marshall's economics, James's psychology, McDougall's and Trotter's social psychology, L. T. Hobhouse's and A. J. Hobson's sociology, and Graham Wallas's political science. When the British sociologist T. S. Simey recently wrote that social science should be an amalgam of "science to give us techniques, and morals to give us a grasp of values," he was defending the position taken in the 1880s against using social science as a justification of existing, but not necessarily desirable, conditions.[43]

It is interesting that despite Marshall's intent, Milton Friedman contends that the *Principles* support a "positive," value-free economics "objective" in precisely the same sense as any of the physical sciences. Friedman is able to make this contention because he separates Marshall's analytical techniques from the explicit ethical and social purposes for which Marshall's economics existed in the first place. In the *Principles* Friedman finds, correctly, that the feasibility of theory can be tested only by its ability to predict, and that hypothetical assumptions, especially in concepts such as perfect competition, are irrelevant to the validity of the conclusions reached.[44] What Friedman fails to understand is that Marshall's use of economic theory and his technical concentration upon selected economic functions, such as prices, were no more than means to the larger end of increasing the quality of life. Jowett read the *Principles* more perceptively than Friedman was to do, and he saw immediately that Marshall had not only resolved the various and conflicting views of economists since the 1870s but the conflict between the "old state of industrial society and the new," by answering "explicitly the question so often asked: 'What is the relation of Political Economy to Ethics?' "[45] Indeed, "ethical considerations" were integral to Marshall's program of economic studies. When the Moral Science tripos at Cambridge was changed in 1897, economics was subordinated to his "ideals and aims."[46] The unity of analysis and ethics was reinforced when Marshall wrote the curriculum for the Economics and Political Science tripos at Cambridge in 1903.[47]

Marshall's revolutionary economics achieved a theoretical case for his ethical, reformist convictions by altering radically the three pivotal concepts of classical political economy: hedonism, utility, and value. Hedonistic psychology had led nineteenth-century political economists to reason that if the distinguishing attributes of human behavior were desire for pleasure and aversion to pain, then motives were measurable by a universal calculus that translated these common behavioral tendencies into "objective" economic criteria of private and public good. Marshall saw that simple hedonism could neither account for the complex behavior of different individuals, nor provide unassailable standards for recognizing what was ethically desirable. It was rather the individual's actual ability to satisfy his wants that decided the utility of any product for him. Marshall defined utility and value as subjective judgments expressed in money: some part of every important problem concerned "those actions and sacrifices which commonly have a money price."[48]

Prices and money could be assessed and compared, but the subjective nature of utility did not lend itself to generalization. Marshall made value depend on an individual's assessment of the final, or marginal, degree of utility that any commodity or service had for him.[49] The marginal utility of money was measured by the degree that income could, at any given time, either overcome an individual's aversion to increasing his efforts or persuade him to continue the discomfort already experienced in his work. Although he assumed that economic choices were based on reasoned experience,[50] Marshall took account of impulses and idiosyncratic desires, opinions, needs, and tastes through the concept of "elasticity of demand," a concept that Marshall did not invent, but which he refined and applied as a major device of economic analysis.[51] For Marshall, contraction and expansion within the economy depended on psychological preferences governed by income and living conditions, while demand responded to both variations in the price and availability of goods and the state of the economy. Although individual motives could never be known, the advantages and disadvantages of a particular economic choice could be measured at the "average of the money value it has for a class of people" to estimate "roughly the relative strength of the forces that tend to increase or diminish the supply of labor" in a particular "occupation *at the time and place*" under study.[52] No blind economic forces coerced the economy. Initially and ultimately everything depended upon the kinds of choices individuals made. Subjective judgments about utility and the actual cost of production were like two blades of the scissors together determining price.[53] When prices coincided with the cost of production, supply and demand tended to stability.

Marshall created a simplified, artificial, and quasi-static model of the economy to examine the role of value and of the forces acting upon value through four different periods of time. To Marshall, a stationary economic state was nothing more than a useful abstraction, a descriptive analytical tool for studying selected economic problems. John Stuart Mill had considered a static economic condition as an actual improvement over existing conditions,[54] but Marshall found such a state to be, not only inconceivable, but undesirable: "man is the end of production; and perfectly stable business would be likely to produce men who were little better than machines."[55] Throughout all his writings, and especially in the *Principles,* Marshall insisted that economic problems are "not mechanical but concerned with organic life and growth." Analogies from physical statics were always limited to the early stages of economic reasoning. Even when he dealt with such traditionally static concepts as the "national dividend" he was careful to define it as an income or flow, a "continuous stream" and not a "reservoir or store, or, in the narrow sense, a fund of capital...." When Marshall did use static methods to relate varying market periods to fluctuations in value, he warned that such analysis was safe only for relatively short periods of time.

Marshall saw the element of time as one of the economist's major difficulties, and the principle use of the static method was to classify economic problems provisionally with reference to the time required for their operation, while freezing forces relatively minor to the particular period of time selected for analysis. Admittedly arbitrary and artificial, this limited method permitted the economist to focus upon certain problems and, temporarily, to ignore others.[56] In the shortest or market period, supplies were fixed and price was determined by demand: in the short-run normal period, supply fluctuated while production remained constant under diminishing returns; during the long-run normal period supply became the amount a facility could produce while existing resources were developed in response to other changes in the economy; and, finally, in the longest period, changes occurred in those external variables such as population, growth, capital, technology, organization, information, efficiency, and tastes that influenced economic judgment and activity. Marshall's technical economics are neoclassical in that all four of his phases describe a fluctuating, but evolving, equilibrium between supply and demand; but Marshall left the classical model entirely when he made economic equilibrium depend

essentially upon the decision of producers and consumers to alter
their lives qualitatively.

Marshall had discovered marginal utility in the 1870s in relation to his "consumer's surplus," the difference between the
amount anyone was prepared to pay for a commodity and the
amount he actually paid.[57] Skeptical about legislation as the
principal corrective for economic problems, Marshall urged that
the consumer's surplus be increased by taxing industries with
diminishing returns to compel them to reduce unit costs, and by
subsidizing industries with increasing returns.[58] In general, Marshall believed that legislation should persuade rather than coerce
for two reasons: his desire to find self-regulatory controls already
functioning in efficient industries, and his fear that individual
responsibility for social reform would be eroded by government
intervention. Neither reason prevented him from supporting
active government aid to education, health, and welfare services,
nor would he condone private interests' denying to ordinary people those conditions of work and leisure requisite for a better life.

Marshall accepted government interference in the economy
only when his "standard of comfort," the minimum condition
necessary for increasing the efficiency of ordinary people in the
factory and in the marketplace, was violated. When an employer
tacitly accepted the economic guidance of a "subsistence level" of
wages, he denied Marshall's standard by treating the poor as if
they were morally unfit when, in fact, they were at an insur-
mountable economic disadvantage. Labor efficiency was not
compatible with managerial exploitation. On the contrary, Marshall argued, when people were deprived of opportunities for pursuing better lives, they became incapable of choosing any goals,
let alone acting upon them. Poverty and inefficiency were inextricably connected.

Marshall never mistook the effects of poverty for their causes.
Since the early nineteenth century, political economists had condemned poor relief as an unscientific and sentimental encourag-
ment of wanton population growth and declining wages. As late
as 1870 Jevons repeated the classical economists' warning against
improving the poor-law medical service since it would only lead

the poor to make "merry with their wages when well and strong, because other people would take care of them when sick and old."[59]

Marshall's position, on the contrary, was that the effect of poor relief was more likely to be "better living, more vigorous and better educated people, with greater earning power." Poverty was no crime but a "thing so detrimental to the state that it should not be endured." Where individuals were overcome by conditions beyond their control, the state must provide remedy. In 1893 Marshall called for an investigation of the entire poor-relief system by a Royal Commission made up in part of workingmen who would also share in relief administration and in the voluntary efforts of private agencies such as the Charity Organisation Society. While Marshall preferred poor relief to be administered by the C.O.S. as a semiofficial agency purged of the oligarchic structure that perpetuated the economic inequalities of an earlier time, he was prepared to accept even government-sponsored universal pension schemes rather "than things as they were."[60] By means of the law, Marshall believed, men could be provided with opportunities for developing their reason sufficiently to make moral choices, but legislation could not replace an individual's active responsibility for the welfare of his community. Socialism, or any other compulsory state support of the able, was undesirable because any impersonal agency of reform weakened further the moral character of both the irresponsible rich and the irresponsible poor.[61] But Marshall never criticized the collectivists' analysis of social problems, only their solution. Although he supported Lloyd George's Budget of 1909 because of its death duties and commitments to improvement in education, sanitation, employment, and recreation, he believed that the effect of purely political remedies was bound to be superficial: even the most specific compulsory legislation would be resisted if it were unacceptable to those it sought to change.

Marshall did not expect from either nature or law a harmony of interests, but he believed that the harmony essential to economic and social progress could be produced by cooperation between employers and employees. Marshall's distaste for controversy made his commitment to conciliation very strong. Rationalist psychology and his desire for an ethical society led him to ignore the growing opposition between industry and labor represented by the extension of trade unionism to the unskilled. There was no anticipation of modern conflict analysis in any of Marshall's writing because such analysis presupposes not only a Hobbesian view of society as an uneasy conjunction of irreconcilable interests but a recognition of human irrationality, as well. L. T. Hobhouse's *Morals in Evolution* (1906) examined the conflict of ideals, but not until Graham Wallas's *Human Nature in Politics* (1908) was there an analysis of the diversities of interest which developed as an intrinsic quality of the new pluralistic democracy.[62] Whenever Marshall encountered conflict, he offered reason, good faith, and the recognition of long-term self-interest as the essential elements of conciliation. During the strikes of 1887, Marshall had proposed that "Boards of Conciliation," composed of employers and employees from different areas, adjust wages after examining the complex conditions prevailing within their industries. The role of the government would be to collect and disseminate economic data required by the board to set fair rates of wages. In case of a deadlock, an independent arbiter would study the economic data and resolve the differences.[63] What was most crucial to Marshall about conciliation was its educational and moral force as a "powerful means of raising the working-classes...[and] their employers."[64] By the late 1890s Marshall had grown increasingly opposed to what he saw as obstructionist efforts by trade unions to restrict economic development,[65] but he always thought of collective bargaining as a legitimate trade-union function because he assumed that the common benefits of productive industry to both capital and labor were greater than the rewards of conflict.[66]

In recasting the "science of Political Economy as the science of Social Perfectability," Marshall's *Principles* attempted to fulfill his community's demand for a new social science.[67] During the same year that the *Principles* appeared, Patrick Geddes, a pioneer in twentieth-century sociology, analyzed the new contents and directions necessary for a scientific sociology according to criteria very similar to those Marshall proposed for economics. Urging a reconsideration of the central role of consumption in determining both the economic role and the nature of the consumer's life, Geddes insisted that the major question of practical economics was how to reconcile evolutionary trends with the maintenance of Marshall's "standards of comfort." His answer was that economics depended upon ethics and that economic behavior would grow increasingly "species-regarding" or "more altruistic, more moral."[68] In Geddes's view, biological and psychological evolution proceeded together. But in order to understand these interwoven processes, different sciences would have to analyze separate parts: the biologist would study the evolution of the species; the psychologist, the evolution of mind; the economist, the parallel development of concrete economic behavior; and the ethicist would examine the subjective meaning of all three phases. And finally, Geddes hoped for a new sociology to synthesize all these efforts successfully, so that complex social problems could be solved.

Marshall rejected sociology as too grandiose an attempt to comprehend and explain experience, let alone to prescribe sufficiently precise remedies for practical problems. Marshall's dismissal of sociology as an effective new social science ignored the similarity between his views and the melioristic social altruism that inspired sociologists such as Geddes and Hobhouse and, when the English Sociological Society was formed in 1903, he would not join. Although crediting sociology with a magnificent "aspiration," it seemed to him that sociologists were concerned either with prehistoric institutions or with the last new fashion in philanthropy, despite their ignorance of either early history or economics.[69]

Despite Marshall's strictures, Geddes apparently knew much more about economics than Marshall knew about sociology. Marshall's concept of the new sociology may have come from the Webbs for whom he had little regard largely because he viewed Sidney Webb as an "anti-theorist" filled with scorn for anything that involved "analytic refinement."[70] Marshall's hostility toward the Webbs was extended to their creation, the London School of Economics, which he mistakenly feared would become simply an institute for Fabian socialist propaganda, a kind of "engine for making people believe that a certain set of doctrines is true." This ran counter to Marshall's view of the university as an open academy where truth was pursued rather than propagated.[71] But despite his dismissal of sociology as an impractical, quasi-professional discipline, Marshall's economics were nevertheless implicitly part of a sociological system that belonged within the meliorist, moralistic social theory dominant in England until World War I.

Marshall's economics served as a liberalizing discipline in the three decades before the war, but the contents and hierarchies of economic priorities after the war inevitably demanded newer perceptions and different solutions. During the late nineteenth century, Marshall's endorsement of free enterprise had been contingent upon a more equable distribution of wealth and opportunities; by the time his last book, *Trade and Industry,* appeared in 1919, he had come to believe that the ideal and the real were coalescing when, in fact, social inequalities were growing. It is undeniable that Marshall clung stubbornly to rationalist theories of behavior which anticipated a genuine harmony of interests to be achieved in time. In order to recognize that his idealistic expectations were far from fulfilled, Marshall should have assessed more carefully not only the forces influencing all behavior but the processes affecting his own thinking. But even if he had returned to his undergraduate interest in psychology, the explanations of mind and behavior prevalent when he was devising the essential structure of his economics would hardly have altered either his assumptions or his ideals. While associationist psychology and utilitarian accounts of motives were being discarded in the 1880s, Marshall had already completed his critique of existing economics and his reformulation of a new system. But the complacency of his later years could not vitiate the genuinely liberal impulse that made him the remarkable founder of an economics with social welfare and self-respect as its ends. Marshall's economics, in common with the new psychology that he ignored, was dedicated unequivocally to moral reform.

PART III
What Can the Matter Be?
Mind, Body, and Morality

6.
Transitional Psychology, 1855-1890

The study of nineteenth-century psychology has suffered from two essentially ahistorical tendencies among historians. One group has arranged individual contributors to a progressively "scientific" development of psychology in a chronological sequence entirely separate from the intellectual traditions and the concrete social, economic, and political problems of the time. This hagiographic genre crudely reconstructs a dialogue between great men and traces their influence by identifying generations of teachers and students. But the hagiographers ignore the purposes and methods that informed particular psychological formulations. Another major tendency has viewed past developments as a mere prologue to the psychoanalytic, behaviorist, gestalt, and holistic theories that burgeoned after World War I. Although these seekers of origins have attempted to analyze the common perceptions, procedures, and conclusions that characterize different psychologies, their imposition of "modernist" principles of selection tends to distort their account. In both cases, historians have overlooked the emergence of a genuinely new psychology in the late nineteenth century as well as the larger revolution in the social and physical sciences of which the new psychology was part.

What actually happened during the course of the nineteenth century is that psychology was transformed from an epistemological study of how the world is known into an analysis of the mind as an active organism influencing its internal and external circumstances. The history of psychology since the seventeenth century falls into stages: the traditional, from the 1680s until 1855; the transitional, from 1855 until 1890; and the new, beginning in 1890.

Traditional psychology, as it developed from the late seventeenth century, included two contradictory models of mind. An associationist model supposed mind to be a collection and arrangement of simple sense impressions "associated" mechanically into distinct ideas and complex wholes. "Faculty" theorists, in contrast, believed that innate faculties or forms existed as the a priori furniture of the mind. By the nineteenth century, the dominant description of mind was derived from association theory, but faculty interpretations persisted too. Both schools imposed a structure on the mind that limited its function to the passive description, analysis, and prediction of the regularities of the physical world. They agreed that the mind passively received sensations that had been ordered so as to conform to the order of the external world.

Association and faculty psychology were both the analogues of the mechanistic and deductive physics that had begun in the seventeenth century. As late as the 1870s distinguished physicists were confidently rounding off the final decimal place in their allegedly complete understanding of a natural order they regarded as regular and wholly predictable. Influenced by this protracted Newtonian model, nineteenth-century psychologists explained mind as a mirror reflecting the objective and recurrent phenomena of the world.

The transitional phase in psychology began in the 1850s. As biologists challenged the physicists' interpretation of reality, psychologists too began to reexamine their assumptions. The genetic sciences, especially biology, rejected the closed mathematical equalities of the Newtonian universe and relied instead on a growing store of partial, novel data that revealed a changing and indeterminate world. In the dynamic metaphors of Darwinian biology, psychologists found a view of reality as a process to which active, adaptive organisms respond. Transitional psychologists learned from biologists to forsake static models, but biology could not offer a description of mind as intellectually and aesthetically complete as the one left behind.

The biologists' view of the world in evolutionary process was re-enforced, after the 1870s, by a new physics, chemistry, and mathematics built upon assumptions of probability rather than certitude and able to utilize incomplete data. When, in the late nineteenth century, William James applied these new scientific attitudes to an inquiry into the nature and interaction of mind and body, a revolutionary new psychology emerged. That new psychology sought to solve the chronic dualism of mind and matter by showing that the active individual mind could control its own development. If mind were indeed a purposive and efficient force in the creation of an individual's conditions and life, then the social scientists' reformist ambitions could be fulfilled.

This chapter deals with the assumptions, methods, and purposes of the transitional psychology that grew out of the successful application of biological techniques to the study of sensation, neural structure, and the brain. Transitional figures such as Herbert Spencer, Henry Sidgwick, A. J. Balfour, and W. K. Clifford confronted similar problems of definition in their attempt to understand and explain thinking and behavior. First of all, they were uncertain about either selecting an appropriate methodology or the "scientific" status of their inquiries. And, when they tried to make psychology a prelude to ethics, they floundered in the old debate over the relation between mind, body, and morality. Transitional psychologists raised questions they could not answer. But their experiments with a variety of apparently irreconcilable theoretical assumptions and empirical procedures led James to develop a psychology centered on the potential of the rational, purposeful individual.

Herbert Spencer was the first transitional psychologist to use genetic and comparative methods to portray the mind as an organism ceaselessly adapting to its environment. But his inveterate system building could not appeal to reformers whose understanding of the events of a changing world precluded any explanatory scheme governed by determined ends. Spencer's substitution of a biologically rooted, allegedly new psychology failed to influence the new social sciences because his a priori convictions about the necessity of progress led him to contort the empirical evidence upon which he claimed to rely. Initially, his psychology rested upon faculty assumptions and then, after 1870, on a form of association theory modified by Lamarckian theories of inheritance. Acquired characteristics, programmed into the nervous system by an aversion to pain and a preference for pleasure, were progressively transmitted to successive generations. In this natural progress, Spencer limited the role of mind to the integration of changing experience through associative mechanisms.

The potentially "new" qualities of Spencer's psychology were restricted by his retention of the static classificatory scheme characteristic of both association and faculty psychology.[1] Needing a theory of mind that would corroborate his a priori belief in progress, he found it initially in phrenology. Franz Joseph Gall had developed phrenology to explain the relation between the structure of the mind and behavior by isolating separate, physically identifiable faculties in the brain. Spencer found Gall's interpretation of faculty psychology useful as a method for resolving the utilitarian conflict between individual good and social good.[2] Through "moral physiology" Spencer combined a belief in an innate moral faculty with a conviction that social development was progressive. Relying, characteristically, on proof by analogy, Spencer argued that both individualism and an organic identity of interest between the individual and society were increasing simultaneously. As individuals became more independent, they necessarily evolved to a "higher" stage, characterized by greater sociality, through the biological mechanisms of differentiation, specialization, and the division of labor.

But faculty psychology, with its fixed forms in the mind, is not really compatible with progressive theory. By 1873 Spencer had almost abandoned it entirely for a theory of mental development modeled first upon embryology, and later upon association theory.[3] A faculty treatment of the dualism of mind and matter appeared in Part I of the *Principles of Psychology* (1873), while in Part IV Spencer argued that the development of both consciousness and matter formed an unbroken series of changes out of which intelligence somehow arises. The model of mind that Spencer ultimately found most attractive was a central railway station with complex switches, shuttles, and lines—one of the few Spencerian theories derived from experience: his own, as a railway engineer.

When Spencer was criticized for constructing an a priori account of mental evolution, he responded that he always gathered data inductively before proceeding to synthetic or deductive interpretations.[4] But there was, in fact, a considerable gulf between Spencer's professed principles and his actual practices, and it is clear that a priori convictions guided his selection of data, analyses, and his conclusions. In the third edition of the *Principles* (1880), Spencer claimed to dismiss "every metaphysical doctrine at variance with ordinary experience,"[5] but Henry Sidgwick correctly perceived in the *Principles* a "large mixture of hypothetical physics and questionable metaphysics."[6]

Spencer contributed to a "new" psychology by transforming the prevailing static theory of mind as a mechanism operating according to the association of ideas into a theory that described mind as adapting to the changes in experience. In applying evolution to psychology, he modified the mathematical model of mind. Although he still saw mind as a mirror, the images it reflected now changed with time. But to avoid the Darwinist implications of accidental change, he tried to prove that the whole evolutionary process, including that of mind, was governed by a determinate, progressive order moving through fixed stages to a known end. Implicit in this was a value judgment about the inherent desirability of his "law of progress."[7] Confusing process with progress, Spencer continued the old social scientists' view of change as a fulfillment of universal moral prescriptions. On the whole, though, Spencer's biological modification for a time strengthened the old mechanistic psychology by making it compatible with evolution.

Unlike Spencer, Darwin never presumed the existence of determined tendencies nor did he deny particular methods of adaptation and survival. Darwin's concept of "variation" had no teleological connotations and meant only that those individuals best adjusted to their surroundings were likely to survive; it did not preclude modification, or reform, of those surroundings. Besides that, the Darwinian "struggle for existence" never predicated any special conditions of competition, so that the struggle could occur not only among individuals and groups but also between individuals and their circumstances.

For the new reforming social scientists, "natural selection" meant only that if favorable variations occurred within a population, the individuals with such variations had a superior chance for survival. They interpreted Darwinian theory as support for their efforts to provide those who were unable to compete because of unfair handicaps with sufficient health, education, and leisure so that they would have an equal opportunity in the struggle for existence. Reforming psychologists turned to biology for a methodology for measuring, classifying, and comparing a rapidly accumulating body of data.

Psychology became a "branch of biology" in the last two decades of the nineteenth century,[8] and nearly every psychological writer used biological metaphors. But few agreed about which, if any, biological methods could be applied to the study of mental phenomena. Methodological disputes were really about the effect of methodology upon the initial selection and ultimate resolution of particular problems. Should psychology rely upon experiment, direct observation, classification, comparative and cultural analysis, or introspection? Should psychologists look for laws of the mind, or should they observe behavior? It was not until a generation later that they clearly understood that one's method both determined and was determined by one's purpose.

In the transitional period from 1855 to 1890, four independent departures from traditional psychology competed for acceptance in the United States, Europe, and England. The first of these methods, introspection, was perpetuated by such influential English psychologists as James Ward and G. F. Stout. The second began at midcentury as the phrenology fad, and it stimulated the first serious anatomical and neurological studies of the brain. Almost simultaneously, in German laboratories under Gustav Fechner and Wilhelm Wundt, psychophysics grew out of the measurement of sensory processes in relation to behavior.[9] And the fourth, or comparative method, was introduced by Darwin in his *Descent of Man* (1870) as the study of animals, infants, and primitives for insights into the origin and nature of more complex civilized adults.

Because they wanted to have an impact upon actual thinking and behavior, nearly every psychological writer after 1870 worried considerably about method. Although differing on many basic questions, they agreed that psychology must be a prolegomenon to the construction of any future epistemology and ethics. For only psychology, they felt, could understand and "investigate its own assumptions."[10] Indeed, until World War I, psychologists investigated the "fundamental suppositions and method" of psychology in the hope that a sound philosophy could eventually grow from psychological roots.[11] The culmination of this kind of effort was early twentieth-century pragmatism, the most systematic and persuasive, as well as the last, attempt to compel philosophy and ethics to depend upon an essentially rationalist psychology.

In their common quest for a method, nearly all transitional psychologists agreed further that the validity of any particular techniques or process had to be determined "scientifically." But the problem was that although the "exact and classificatory sciences, by the brilliance of their methods and results" filled the psychologist with "envy" as J. A. Stewart observed, mental phenomena were in fact "not definite enough to be the objects of a science." One solution was to define psychology exclusively as a method or "*critique*" in the sense of "a certain thoughtful attitude" which did not have to meet the rigorous criteria characteristic of the "exact" sciences.[12] This solution was unacceptable to many late nineteenth-century psychologists because they continued to hope that psychology could, like the deductive sciences, provide a "clear" and "unambiguous" explanation of events "as they successively present themselves" to the observer.[13] This traditional expectation was confounded by the growing recognition that there were no longer any universally recognized "clear" and "unambiguous" explanations even in the physical sciences, and that the concrete phenomena were rarely so accommodating as to arrange themselves in orderly series.

Having lost confidence in the certainties once accepted as corollaries of religion and mechanistic science, transitional psychologists groped for some quasi-objective criteria in the subjective realm of choice where they had been marooned. Since the most promising sources of such criteria were the new experimental sciences, it was natural to seek justification by experiment. But when experiment was introduced into psychology in the 1860s, it was limited narrowly to the German psychophysicists' isolation of behavioral phenomena. The Germans and their disciples in England and the United States were enormously successful in developing techniques for collecting data, but they were reluctant to generalize. Furthermore, they had no theoretical apparatus for interpreting or applying that data. Beginning with the appearance of Fechner's *Elemente der Psychophysik* (1860), psychological experiment was equated with the measurement of sensations. Even in the subsequent work of Wundt and the students who flocked to study with him from all over the world, Fechner's influence resulted in an exclusive concentration upon method, so that ends were either confused with means or indefinitely postponed. When in 1887 W. S. Hall launched his *Journal of Psychology* to serve experimentalists, William James complained, with some justification, that psychophysicists thought that the way to save "their souls psychologically lies through the infinite assimilation of jaw-breaking laboratory articles. If you try to draw any expressible theoretical conclusion from any of them, they won't hear of it."[14] The masses of measurements collected could not be interpreted without some explicit theoretical apparatus. Prewar British sociology suffered from exactly this predicament when theory and practice confronted each other with hostility. Most sociologists indiscriminately considered any theory as a form of positivist hypothesis and they limited their enterprise to the mere gathering of masses of undigested facts.

This was not the case, however, with British psychology. For although psychophysicists claimed to disavow theory, they did accept, at least tacitly, the associationist view of mind. Then, at the very time that association psychology appeared least tenable, it was given new life by researchers in anatomy, brain process, and neurology. In experiments that were largely self-fulfilling prophecies, these investigators found mind to be explicable through the same kind of mechanical laws that had so successfully explained classical physics. Experiments challenging these expectations were difficult to justify because no sufficiently elaborated theoretical structure yet existed with such satisfying completeness as that of association psychology.

British psychophysicists insisted that their freedom from theoretical assumptions enabled them to make new empirical discoveries. But their work depended upon those physiological and neurological studies that supplied physical evidence of associative mechanisms. When Camilio Golgi drew an anatomy of the brain in 1875, he showed an interrelated network of associated cells that supported independent experiments in England done by David Ferrier and by Hughlings Jackson from 1873.[15] Even though physiologists dropped association theory by the next decade — the last physiological defense of an associative mental and neural structure occurred in Charles Mercier's *The Nervous System and the Mind* (1881) — the psychophysicists continued to rely upon it, at least implicitly, as an accurate description of the physical structure of the mind. G. J. Romanes, for example, used associative mechanisms to explain learning processes in his *Animal Intelligence* (1822) and in his *Mental Evolution in Animals* (1883), and association theory survived as an explanation of "learning" until the middle of the twentieth century.[16]

Each type of psychologist warmly defended the particular method that agreed with his understanding of what psychology ought to be. At one extreme were those who viewed psychology mainly as the epistemological side of philosophy; at the other were those who saw it as merely the practical study of character, behavior, and institutions. One's position in this spectrum of opinions was determined directly by one's view of the mind either as active or passive as well as by the role assigned to reflex, instinct, habit, and consciousness. Underlying these disputes was the basic issue of whether mind could be considered apart from other natural phenomena. If nature was uniform, as classical physics demonstrated, then mind was part of nature and obedient to natural laws. The effect of this materialist view was that mind was reduced, in the end, to mindless matter. Distinctions between subject and object, thought and feeling disappeared, and the consoling illusion of free will vanished.

Psychologists of all schools — traditional, transitional, and new — shared the conviction that free will would stand or fall upon the verdict of psychology. But ethical responsibility had been threatened "scientifically" by deterministic interpretations of mind and behavior as early as 1835 when Quételet bound human conduct to the constant and predictable laws of probability. But it was in Robert Chambers's *Vestiges of the Natural History of Creation* (1844) that the idea of psychological and ethical necessity was given perhaps its most extreme nineteenth-century formulation. Chambers's contention that all of nature, including man and his mind, was subject to natural law was hardly original, but it had never before received such extensive publicity. The *Vestiges,* selling over 25,000 copies before 1860, accelerated an ancient debate about intellectual and moral accountability that has not yet ended. Scientific determinism was further strengthened in 1847 by Helmholtz's extension of the theory of the conservation of energy to all physical processes.[17] And then in 1848, E. du Bois Reymond subjected physiological processes to invariable physical laws in his "researches on Animal Electricity."[18] When Darwin's *Origin of the Species* appeared in 1859, it seemed to critics like Bishop Wilberforce still another "scientific" assault upon individual moral autonomy.[19]

Determinism had been challenged throughout the century by the two major schools of English ethics. Both schools continued to be corollaries of the two traditional divisions among psychologists: utilitarian ethics was derived from association theory, while intuitionist ethics relied upon the notion of a built-in moral faculty. Neither account explained why people behaved as they did or why virtue was intrinsically preferable to vice. Moreover, neither association nor faculty psychology provided the altruistic individual with any assurances that his rational goodwill was a force sufficient to reshape the obstinate and unjust realities of social existence. The inadequacies of English ethical traditions led some thinkers to confuse gratuitous success with inherent merit, while others resigned themselves to the sway of unpredictable chance. Neither of these alternatives was reassuring to reforming social scientists who wanted to find psychological evidence of an intelligent, unified personality guided by a conscience that was increasingly social.

The failure of every variety of utilitarian and intuitionist theory to explain obligation and motive, or to resolve the conflict between individuality and altruism, in the end compelled the reformers to abandon the traditional psychology upon which utility and intuition both rested. Instead, they turned to evolution in the hope of discovering an emergent ethical sense growing simultaneously within the individual and within society. The conviction that the evolutionary process was beneficent and progressive gave the individual the reassuring feeling of a true believer acting in concert with an inevitable movement toward desirable ends. Many clung to this evolutionary optimism even after it became clear that it was blatantly at odds with experience. For, in a time of multiplying uncertainties, the feeling of cooperating with beneficent natural laws was a far greater spur to reforming activity than a paralyzing admission that random and overwhelming forces, imperfectly understood, had reduced the individual to impotence. But, conversely, even a conviction that ethics were evolving progressively could not provide the most energetic reformer with a method for distinguishing the desirable trends from the undesirable.

Spencer, perhaps the most convinced of all the evolutionary optimists, had tried to explain the inevitable growth of ethics by arguing that as individuals progressed within the evolutionary scheme, their behavior grew increasingly moral. Conduct thus depended entirely upon the relative efficiency of an individual's adjustment to his physical and social surroundings. If we understood how society changes, we should be able correctly to predict the kind of conduct appropriate to that level of social development. Just exactly how Spencer intended to make this deduction was unclear, but it led him to argue that moral rules, naturally produced by the evolution of society, were learned by individuals intuitively. The dual result of this process was a greater identity between the individual and the interests of society as well as the individual's awareness of that identity. Eventually, evolutionary progress would result in the merging of private and public goods. A facile presumption that the individual would necessarily develop in progressive moral harmony with society was converted into an increasingly deterministic reading of evolution that tautologically supported not only Spencer's psychology but his antipathy to any political remedy that attempted to compensate for individual and social failings.[20]

Neither Spencer nor any of the other evolutionary moralists after him were able to demonstrate that either individual intelligence or moral discernment were actually increasing. Moreover, even if it were true that morality developed in proportion to the evolution of mind, what were the elements within that process that provided individuals with tests for their moral judgment? Evolutionary moralists failed to demonstrate that conduct was either intrinsically better or socially more beneficent later in the evolutionary process. Nor were they ever able to extract compelling ethical norms from evolutionary tendencies.

Spencer was repudiated by Henry Sidgwick, one of the earliest and most persistent critics of those who sought to turn evolution into scientific prediction. Although ill at ease with utilitarian ethics, Sidgwick could not accept evolution as an alternative source of ethics because of its self-fulfilling prophecy: "The believer in a 'good time coming,'" he pointed out, "often seems inclined to believe that what is coming is good because it is coming."[21] Besides, even if the future could be known, Spencerian evolution did not necessarily carry with it an increase either in individual morality or happiness.[22] Although Sidgwick's criticism was well taken, his own ethical theory was hardly more satisfactory as it vacillated, on the one hand, between a utilitarian definition of the good as the greatest happiness of the greatest number and, on the other hand, a reliance on intuition or good conscience. But Sidgwick knew only too well the implicit conflict in utilitarianism between individual and social goods, and he tried, with misgivings, to discover an altruistic solution in the unproven, and in any case irrelevant, assertion that we have no rational grounds for preferring our own to any other's happiness.

Despite the inadequacies of religious, utilitarian, or intuitionist ethics, Sidgwick could not accept evolutionary ethics as a substitute. Because of an overwhelming dread of uncertainty, he resisted the notion that ethics was evolving, since this implied first, that it was incomplete, and second, that the direction of the movement was by no means assured. Although he shared the new psychologists' desire to improve the quality of thought and behavior, Sidgwick remained a transitional figure, intellectually bound to an earlier period. He continued to believe that given the failure of traditional religion and philosophy to provide an intellectually respectable degree of certitude, the only plausible alternative lay in a scientific demonstration that there was an intelligible and coherent Cosmos from which ethical principles could be deduced.[23]

Sidgwick's passionate search for ethical sources was characteristic of the transitional thinker's need to find a consistent and compelling explanation for the meaning of human life. His quest involved him in intense psychical research, but when he could find no empirical evidence of the individual's continued existence after death, he fell into deepening pessimism. If he were to admit that moral sanctions were ultimately mundane, then how could he reconcile the concepts of duty and happiness that utilitarianism had left in such unnatural tandem? Searching desperately for higher sanctions in revelation, reason, intuition, evolution, and empirical science, he never found them. It occurred to him in midstream, as to so many others in his generation, that he did not have sufficient grounds for holding any ethical system.[24] When he rejected the idea that ethics developed as part of evolution, he ignored the effect of historical change upon standards of conduct, and he never considered what Frederick Pollock called the "genesis of those feelings which contributed to ethical sanctions."[25] It never occurred to him that a study of the origin and actual development of moral beliefs and practices might result in an analysis of the content and validity of moral ideas. To be fair to Sidgwick, it was really a matter of emphasis. What he wanted to avoid was the notion that the mere survival of certain rules of conduct demonstrated either their value of their necessity. Sidgwick was unwilling to equate historical success and inherent merit, and in this he represented the intellectual and ethical commitment of his time. None of his friends, not even Pollock, was content with the status quo and they all believed that people and institutions must be changed for the better. The new psychologists adopted their criticism of evolutionary ethics from transitional psychologists like Sidgwick, who hoped that a more scientific, more complete, study of mind would yield a prescriptive theory of conduct or at least a general glossary of values and judgments.

Sidgwick tried to transcend utilitarian ethics, too, as well as its psychological justification, by encouraging Cambridge students to study psychology as an experimental explanation of the relation between mental, physical, and ethical phenomena. In 1875 he set out to make psychology the prelude to subsequent metaphysical and ethical inquiries; first, as praelector in moral and political philosophy, and then as the revisor of the moral science tripos in 1881, Sidgwick worked out the first comprehensive program in psychology at any university. This was done by separating traditional epistemology from psychology. To epistemology, Sidgwick reserved the investigation of *"real* or *valid* thoughts and perceptions," while he made psychology the field of the "illusory and invalid," through which the human mind would reveal itself. The new discipline of psychology would study "cognitive acts or states" as part of the "stream of consciousness" of "certain particular minds, whose processes the student is able to observe directly or indirectly."[26] The revised tripos went into effect in 1883, the year Sidgwick assumed the professorship of moral philosophy. But from its introduction until the 1890s, few students at Cambridge, or for that matter at any other British university, were examined in this optional subject.[27]

Sidgwick hovered on the periphery of the new social science of psychology just as he had done in the new economics. He came closest to the new mood in his recognition that psychology was changing rapidly, his insistence that psychophysics was vital for an understanding of the relation between mental and physical changes, and his support of every kind of experiment. But his reforming enthusiasm could not compete with his longing for certainty or his recurring bouts of bleak pessimism. A discontent with "merely empirical generalisations"[28] and a rejection of both evolutionary methods and evolutionary conclusions prevented Sidgwick from participating fully in the contemporary revolution in social thought. More concerned with abuses than with remedies, he feared that reformers would accept all change uncritically, instead of testing particular cases by criteria of ethical quality and social desirability. Although radically discontented with the social and economic conditions and moral climate of his time, Sidgwick was instinctively uneasy about radical change because of his inability to transcend utilitarianism completely. The new social scientists, on the other hand, were concerned to interpret, to structure, and to control change so that it would be neither random nor radical. Having challenged utility and its psychological justification, they were compelled to find a rationale for their thought and conduct compatible with the social, economic, and ethical reforms they considered necessary.

Despite the small number of students actually taking moral science at Cambridge, Sidgwick's earnest, open, and painful search for certainty attracted distinguished pupils who shared his purposes but tried to shed his doubts. His enormous personal influence at Cambridge was due, in great part, to his honesty about his ethical and intellectual problems. He made his own dilemmas about thought, responsibility, and conduct so important to his students that many felt compelled to transcend them. Those students included Alfred Marshall, the psychologist James Ward, the historian F. M. Maitland, the economist John Neville Keynes, the father of John Maynard, Sidgwick's successor Sorley, and the Conservative party leader and theist A. J. Balfour, whose sister Sidgwick married.

While his other students eventually went their own ways, Balfour followed Sidgwick in his most characteristic departure from traditional psychology. Both men accepted a psychological explanation of the human need to believe because they were convinced that natural science, evolution, and history had nothing to say about problems of meaning or value. Balfour separated philosophy and psychology, much as Sidgwick did in his argument for the new moral science tripos, by assigning to philosophy the justification of beliefs, and to psychology the investigation of its causes or antecedents. For Balfour, solution of the moral problem of obligation depended upon a thorough psychological examination of the etiology of beliefs. His examination concluded that a priori beliefs, so long as they were only provisional, were preferable to experience when they filled distinct emotional needs.[29] Balfour argued his case most completely in *Foundations of Belief* (1895), a plea for permitting feeling or nonrational factors to support our sense of conviction, especially since all naturalistic systems were entirely inferential and never demonstrable. Balfour's own feelings led him, as Sidgwick's ultimately did, to take refuge in a theistic source of morality.

Sidgwick himself accepted theism eventually on the same grounds "on which important scientific conclusions have been accepted," that is, on the basis of belief that a "sufficient strength of reasoned conviction justified calling one's conclusions a 'working Philosophy.'"[30] This did not imply either a predictive science of ethics or grounds for the verification of a particular ethics. Since Sidgwick could not achieve the certainty he wanted and at the same time remain intellectually honest, he compromised by accepting a provisional certainty in "reasoned conviction."

The question of the nature of belief was central to any late nineteenth-century discussion of psychology and ethics. In the hiatus between the disappearance of traditional certainties and the postwar discovery that certitude was unnecessary, belief was treated as no more than a psychological condition of thought and action. This was a reaction to the traumatic discovery that universal laws often failed to be compellingly universal. John Stuart Mill's a priori guarantee of scientific laws on the basis of the uniformity of nature had actually been tested by the same kind of laws that remained to be proven — a circular argument that maintained that every individual inherited a predetermined world and, that in order to live and work within that world, he had to learn its absolute laws. "Such specific experience as we can have," Mill wrote, "serves only to verify, and even that insufficiently, the conclusions of reasoning."[31] Reasoning was the process by which the order of the world was disclosed. When Spencer read Mill's *System of Logic* (1843) at midcentury, he saw immediately that Mill's universal laws were universal only if one believed in them absolutely.

In an effort to tie belief and certainty closer together, Spencer had developed his "Universal Postulate" in 1853: If it is impossible to reject a belief or to conceive of its negation, then what remains is an ultimate criterion for certainty. Then, by defining understanding as the connection between the individual and the world he confronts, Spencer transformed certainty into a relative concept. But since "Absolutes" cannot logically be relative, they were exiled to a dimension beyond understanding, to an area of necessary ignorance, that he called the "unknowable."[32] Beginning in his *Psychology* (1855) and ending in his *First Principles* (1862), Spencer used this unifying concept of "unknowability" to catch up the loose ends of science, religion, psychology, and certitude. When William James devised his revolutionary psychology, he choked upon this theory of futility because it restricted his own intellectual and moral aspirations. It was precisely to overcome Spencer's legacy that James appealed to the individual to think, experience, and act so as to understand and master the unknown.[33]

For those who sought a source of ethics beyond evolution or the defunct utilitarianism that evolutionary ethics tried to replace, the turn of the century produced G. E. Moore's description of "goodness" as a simple, unanalyzable, nonnatural property. Moore, too, rejected evolutionary ethics and utility, but he did not turn to psychology. Instead he argued that we easily recognize what is "good" even if we have difficulty in defining the concept. Since judgments of value are unique, they cannot be deduced from facts nor verified in the observable world.[34] One must act, essentially, on the basis of an unanalyzable feeling for the "good." Moore's confidence in the necessary simplicity and rightness of value decisions may have supported self-approval among Cambridge undergraduates, but this variation of intuitive ethics was of no more help to reforming social scientists than utility or evolution since it never explained how we learn to recognize good or the relation between recognition and implementation. Moore failed to explain, moreover, why even if one could discriminate between competing claims to "goodness," that would compel one to act morally. And how would one weight different kinds of "goods" in any scale of priorities?

The search for an intellectually satisfying basis for ethical choice in a changing and troubled society was a common concern of the community to which the transitional and new social scientists belonged. A whole unique generation, coming to maturity in the eighties and nineties, were eager to find both psychological and moral justification for their faith in reform. From the late 1860s, the brightest young university men had dedicated themselves to a "complete revision of human relations, political, moral, and economic in the light of science" and, secondarily, of history. They were guided by "comprehensive and impartial sympathy" to reform unsparingly "whatever was pronounced to be not conducive to the general happiness."[35] The only difficulty in the familiar utilitarian quest lay in the pronouncing. By the 1880s it was clear that a concept of reform limited to piecemeal tinkering with glaring social injustices was not acceptable. Nothing less than a reform of "character," of thought, motives, and conduct, would satisfy this generation of moralists who, whatever their intellectual differences, agreed essentially on the necessity of ethical conduct.[36] But, except for G. E. Moore, everyone who talked about morality eventually became involved in the debate over the relative strength of free will and determinism in the decision of ethical issues.

The relation between mind, body, and morality did not become the center of a long, acerbic, international controversy until the mid-1870s. This was the result of two factors that had not existed in the 1830s and 1840s. First, there was the newly accepted legitimacy of biology as an essential source of knowledge; second there was T. H. Huxley's notorious 1874 address to the British Association, "Of the Hypothesis that all Animals are Automata." Huxley's eminence as a biologist and his enormous popularity in the lecture hall meant that any subject he introduced would immediately be magnified in importance. His discussion of reflex action in headless frogs challenged what had traditionally been understood as purposive action. "Our mental conditions," Huxley contended, "are simply the symbols in consciousness of the changes which take place automatically in the organism; and . . . the feeling we call volition is not the cause of a voluntary act, but the symbol of that state of the brain which is the immediate cause of that act." Men, he concluded, are but "conscious automata. . . ."[37]

The obvious and dramatic implication was that the weight of physiological and evolutionary evidence had crushed the possibility of a voluntarist-rationalist psychology along with its moral adjunct, free will. Huxley's mindless frog spawned a robot psychology, perpetuated into the present in psychoanalysis, learning theories, neobehaviorism, and computer models of the brain and behavior. There are clear and substantial differences between these theories, but all in common treat the individual as an organism *reacting* to impinging stimuli through either innate or learned mechanisms. Only recently, in a variety of new psychologies ranging from neo-Freudian "self-realization" to encounter therapy, and including phenomenological, epistemological, developmental, and sociological psychology, has the individual reemerged as an active, creative agent.[38]

The classic repudiation of automatism, incorporating all these recent kinds of criticism, was developed well before the mid-twentieth century. As early as 1878, William James presented a powerful case against any form of robot psychology. Left paralyzed with despair by an emotional and physical collapse in 1870, James discovered in the terrifying abyss of his own being a psychology of individual capacity. Originating as a personal remedy, his psychology of will grew into a coherent view of mind, body, and behavior that left transitional psychology behind by providing the prewar generation with the theory that individuals could influence even evolution. James's psychology did not reach a wide audience until the publication of his *Principles* in 1890. But from then on, any English reformer could go to James for reassurance that they could participate effectively in a society where ethical choices have real effect upon the quality of life.

Prior to 1890, the automata controversy was fought principally in the pages of *Mind,* the first forum anywhere open to every variety of psychology. *Mind* became, to mix a metaphor, the heart of British and American psychology. No American journal existed until James's heretical student Stanley Hall began the *Journal of Psychology* in 1888 as an organ for psychophysical and experimental studies. Determined to eliminate interminable conundrums from psychology, Hall convinced many American psychologists to ignore philosophical questions of any kind. It was for this reason that James found a more receptive and congenial audience in England than he did at home. Hall's journal excluded not only James but psychologists such as John Dewey and James Mark Baldwin who were interested in theoretical questions. Even an American experimentalist like James McKeen Cattell preferred to publish his experimental work in *Mind.*[39]

Mind was founded and underwritten in 1876 by James Bain, an association psychologist who, in his belief that mind should be studied exclusively through introspection, represented British psychological orthodoxy from the 1850s to the 1870s. Until 1876 the only British outlet for psychological articles was the *Fortnightly Review,* created by George Henry Lewes in 1866 and managed by John Morely from 1867.[40] But the *Fortnightly's* enthusiasm was limited generally to essays that supported the agnostic implications of the new sciences. *Mind,* on the other hand, was intended to provide publicity for the widest possible range of psychological and philosophical thought and practice. Even more, the new quarterly set out to stimulate public acceptance of psychology as a "scientific" subject. It was no coincidence that *Mind* was begun after the Royal Commission on Scientific Instruction in 1876 deliberately omitted from their survey the "Mental and Moral Sciences" on the grounds that they were not of sufficiently serious scientific interest.

Bain's student, G. Croom Robertson, Grote Professor of Mind

and Logic at University College, London, became *Mind*'s energetic and ecumenical editor. Never permitting his own opinions to influence either contributors or their subjects, Robertson was interested in transforming psychology from a subject of random, leisurely, and peripherally amateur interest into a professional activity. He expected psychological inquiries to transcend the academic speculations of such earlier writers as Mill, Spencer, and Bain so that they might effect the contents and development of ordinary thinking. Robertson treated psychology as a "kind of common ground" where different philosophical schools could be brought as "far as possible to their psychological base."[41] Rejecting uniformity or agreement, *Mind* provided an outlet for such developing and diverse concerns as human and animal neurology, language, pathological behavior, anthropology, animal psychology and, the relation between psychology, biology, and the physical sciences. *Mind*'s great influence came from its freedom from both old traditions and new dogmas.[42]

More than thirty articles on the conscious-automata debate were published in *Mind* from 1876 to 1881, and the debate became the focus of all D. A. Spalding's book reviews in *Nature,* and of important articles in the *Fortnightly* and the *Contemporary Review*. In this crucial psychological question, the materialist position was advocated most ably by the brilliant Cambridge mathematician, W. K. Clifford, while William James defended freedom of consciousness. James's epochal *Principles* dealt essentially — as reply, correction, refutation, extension, and amendment — with the issue of free will first raised in the pages of *Mind*.

Clifford was a genuine revolutionary in mathematics, but his transitional role in psychology was similar to Sidgwick's. Both men pioneered the theoretical transition from an older tradition to a new form of thinking without fully recognizing mind as an active, malleable, and emotional entity. Clifford came very close to the new psychology in his understanding of mind as constantly inventive within a world known only through probable laws. But he remained a transitional figure because he believed absolutely in the existence of a value-free truth. Clifford adopted the view from Spencer that mind grows more differentiated and more integrated simultaneously in its relation to other minds and external things, but he altered Spencer's view of the mind as an assimilative agent by making mind creative. He also gave up certainty, but not for Spencer's area of unknowable ignorance. Instead, Clifford interpreted reality as a continuous disturbing flux that could be known only in a proximate sense. He made mind part of the physical world because, as a militant agnostic, he worried that exemption of mind from physical causality subordinated human activity to some *deus ex machina* that overruled human efforts and guided "history to a foregone," and not necessarily desirable, "conclusion."[43] In Darwinian evolution, Clifford found a reconciliation of physical necessity and morality. It was not that later stages in evolution were inherently superior to earlier ones, as Spencer had believed, but rather that social life created progressively higher moral standards and protected them through social institutions. Morality was compatible with physical law because motives and conduct were governed by social instincts developed through centuries of social life. In Darwin, Clifford discovered a "scientific" explanation for the continuous progress of consciousness through which mind and body constituted a unified self-propelled mechanism.

To Clifford evolution meant that the world, the mind, and knowledge were in a process of constant change and growth. Hypotheses, initiated as theoretical guides in one period, had to yield to changed circumstances and improved understanding. Moreover, the original hypothesis did not necessarily affect the proof of the truth of scientific laws. Since mind was continuously adaptive and creative, rather than simply assimilative and acquisitive, theoretical formulations from the past were never binding.[44] Clifford subjected "laws" to the same statistical test of probability that contemporary physicists were using to explain gases, electricity, and magnetism. Although he expected every rational question to have an intelligible answer, that answer depended upon the application of past experiences to new circumstances, rather than any absolute laws. Explanation meant no more than the description of the unknown and unfamiliar by reference to known and familiar; it did not mean that new information must be added progressively, as Mill and Spencer had asserted. A law could be thought of as "practically universal," Clifford argued, when its results are more exact than those arrived at by experiment alone. Besides, no law could be considered absolutely universal since one could never know whether it was true in all possible cases. One assumed practical universality only because it "pays" to do so; uniformity was a logical requirement for inferring the general rules necessary in a science.[45]

Clifford's mathematical disciple Karl Pearson extended his mentor's use of probability by maintaining that the uniformities or "laws" we experience, the supposedly invariable sequences of natural phenomena, are only the sequence of our sensations. What we call "invariable" is nothing more than the result of our experience projected into a probable future. The so-called laws of nature are really laws of thought dependent upon the ordering powers of perception and not upon either sensations themselves or upon laws of matter. Every "natural law," then, is a description of the way in which our sensations occur; it is never their cause.[46]

Pearson and Clifford both rejected absolute knowledge, but they believed absolutely in truth to be reached through disinterested, objective, value-free scientific methods. Clifford asked, not "What conclusion will be the most pleasing or elevating to my feelings?" but, "What is truth?"[47] His thorough materialism prevented him from even considering the kind of psychological investigations that his contemporaries were conducting under the rubric of psychic research. Without a brain there is no mind. Clifford was unequivocal about the scientific dangers of "belief": "It is wrong in all cases to believe on insufficient evidence; and where there is presumption to doubt and investigate, there it is worse than presumption to believe."[48]

Clifford strenuously promoted the nineteenth-century conviction that science, including even Huxley's twitching frog, was benevolent. It is "idle to set bounds to the purifying and organizing work of science," he proclaimed with great confidence. "Without mercy and without resentment she ploughs up weed

and briar; from her footsteps behind her grow up corn and heal-
ing flowers; and no corner is far enough to escape her furrow."
The individual's assignment was "to speed the plough."[49] But to
fulfill benevolent ends, science had to order mystifying, random,
or incomprehensible forces, and it had to escape the constraints
of a static view of the material world. Where James rejected Spencerian and Kantian limits upon knowledge because they prevented people from inventing more satisfying lives, Clifford
found any "unknowable" unacceptable because it narrowed the
range of science.[50] Clifford's definition of science, "the getting of
knowledge from experience on the assumption of uniformity in
nature, and the use of such knowledge to guide the actions of
men," came from his interpretation of evolution as a process dependent upon human effort.[51] Ethical views are not determined
by, nor do they depend upon, the vagaries of individual choice.
Clifford advised moralists to study the source and substance of
ethics scientifically, through an analysis of institutions and the
way they perpetuate certain values while rejecting others.

Beginning in 1878 with his response to the automata controversy, William James tried to resolve the conflicts and ambiguities
of transitional psychology by creating a new synthetic study of the
entire person in a particular time and place. By 1890 Jamesian
psychology combined physiological, neurological, introspective,
and behavioral studies in a revolutionary new psychology that
examined every facet of knowing, personality, and behavior to
conclude that intelligence could compel reflex, instinct, habit,
emotion, and even heredity to serve rational and moral purposes.

7.

William James and the Revolution in Psychology

The revolution in psychology was accomplished in England when William James's *Principles* shifted the psychologists' focus from a study of mind as a receptacle filled by experience to a study of the individual actively directing his own psychic and physiological processes. For the reforming community, the implications were encouraging and liberating: successful reform could be planned and executed when people understood their own motives and habits better. James's psychology, like Marshall's economics and Wallas's political science, was written to provide ordinary people with the insight and information that would allow them to scrutinize their own thinking and behavior critically. Each of the revolutionary social scientists made reform depend initially and essentially upon the reasoning, well-informed individual, guided by moral imperatives.

In psychology the revolution began when the young William James discovered that his deterministic theories were contradicted by the strength of his own will. All his life, William James suffered from serious ailments that totally debilitated his mind and body. Neurasthenic diseases marked by crises, depressions, and long periods of idle recuperation were a cultural phenomenon among Victorian intellectuals: Charles Darwin, John Stuart Mill, Florence Nightingale, Elizabeth Barret Browning, Herbert Spencer, W. K. Clifford, Henry Sidgwick, and even Alfred Marshall were struck down periodically by neuroses and hysteria. But James differed from these eminent Victorians in two striking ways. First, he endured an unusual variety of plagues; there were spinal problems, occasional blindness, black periods of depression that nearly drove him to suicide, crippling, recurring neuroses that he recognized only too well and, finally, the heart disease that killed him. Second, he found a practical and decisive, if difficult, solution to his psychosomatic illnesses in a voluntaristic psychology of choice.

Recovery was nearly as traumatic as illness because it left James with the problem of being unable to reconcile his voluntarist experience with his deterministic beliefs. Then, in 1870, he read the French philosopher Charles Renouvier, who repudiated determinism by contending that all thought originated in the "theater" of the will. From that moment, whenever he found himself on that familiar, frightening road to psychosis, James chose instead to be sane, not by ignoring emotions but by controlling them.[1] His illnesses never soured him. Every page James wrote reveals a warm, witty, ebullient man of enormous and generous vitality. He learned to "stand this universe," not out of a sense of either humility or necessity but because the effort this demanded was the "one strictly underived and original contribution which we make to the world." The proper course for him always lay in the puritanical "line of greatest resistance" — which meant active, not passive, living.[2] James never accepted Freudian theory, but he came close to it in his belief that civilization rested upon the subduing and overcoming of impulses no matter how attractive or pleasant they might be.

To Renouvier's psychology and his own experience, James added a reading of Darwinian adaptation that made mind responsible for adjusting the environment to the organism. Darwinian theory persuaded him that nature was a "sort of table on which dice are constantly being thrown," but the individual always had the opportunity to reduce immensely the number of "stray shots."[3] James found that the brain evolved as it set both the ends and the means for reaching them.[4] Even his theory that emotions follow physical changes was meant to demonstrate that emotions could be directed, and even repressed, by rational, purposeful conduct.[5] In his account of emotion as the result of specific physiological reactions, James provided the first holistic description of the individual organism as a "sounding-board" in which every change in consciousness, however slight, reverberated.[6] Since free will was neither measurable nor predictable and could not be asserted or denied through objective physiological or psychological evidence, James chose to believe it entirely on ethical grounds as an act of faith. The illusory security of determinism requires the individual to be an absolute optimist moving along a set course toward good ends; but a genuinely moral act requires an individual to choose among equally possible alternatives.[7]

James's psychology of choice explained every kind of belief, disbelief, and doubt, including those that are pathological, as acts of emotional consent. Those things intimately connected with a person's life are undoubtedly real: people choose to believe whatever answers their active, emotional, intellectual, or aesthetic needs. James saw in the 1870s what many psychologists accept today, that those whom we call "insane" have chosen to escape from a given world that they find unbelievable into the greater security of a contrived reality. In the debate between Clifford and James over the validity of belief, Clifford emphasized the "unscientific" consequences of belief, while James was more interested in its psychological origins and purposes. To James, belief was necessary both for scientific discovery and for individual sanity in a complex and capricious world; it was sufficient for decision, judgment, and activity.

Decisions have to be made, whether we like it or not, even though the evidence might be far from satisfactory. People act upon such decisions when their "sentiment of rationality" persuades them that no further justification or explanation is necessary.[8] Since belief is initiated whenever a problem has to be solved, one constantly has to act on hypotheses based upon necessarily inadequate scientific data. Conversely, no idea or thing has practical reality for anyone unless it is "both *interesting* and *important*" in his emotional and active life.[9] When the senses bombard mind with conflicting or differing impressions, "then the one most interesting, practically or aesthetically, is judged to be the true one."[10] To "*conceive with passion*" is "to affirm."[11]

The truth of any idea lies in its function of continuing the purposive processes of thought in a direction selected by the individual. If ideas diverge from that direction, they become "false" by their inconsistence, purposelessness, and therefore, uselessness.[12] Belief grows gradually; if we continue to act as if something were real, then it becomes so much a part of habit and emotion as to be, in fact, real. Moreover, we never disbelieve anything except to believe something else that contradicts or replaces what was believed before.

Belief and disbelief are successive phases in a continuing rhythmic dialectic characteristic of the mind's operation. From birth, the individual's evolving purposes determine all his feelings, thoughts, and activities. Out of his personal consciousness, "an undistinguished and swarming continuum," he chooses only those things that are objectively real for him.[13] James's metaphor of a "stream of consciousness" described the contents of mind, flowing and changing, while the brain's structure grew continuously "different under the pressure of experience."[14] Everything within the mind and in experience contains both past and future elements so that the present is actually "specious," and no more than a *"short duration of which we are immediately and incessantly sensible."*[15] The traditional and transitional psychologists preceding or paralleling James understood consciousness to be a stable property of mind; he portrayed it as continuously flowing, unimaginably complex and, above all, selective. Mental life alternates between "substantive" or resting places, and flights or "transitive" phases whose main end is to reach another substantive rest after being forced to leave the previous one.

Of the many implications to be drawn from James's imagery, the most revolutionary was that certainty was a temporary halt in a thinking process whose one constant was change. While transitional, social, and psychological thinkers such as Spencer and Sidgwick searched futilely for certainty, James insisted that certain belief was not only impossible, but that progress occurs only when beliefs are challenged. This view of progress was crucial to the revolutionary social scientists' theory and practice. Beginning in protest against the apparent finality of positivistic economic, social, and political theory, mechanistic psychology, and utilitarian ethics, the revolutionaries suggested tentative assessments and methods that were expected to change as knowledge and experience changed. And they agreed that purpose must guide every stage of development.

James contributed an important concept to this strain of revolutionary thinking by maintaining that thought itself is entirely teleological. But if that is true, then what happens to the concept of objectivity? Unwilling to reduce reality to a set of wholly subjective constructs, he argued instead that external or objective events do indeed determine an individual's thought and experience, but only if he is receptive to them. When confronted with even so objective a phenomenon as fixed optical sensations, an individual's unique experience leads him to select some as more important or more "real" than others. Yet, despite the apparent subjectivity of James's psychology of belief, he always insisted that no concept will continue to be believed unless it refers at some point to orderly, sensible objective experience. Moreover, he saw no problem in distinguishing objective reality from subjective fantasy because the ultimate test of truth is the sensations, and they come from a different neurological source than imagination. Common sensible things, the "only realities we ever directly know," are the "first and last limits of the mind." Every belief, no matter how selective, must be verified through a practical conclusion "of a sensational kind."[16]

But despite James's reliance upon demonstrable sensational tests, he still believed with the rationalists that the mind always creates more than the senses give it. Although his pragmatism was essentially an attempt to mediate between the a priori categories of rationalism and pure empiricism, James was always closer to rationalism. Although he understood that we often deceive ourselves by pretending that our irrational notions are actually rational, a process Wilfred Trotter later described as "rationalization," he did not ascribe this deception to any fundamental human irrationality. Instead, he argued, we are often misled because there are no properties absolutely essential to any thing, and rational conception, like classification, is a purely teleological tool. In effect, there are no solid boundaries between reason and belief, and we call a property "essential" only when it is so important for our purposes that we neglect or subordinate other properties.

James's discussion of belief was hardly academic. It was integral to his theory of moral choice because he identified will and belief as the same psychological phenomena. He had disavowed utilitarian psychology because it rested on the hedonistic calculus of behavior as a response to pleasurable and painful stimuli. Admitting that pain and pleasure are compelling sensations, James made them subordinate to the more compelling passionate excitement he found especially intense in ethical issues. We must regard ourselves, James wrote, as "actively combating each for his interests in the arena"; it is impossible to be an "impotent paralytic spectator in the game."[17] Fence-sitting is no way to acquire iron in one's soul. In moral questions, one cannot be a skeptic: "The Universe will have no neutrals . . . who is not for is against."[18] For this reason above all others, doubt and inquiry, the opposites of belief, lead us uncomfortably from one belief to another. Whenever we think, we move through the realities and illusions or "subuniverses" of authority established within our private and social experience. Depending upon the particular problem facing us, we select our primary source of belief or authority from either common sense, science, abstract and a priori assertions, pervasive prejudices, individual opinions, or even pathological perceptions. Once a selection is made, it becomes an ultimate reality from which no appeal is possible.[19]

The conscious-automata debate that led James to develop a new psychology revived another aspect of the mind-and-body paradox by questioning the relative influences of reflex, instinct, and consciousness. No one denied that human reflexes were as automatic as those displayed by decapitated frogs. Although G. H. Lewes contended that as part of the neural process reflex was "latent consciousness,"[20] few psychological writers confused reflexive and conscious activity. But the role of the instincts was less clear. Did they contribute to automatic or to conscious behavior? In the last two decades of the nineteenth century, instinctual impulses were assumed to be quasi-conscious phenomena.[21] James provided a coherent and empirical treatment of instinct by using evolutionary theory to narrate the biological origins and decline of instinct in the education of the species and the individual. Instinct was a primitive source of reason and habit. As reason matured and useful habits developed, the importance of instinct declined. James found evidence in contemporary neurological studies that the evolving brain had differentiated itself into a merely automatic or reflex portion and a part increasingly intellectual and decreasingly instinctual. In James's psychology, then, conflict between mind and body, consciousness and instinct, intelligence and reflex was impossible. Not only were automatic neurological processes, on one side, and states of consciousness with their instinctual origins, on the other, part of the same natural evolution, but even automatic behavior could be consciously regulated.

James made instincts the evolutionary prelude to habit, "the enormous fly-wheel of society." Instincts, such as sympathy, acquisitiveness, recreativeness, cleanliness, sociability, shyness, and imitation, become habitual when acted upon and then, without any further role in the psychical economy, they fade away. In a well-rounded person, a balance of these instincts create habits that benefit the individual in his attempts to resist stress and undesirable impulses. The practical conclusion that James reached was that from infancy the nervous system must be made "our ally instead of our enemy." In common with the other new social scientists, James saw man as "*par excellence* the *educable* animal,"[22] who could learn to create unprecedented opportunities for his own development. But unless real social opportunities for exercising choice exist, an individual's development will be thwarted. If poverty or educational deprivation starve natural instincts, then psychic development will be so constrained that no future experiences will ever be able to enlarge it. James observed further that individuals suffer considerably when their instinct for sociability is violated, but he drew none of the social or political implications from his recognition of a social instinct that would be apparent to crowd psychologists in the early twentieth century. It was not until 1908 that McDougall and Trotter, troubled by the potential of a coercively irrational "crowd instinct," created a social psychology to combat it.

In James's psychology there was no conflict possible between a higher and a lower self. But on the continent, psychologists, from Jules and Pierre Janet to Freud, had translated the traditional Christian dichotomy between spirit and flesh into an internal struggle in which unconscious irrational impulses thwart deliberate rational purposes. Unlike his continental colleagues, James treated all parts of the self as conscious, continuous, and subordinate to the individual's teleological intelligence. Other psychologists' findings that the "self" could change radically and unpredictably, was to James only proof of psychological aberration.[23] His concept of a hierarchy of levels of consciousness, each subject to reason and will, permitted pre-Freudian Americans and Englishmen to acknowledge the existence of the irrational without granting it sovereignty or conceding that it might be stronger than their own rational determination to think and act purposefully. To James, the mind was, at every level, Renouvier's "theater of simultaneous possibilities" in which consciousness selectively worked whatever data it received, as a sculptor worked a block of stone. In a sense, the statue he would create had stood there "from eternity," but there were "a thousand different ones beside it" and the "sculptor alone extricated this one from the rest."[24]

While the theory of automatism was being challenged conceptually, the physical evidence upon which it rested was also undermined. Cerebral research, begun by Gustav Fritsch and Eduard Hitzig as early as 1870, suggested that mind was not mechanistic.[25] The case for rational consciousness was developed further through comparative animal studies conducted in the 1890s by the "new" psychologists Conway Lloyd Morgan and L. T. Hobhouse. Morgan's pioneering work on animal psychology led him to describe learning as a process of conscious stages, while Hobhouse's more careful experiments at the Manchester zoo bore out the thesis of increasing rational learning in higher animals.[26]

Each man concluded independently, as James did, that reflex and instinct both contributed to the evolutionary development of rational consciousness.[27] And, in 1899, Alfred Binet's research in unicellular organisms convinced him that some measure of conscious choice, and not just cellular irritability, moved even such simple forms of life.[28] Even Huxley tried to bury his redoubtable frog at the century's end by insisting that conscious choice remained the decisive factor in human affairs.[29]

The experimental work of Hitzig, Fritsch, Morgan, Hobhouse, and Binet reflected the significant changes in the conceptual climate of the scientific world. The biologists' emphasis upon development, process, and variation was no longer contradicted by an exclusively static description of the physical world. Physicists themselves were abandoning absolute distinctions between passive subjects and active objects and increasingly formulating their knowledge, and the world itself, in probabilistic terms. Among psychologists, the transitional James Sully urged in 1885 the abandonment of the mechanistic, stationary view of mind derived from concepts that were being rejected in the new sciences, for a rehabilitation of the "volitional factor in thought."[30] The rehabilitation of the will would be the distinguishing characteristic of every kind of innovative thought until the war.

Yet it is ironic that the techniques developed by the new scientists turned out to be as useful to the deterministic revisionists as to the voluntaristic revolutionaries, especially in the study of genetic inheritance. Francis Galton, whom many contemporaries mistakenly thought of as a "new" psychologist because of his inventive use of new techniques, began the study of heredity in the 1870s with a questionnaire to eminent scientists designed to discover that heredity determined outstanding success and genius.[31] During the next decade Galton measured the performance and stamina of the various physical senses, while at the same time conducting an introspective examination of his own mental processes. By 1884 he was prepared to assert that "man is little more than a conscious machine, the larger part of whose actions are predictable." The more he examined hereditary similarities and the histories of twins, the less likely it seemed to him that there was any "residuum" that was not automatic.[32] If there was indeed an inherited, mechanical structure in the mind which processed the material provided by the senses, then mental functions could be measured precisely enough to predict behavior. In Britain and the United States, Galton's a priori conviction became the first law of experimental psychophysics.

Until he became a convert to eugenics in the final decade of his long life, Galton never discussed the ends to which his techniques were to be put. Although concentrating exclusively upon the physical qualities without any apparent ulterior purpose, the qualities he chose to study revealed his a priori assumptions. After his questionnaire to scientists, Galton isolated "energy" as their most important common quality.[33] Beginning in an Anthropomorphic Laboratory at the London International Health Exhibition in 1884, and continuing at the Kensington Museum until 1889, Galton measured the "energy" of volunteer subjects through the performance and stamina of the various senses. This was pioneering work. But while Galton's methods were capable of precise refinement, his conclusions were inadequate because they lacked a theoretical explanation. The practical effect of Galton's measurements, based as they were upon A. J. Quételet's deductive averages and laws, was to minimize individual uniqueness.[34] This weakness was especially evident in the mental-testing movement whose roots lay in the Anthropomorphic Laboratory's attempt to collect data about different physical and mental attributes. Galton expected that intelligence, like height and weight, could be measured exactly, and in 1903 he launched a project to develop and make standard tests of intelligence and specific abilities in schoolchildren.[35] Even when ranking in quartiles was introduced subsequently, intelligence tests tended to reveal more about the mind of the tester than about the intelligence of those supposedly tested.

Galton's cultural perspective was hopelessly parochial, and his methods of measurement were simplistic. In ignorance of contemporary developments in mathematics, Galton adopted Quételet's aesthetically pleasing arrangement of statistics into a "bell" curve. Statistics was Galton's means of subjecting the disturbing flux of experience to a regular form.[36] Behind Galton's attraction to Quételet's statistics lay an unstated presumption about the desirability of social equilibrium that was central to revisionist thinking. But even if this were a social value, the question remains as to who should determine the nature, form, or content of such an equilibrium. The answer to that kind of question cannot be derived from any study of averages, however arithmetically precise.

When Karl Pearson refined Galton's crude techniques through a mathematics of correlations and skew curves, he created a behavioral psychology that found high correlations between measurable factors in behavior. From its inception, however, behaviorism treated measurable problems as if they were the only problems. Pearson's refinements and a relentless series of statistical studies from the Galton Laboratory and the Biometric Institute at the University of London reenforced Galton's deterministic genetics. All these publications were in the deductive tradition of Galton's *Natural Inheritance* (1869), yet they were presented as the inductive results of precise and sophisticated techniques of statistical inquiry. The eugenics establishment, firmly entrenched at the University of London, weathered even the rediscovery of Mendelian emphasis upon individual variation.[37]

Although even so dubious an experimental psychology as that practiced in the eugenic laboratories at the University of London readily withstood criticism until after the war, traditional association theory and its mechanistic description of a passive mind, covertly incorporated into eugenics, could not survive attack in the late 1870s and 1880s. During these years, James struck the first shattering blows against both associationism and the faculty description of built-in categories in the mind. In this attack he was supported by the Cambridge philosopher-psychologist James Ward's famous essay on "Psychology" in the 1883 edition of the *Encyclopaedia Britannica*. Ward was hailed as a "new" psychologist because he rejected passive descriptions of mind to emphasize the creative and unitary function of intelligence as it actively encountered experience. But he remained a transitional psychologist because he was convinced that psychology must be subjective and introspective, rigorously excluding the study of emotion, ethics, and social conflicts. As other psychologists moved toward inquiries into the relation between mind and body, Ward sought the sanctuary of metaphysics. There was no genuinely new psychology in England until James's theoretical and empirical synthesis.

Ward's ponderous essay was received and discussed as if it were a major book because it described psychology through metaphors borrowed from biology and from the theory of dimensions in the new physics. Indicating a new direction, Ward defined psychology as the science of "individual experience" and experience as the "process of becoming expert by experiment."[38] Biological processes accurately described the "unfolding of consciousness," and the place of mind within the objective continuum of experience; the static images of association psychology did not. Ward adopted biological rhetoric because his thought was essentially, if not explicitly, genetic. But he dismissed biological methods as irrelevant to psychology.[39] Ward's psychological method was "subjective idealism": while true for everyone, it remained "subjective," because it assumed a unity of subject and object.[40] He combined this method with a theory of inheritance: individuals inherit an a priori "psycho-plasm," from which the mind carves a personality in a process which represents the individual both as he is and as he strives to be.

Despite their skepticism about the possibility of a physiological psychology, Ward and the logician John Venn had tried unsuccessfully in 1874 to establish an experimental psychology laboratory in Cambridge. In 1899 Ward appealed to the Cambridge University Association for funds for a reader in psychophysics and for a modest laboratory to consist of a dark room, and a room each for optics, acoustics, and haptics.[41] He was willing to support the measurement of sensations, and he never denied a connection between the mind and the nervous system, but he argued adamantly that the nature of that connection could never be known. Psychology was limited to the analysis of developing individual experience as it existed for the individual experiencing it. So far as Ward was concerned, the real problem of psychology was first, the discovery of the constituents of experience as they appeared to the individual; and second, an explanation of how those elements combined and interacted.[42] Ward wanted psychologists to study only the subjective certainties in consciousness. The objective basis for this delimitation lay in the fact that individual experience included both the self and sensible things. Experience was given to the individual, not created by him. Ultimately Ward's criteria for objectivity came from the consensus he expected introspective observers to reach.

Although dubious about physiological psychology, he contributed to the new psychology by calling for a correlation between introspection and an evolutionary treatment of mind. But although Ward recognized that evidence accumulated in the various sciences had eroded the religious certainty and mechanistic science that had together presented such a complete and comfortable portrait of man and the world, he was convinced that psychology had no answer for what Frederick Myers described as painful and irretrievable loss.[43]

What Ward missed was that the new psychology began precisely as an effort at consolation and replacement. Ward's Spencerian notion of inherently unknowable areas had been challenged in the late 1870s by the argument that ignorance is directly proportional to the absence of scientific investigation. The new psychology started with the conviction that a sense of personal desolation is tolerable only when its source is understood. The new psychologists were hardly alone in their attempt to fill the void in identity. While entirely dissimilar in every other way, psychical research and philosophical Idealism both were launched, as was the new psychology, in a common search for convincing grounds for values. In England and in America, members of the Psychical Research Societies, including William James, appreciated that the immediate experience of mind and nature is "everywhere gothic, not classic . . . a real jungle where all things are provisionally half-fitted to each other, untidy."[44] Still, James and the other psychical researchers such as the Sidgwicks, Arthur Balfour, and Lord Rayleigh, searched for a rationalist and voluntarist explanation for what was apparently irrational and mysterious.[45]

The Society for Psychical Research, begun informally in May 1874 among a group of Trinity College, Cambridge friends, established itself formally in 1882 to investigate "debatable phenomena" through scientific, "exact and unimpassioned inquiry."[46] Three years later, an American society was founded. The force behind it was William James, who shared with his English friends the notion that science could not be confined to measurement: the "sense of possibilities that can never be disproved is capable of exercising pervading effect on the human mind which is absolutely irrelevant to any numerical estimate of odds. . . ."[47]

A generation after the society was founded, Sir Edwin Ray Lankester told the British Association that the emergence of "a definite line of experimental research" in psychology was an important step in the progress of "Science in the past quarter century," and he lauded the "scientific" psychophysicists in contrast to the amateurish "enthusiasts" of the Society for Psychical Research.[48] Lankester's accusation was unfair and inaccurate because the S.P.R. did original and important work in psychology. Henry Sidgwick would hardly have been the guiding spirit of the group if it had been no more than a collection of passionate partisans and peripheral cranks.[49] Within a year of its creation, and despite stiff dues of two guineas a year, there were 156 members. By January 1900 the membership numbered 707. The governing council rid itself of credulous believers in 1887, and those remaining included that cross-section of prominent men so characteristic of English intellectual life until World War I. Although it is difficult to establish the exact motives of every member, it is clear that the leaders wanted to overcome religious and philosophical uncertainty by applying experimental techniques to phenomena that were obscure only because they never had been investigated scientifically. Through extensive questionnaires and random sampling, the society carried out original and seminal analyses of such little-understood phenomena as hallucination, hypnosis, and multiple personality.[50] Even more important work might have been done, but many projects never passed beyond the planning stages, and, as F. C. S. Schiller complained to James, the society often missed excellent opportunities to show that they "could really do valuable psychological work."[51] The S.P.R.'s failure to maintain an aggressively scientific image led people like Lankester and Benjamin Jowett to condemn it as a group of ghost hunters. When the Master of Balliol learned of the absorption of Cambridge people in psychical research, he warned the Alfred Marshalls that such pursuits interfered with "higher interests."[52] What Jowett did not understand was that the members of the society, although often troubled, were deliberately rational and terrifyingly earnest. They were attracted to psychical research by exactly those "higher interests" Jowett was so concerned to cultivate.

Another alternative to the acute uncertainty that many late-nineteenth-century intellectuals found unbearable, was provided by the Idealist view of mind, body, and society. As John Grote, professor of moral philosophy at Cambridge, explained in 1865, Idealism allowed people "to feel at home" in a universe that was the kind of rational system we might have created for ourselves if only we had such power.[53] Alfred Marshall and Sidgwick were among the uncertain young men who, after suffering religious crises, came to Grote's home to discuss moral problems. While most of them would ultimately reject Idealism, their initial feelings of loss led them first to its satisfying and coherent simplicity. At Cambridge, two generations of Idealists from Grote to G. E. Moore, four decades later, found the world a reasonable club of congenial, intelligent, and amiable friends "at home." A more abstract and Germanic Idealism was asserted at Oxford in the 1870s and remained the dominant intellectual current there until the war, easily triumphing over the dissenting "humanists," inspired by James's pragmatism.

F. H. Bradley, the least pretentious of the Oxford Idealists, knew that his Idealism came from an unwillingness to conceive of the world in any other way. Starting from a position close to James, Bradley defined metaphysics as "the finding of bad reasons for what we believe upon instincts."[54] He understood, too, that science consisted essentially of convenient fictions. But despite these perceptions, he craved absolute truth. Since neither religion nor science could fulfill his need, he turned to Idealism with its metaphysical Absolute, and its internally self-consistent, completely harmonious and comprehensive unity of experience, reality, and morality. Where James wanted Idealists to admit that every philosophy, including theirs, was no more than one hypothetical answer among a diverse variety of psychologically rooted beliefs, Bradley saw metaphysics rather as a common human need.

For James, Idealism was untenable because it glossed over the frightening aspects of practical living and because it denied the free will necessary to stand life. The Idealist's "through-and-through universe" suffocated James, making him feel that he "had entered into a contract with no reserved rights." It was, he wrote, as if "I had to live in a large seaside boarding house with no private bedroom in which I might take refuge from the society of the place."[55] James found Idealism psychologically paralyzing, intellectually false, and morally evasive. The Idealists' division of reality into categories of negations and affirmations beyond individual control vitiated will; and their reconciliation of the contradictions of experience into the convenient mechanism of an Absolute ignored both the problem of evil and the obvious distance between the ideal and the actual. The only reason for anything to exist, James insisted, is that "it is wished."[56] Bradley rejected James's emphasis upon individual will, but was prepared to admit that the "doctrine of truth is what satisfies the intellect and if one could find the doctrines required to satisfy the rest of our nature then I think we might hold them to be true also. . . ." However, he found James's stress upon "conduct" to be "excessive" and "mistaken." But the central issue between the Idealists and James turned upon James's definition of human nature and conduct in primarily moral terms. Bradley objected vigorously to accepting "mere morality" as "our main nature."[57] Like T. H. Green, he preferred to leave problems of conduct and the control of individual impulses to the social structure with its well-defined rules and functions.

In contrast with the Idealists' metaphysical escape from the disturbing conflicts in experience, James wanted to understand how and why people thought and acted as they did within concrete circumstances. James's psychology was genuinely "new" in its analysis of the effect of actual possibilities, options, and constraints upon mind and body. He saw that an individual's psychological needs govern his selection of problems, the methodology to be applied to their solution, and even the answers he will accept. Such needs, the individual's total personality, and his values are shaped, James suggested, by increasingly demanding and competing levels of authority that begin with family, home, and property, and culminate in rational, purposeful, and moral imperatives. To be consistent, James should have argued that conflict among these various levels would be decided according to those ends that best serve someone's purposes at the moment he is compelled to act. But for James, as for the other new social scientists, progress depended upon those individuals who set successively higher goals for themselves.

Selection, a central concept in Jamesian psychology, is governed by "acquired" perceptions: those things already labeled guide us through the intellectual world. Concrete and singular things are the really valuable parts of experience, but these constitute a flux that is incomprehensible until translated into convenient invented and petrified terms. When the mind acts on sense data, it transforms the order in which experience is given into the entirely different order of a conceptual scheme that serves as a "sieve in which we try to gather the world's contents."[58] In the ancient nominalist-conceptualist controversy carried over from epistemology into psychology, James chose the conceptualist side because it gave mind control over experience. This did not mean that the senses are necessarily misleading: confusion comes rather from our intellectual interpretation of what the senses supply. Since each new experience tends to be filed under old and familiar categories, we often are unable to use the new impressions we receive. The regrettable result is that whatever upsets our traditional ideas is usually ignored, independent of its merit or accuracy. Only the rare individual feels curiosity about things he is unable to measure or explain through known standards and concepts.

Selection and decision are different aspects of the same process in Jamesian psychology. In both cases he was concerned as much with how people actually chose as with how they ought to choose. Like Marshall and Wallas, he treated the preoccupations of the energetic, moralistic, and reforming community to which he belonged — an extraordinary group — as if they were universal. An introspective anatomy of his own processes of decision was stretched to fit the dimensions of general behavior. While all the new social scientists lived intellectually and emotionally within a narrow community from which they drew their values and purposes, their perceptions of economic, social, political, and psychological problems were sufficiently general to attract a broad reading public. Indeed, the great appeal of James's psychology of the active will was due to his correct perception that even his most personal and painful experiences were not unique. In his own life he had seen that decisive changes followed from a commitment to a particular end that would make "slumbering potentialities" actual.[59] Once a decision was reached, action had to follow: no one could bear for long the tension of doubt and hesitancy characteristic of inactivity. Although people might dread the irrevocability of their acts, the need to act was always stronger than any fear of consequences. The only uncertainty, for James as for the other new social scientists, had to do with the question of timing.

James saw that, in practice, there was a wide gulf between his ideal of the judicious weighing of evidence according to stable, morally valuable criteria and the realities of daily choice and conduct. People drifted most often in directions accidentally determined by events, and then justified their failure to decide by assuming that things were bound somehow to turn out well. More common still were automatic, random, and unpremeditated responses to irrational inner compulsions. James accepted the irrational only if it concluded in self-knowledge and responsible behavior. To solve the dilemma created by the distance between the ideal he desired and his actual observations, James turned, as the other social scientists did, to the various theories of mental evolution in the hope that the evolutionary record would demonstrate increasingly rational thought and behavior. He persuaded himself that evolutionary history indicated the progressive inhibition of impulse, but he found no evidence of any necessary or predetermined message. On the contrary, he saw psychology itself as an evolving account of the emergence of a plastic reality and a malleable mind, both selectively acted upon by people with specific problems to solve.

The late nineteenth- and early twentieth-century attempt to discover evidence of the evolutionary growth of mind, free will, and morality did not confuse process with progress, as Spencer and the earlier evolutionary moralists had done. Instead, turn-of-the-century thinkers claimed only that the evolutionary process created opportunities for individuals to apply rational concepts of the good that they derived from practical and social experience. When Darwin had earlier discarded the hedonistic search for pleasure or happiness as a basis for ethics, he had suggested that morality was a fundamental social instinct developed through evolution for the welfare, first, of the community and, ultimately, of the race. In the last decade of the century, the eroded unity of man, nature, God, and society was replaced by an equally organic view of the necessary interdependence of the functions of mind, body, and society, But, although the reforming social scientists all agreed man is part of the evolving phenomena of the universe, as a "moral agent" he is not "under the necessity of nature."[60] James added substance to the social scientists' reliance upon free will by presenting experimental and theoretical evidence that suggested that mind had to be more than the brain and nervous system. If mind and brain were the same, then every human act would depend upon those laws that determined neurological behavior. James and the other new psychologists accepted an account of evolution through natural laws, but they also conceived mind as developing voluntarily through an individual's intelligent and deliberate manipulation of changing private and social events and structures. Variations on this theme appeared in Marshall and Wallas, in the founding sociologists Westermarck and Hobhouse, in historians like Mandell Creighton, and in the social psychologists Trotter and McDougall. Only the social psychologists found evidence in the evolutionary history of morality that human behavior was conditioned by mechanisms beyond the control of most people.

Evolutionary studies provided James with evidence of the efficacy of individual purpose and with an "entirely new quantitative imagination" that led to the amassing of new data on an enormously greater scale of time, space, and numbers.[61] James was excited about this transformation of the "outer shape" of psychology, and he expected that new questions would be asked of the accumulating data so that the answers could be applied directly to the remedy of both personal and social problems.[62] But to his great disappointment, James found only narrow and self-limiting purposes among the laboratory psychologists collecting data. He envisioned a fruitful union between physiology and psychology, but he could hardly accept the validity of a "so-called scientific psychology" that ended in a rigid system.[63] It was not that James misunderstood laboratory work, for he had trained in medicine, and from 1875-1876 taught experimental psychology in the first formal psychological laboratory existing in any university. He continued sporadically to do original physiological experiments and, in 1881, he discovered the correlation between dizziness and the semicircular auditory canals.[64] All his active professional life he kept in close personal contact with every form of psychological inquiry and experiment.[65] Yet, it was with enormous relief that, in 1892, James relinquished his small Harvard laboratory to Hugo Munsterberg. The results of all "this laboratory work" seemed to him to "grow more and more disappointing and trivial" because no "new ideas" came out of it.[66] It was temperamentally impossible for James to isolate those narrow segments of experience that must necessarily serve as the subject of laboratory analysis. Instead he felt compelled to consider the whole person in the midst of complex, changing, and indeterminate experiences that could never be cut into segments small enough to get through the doors of any laboratory.

By the early twentieth century the collection of behaviorial data was threatening to become the whole enterprise of psychology. When James attended the international Psychological Congress in 1904, organized by Münsterberg in St. Louis, he found the prevailing mood to be "pure love of schematization running mad."[67] His fear about the absence of explanation in experimental psychology was well founded. Especially in the charting of sensory performance, James saw in 1890 "little theoretical fruit commensurate with the great labour expended."[68] As late as 1906 so enthusiastic a supporter of psychological experiment as Lankester, the president of the British Association, had to concede that psychology was still in an early phase of assembling accurate observations and measurements that were not yet ordered by "great guiding hypotheses and theories."[69] A psychology that never went any farther than data gathering could hardly satisfy the expectations of James or the community guiding English thought and institutions. They expected that increasingly precise information would be applied to the solution of the ancient conundrums in psychology, including the relation between mind and body.[70]

James never intended his psychology to provide final or complete answers. His *Principles* were meant to be only a "mass of descriptive details" in an "unfinished-seeming" psychology that would change as new data and theory grew.[71] In common with the other new social scientists, James wanted to solve immediately pressing problems for the time being, instead of debating ultimate solutions to eternal questions. He hoped that psychologists would continuously test, amend, and correct their observations and interpretations. But during the prewar period, James alone examined the competing assumptions, methods, and purposes of various psychologists and discovered the "psychologist's fallacy": the confusion of the observer's own attitudes and thought with those of the subjects under study.[72]

In the psychological revolution James acted as a sensitive catalyst, sympathetically responsive to the vagaries of the human predicament. Through a synthesis of brain studies with those of the physiological and neurological sources of experience and conduct, he arrived at a definition of mind as a teleological consciousness pursuing future ends by choosing the means best suited for reaching them. Though he continued to regard experience as the source of knowledge, James had no doubt that experience was altered constantly by individual decisions about its meaning. Above all, his psychology provided the kind of practical assurances about the efficacy of human reason and will that encouraged reforming aspirations.

The physiological and psychological evidence mustered by James demonstrated the primacy of individual decision over instinct by retaining the traditional nineteenth-century assumption that instincts, as J. S. Mill had said, could be modified or completely subordinated by "other mental influences, and by education."[73] Spencer's *Principles of Psychology* (1855) had extended Mill's argument, maintaining that within the nervous system instinct was converted into organized habits, "which became second nature and the permanent elements of all thought."[74] James rejected Spencer's mechanism to portray a plastic nervous system characterized by dynamic habit-forming tendencies that made possible the increasing complexity and creativity of consciousness.[75]

Despite James's efforts to refurbish the traditional intellectualist insistence upon the dominance of reason, deterministic interpretations of instinct and heredity grew. In 1908 an avalanche of publications tried to document the coercion exercised by inherited instinct over reason: D. F. Treadgold's textbook on mental deficiency, William McDougall's *Introduction to Social Psychology*, Wilfred Trotter's first essay on herd instinct, and the Report of the Royal Comission on Mental Deficiency. These studies were supplemented in the next six years by relentlessly statistical polemics from the Galton Laboratory and the Biometric Institute.[76] If these demonstrations of the role of irresistible compulsions were "scientifically" accurate, then the new social scientist's plans for substantial individual and social reform were hopelessly utopian. Nor were the calculated projects of the social scientists encouraged by the intellectual's susceptibility to Henri Bergson's celebration of irrationality in his *L'Évolution Créatrice* (1907). The "burning topic" of instinct versus reason roused the early twentieth-century British psychological establishment to a defense of intelligence and environment over instinct and heredity.[77] In a weekend symposium in 1910, the British Psychological Society, the Aristotelian Society, and the Mind Association joined forces to assert the new orthodoxy. Every participant would be a decisive figure in the future of English psychology and, despite their differences, they all affirmed James's legacy unequivocally, insisting that the evolutionary development of instinct was increasingly directed by informed, responsible, purposive, individual intelligence.

The meeting was opened and adjourned by Charles Samuel Myers, who, as director of the Cambridge Psychological Laboratory established in 1913, would train the first generation of Cambridge psychology students. Myers's position was that the psychology and the physiology of instinct were inseparable from the psychology and the physiology of intelligence. Together, instinct and intelligence formed "one indivisible mental function" as different sides of the same mental process of "instinct-intelligence." But these aspects, though inseparable, were unequal, because instinct was subordinate to reason. Free will, the moral expression of reason, grew within the evolutionary process as individuals were increasingly conscious of desirable ends. The result was that mindless, lower reflexes steadily yielded to higher stages of consciousness, represented first by instinct and then by intelligence. Mind then became more complex in its ability to modify existing needs and to invent new ones.[78]

Another participant in the symposium was Conway Lloyd Morgan, the experimentalist who made animal psychology a study of the origins of human behavior. Morgan's experiments served as a basis for modern learning theory, and they led him to a theoretical analysis that found instincts subservient to consciousness. The conscious-automata controversy, begun in the 1870s, was revived vigorously in the 1890s by the Darwinian-Lamarckian differences over the role of selection and inheritance. Morgan's most important book, *Habit and Instinct* (1896), offered a Jamesian reconciliation by arguing that mental evolution had transcended both natural selection and organic imperatives to become a matter of conscious choice. It did not really matter whether individuals who adapted to a more conscious level of existence were "selected" to transmit their powers or that acquired powers of conscious adjustment were "transmitted" from parent to child. The crucial factor, Morgan argued, was conscious adjustment. When August Weismann's theory of "germinal selection" suggested a third reading of evolution, Morgan assimilated that too into his rationalist-voluntarist psychology by making individual behavior depend more upon the cultural community than upon biological phenomena.[79] Even the relative strengths of reflex, instinct, and habit are determined by conscious choice rather than by biological accident. Morgan's predecessor in animal studies, G. J. Romanes, although careless about assumptions and methods, had concluded that consciousness exists when the "observable" profits "by experience."[80] Morgan accepted this and made it conform to Jamesian psychology by defining consciousness as the "exercise of choice and the way in which that choice was carried out." Morgan's purpose was to distinguish clearly between automatism of any kind and the "controlled action" that always indicates choice.[81]

At the symposium, Morgan came to the same conclusion as Myers, but by another route. Beginning with the premise that all intelligent behavior had instinctive origins, Morgan reasoned that instinctual and intelligent ends could never conflict. In his famous study of moor hens in 1909, he explained the behavior of a chick, who instinctively dove into water to escape the sudden frightening appearance of a puppy, as a demonstration of learning.[82] Such learning depended upon the way in which the nervous system was altered in the course of "that individual preparation we call the acquisition of experience." Morgan's description of this learning process as "backstroke" came from James's theory of the emotions.[83]

So unlikely a partisan as Bergson was brought partially into the rationalist-voluntarist tradition by H. Wildon Carr, a businessman who became professor of philosophy at King's College, London, in 1918. Carr represented the French vitalist as understanding instinct and intelligence to be two radically heterogeneous, though complementary, psychical activities proceeding harmoniously along different evolutionary paths. Instead of competing with intelligence, instinct provided an entirely different kind of cognition characterized by intuitions or visions of reality beyond the limits of intellectual understanding.[84] Carr's anglicization of Bergson supported the separation of instinct from automatic or reflex activity, but he diverged from the other participants in his introduction of irrationality as a source of knowledge that paralleled and equaled rationality. Yet James's own view of the importance of irrational belief in informing judgment was actually more consistent with French vitalism than with the exclusively rationalist views of those who accepted his psychology while ignoring the pragmatic philosophy to which it led.

At the symposium, the most traditionally intellectualist defense was made by George Frederick Stout. Throughout a long, perambulating career, Stout supervised the establishment of psychology at nearly every British university. At Cambridge he controlled the psychology program from 1884 to 1896, and in 1898 he became the first Wilde Reader in mental science at Oxford, where he introduced psychology into the Greats school. Stout accepted James's and Ward's rejection of associationist psychology along with their emphasis upon the unity, continuity, and creativity of mental life. In *A Manual of Psychology* (1898), Stout's portrayal of mind as an active entity striving for control over its circumstances reveals James's unmistakable influence.

Stout assigned instinct a place several rungs behind intelligence where it would be abandoned in man's upward climb to greater reason. Instincts served animals both as a substitute for intelligent learning through experience and as a didactic means of providing experiences useful to the animal who learned only what it needed. Men, however, were differentiated from animals by their "instructability." In effect, this meant that few "well-marked instincts as distinguished from special capacities for learning by experience" remained in men.[85] Stout upheld the rationalist-voluntarist tradition by finding a critical evolutionary distance between instinctually dominated animals and intelligently decisive men.

Even the "instinctualist" William McDougall, cofounder of social psychology, endorsed the power of reason and will but con-

fined their operation to an elite few. McDougall was part of the
new group of psychologists which included C. S. Myers and William Halse Rivers. All three had gone with the zoologist-anthro-
pologist Alfred Cort Haddon on the celebrated Torres Strait expedition of 1898 to study the "mental characteristics" of primitive
people "by the methods of experimental psychology."[86] Then,
from 1902 to 1908, McDougall and Myers had participated in the
Anthropomorphic Committee established by the British Association for the purpose of listing personality traits. By 1904
McDougall had succeeded Stout as Wilde Reader. Despite the
efforts of the chair's founder to eject him for his supposedly
experimental bent, McDougall began the laboratory work that
marked his Oxford tenure until 1920 when he left for Harvard.[87]
McDougall's controversial reputation was made by his *Introduction to Social Psychology* (1908).

Unlike the other symposium speakers, McDougall wanted psychology to be the study of complex, composite instincts. He was
interested especially in the "essential similarity of human instincts
to those of animals,"[88] and subscribed to the prevailing agreement about the evolutionary continuity between animals and
men that culminated in the emergence of rational and moral responsibility. Where he diverged from the other members of the
psychological establishment was in his assumption that since individuals developed unequally within the evolutionary scheme,
most people would follow instinctual imperatives unless guided
by those special few whose intelligence was able to subdue their
instinctual demands.

It was evident in the symposium that James's influence upon
twentieth-century psychology was decisive but never monolithic.
In spite of his synthetic efforts, psychological theory and practice
continued to develop according to separate sets of criteria; and
the intellectual community, especially in England, was very slow
to recognize psychology as an independent discipline.[89] James's
Principles had attempted for psychology the same kind of practical resolution of irreconcilable conflicts that Alfred Marshall accomplished for economics. Each man devised an innovative discipline, revolutionary in its breadth, in its mediation of past tradi-

tions and contemporary developments, and in its intention of providing individuals with the practical information that would equip them to master their lives. Each set out to create a professional discipline in which theory and practice were mutually dependent. The strength of both men lay not only in their originality but in their ability to write eminently readable books that were widely read. Marshall explained economic motives, practices, and institutions so that ordinary people could improve the conditions under which they labored and lived. James went beyond economic conditions and behavior to explain that as every condition and activity was a response to an individual's immediate emotional, rational, or aesthetic needs, individuals could plan and achieve more satisfying private and public lives.

Even though there were serious differences among psychologists, psychology came out of the 1890s with a sense of subject and of profession that had never existed before.[90] Until After World War I, psychological controversy was relatively quiescent in England. Freudian psychology was not yet reputable, and there was no other major challenge to the voluntarist-rationalist tradition to which James's *Principles* was the last monument. In the United States and on the continent, where there were more professional psychologists than in Britain, the greater distances encouraged disputes so that hostile camps developed. Neither the continental reduction of behavior to irrational and unpredictable compulsions nor the evidence for genetic and instinctual coercion was acceptable to English reformers. They had not rejected the old associative and faculty views of mind in order to let themselves be bound by some other deterministic theory. In the prewar period, only Jamesian psychology provided a theoretical and practical alternative to both the old and the new determinisms. By insisting that his own theory met sensational and experimental tests, James answered the demand for a "scientific" study of mind and body. Most important, by portraying mind as an active entity able to create more than the senses and experience gave it, James provided a psychology that supported the reforming, moralist temper of the new social sciences. And when Jamesian psychology was applied directly to the observation of political behavior, political science emerged.

PART IV
Politics, Science, and Reform

8.
Liberal Reactions to the Failures of Democracy

In the prewar generation of revolutionary social scientists, nineteenth-century liberal individualism was modified so as to remain fundamentally the same in spite of altering circumstances. Marshall's economics were intended to inform the individual so that he could satisfy his needs in a classical free marketplace, while James's psychology revealed the compulsions of belief and emotion which must be overcome so that the individual is able to recognize what his needs are in the first place. When Wallas applied Marshall's quantitative methods and James's psychological perceptions to an inquiry into the conditions necessary for individual survival in a mass, urban society, he created a modern political science. Wallas's new discipline attempted to sever liberalism from psychological assumptions in conflict with political experience. While many social critics were isolated from frustrating encounters with social problems, Wallas's active role as a practical politician, administrator, and educator led him to a sense of urgent crisis at the century's end. But serious doubts about the future of Western civilization were shared increasingly by British and continental observers in common rooms, in government, and on the streets, as 1914 approached. Among them, Wallas stood out in his determination to find a more durable foundation for the rational, liberal values threatened at the polls.

In England, turn-of-the-century social thinkers insisted upon the necessity of progress toward increased material well-being. A romantic vision of a simpler, more secure past lingered only in the hearts of the true believers speaking exclusively to one another. Generally, social reformers worked for an extension of comfort; social, economic, and political opportunities; and the kind of education that would promote reasonable and altruistic activity. But those eager to improve the quality of life, especially in neglected urban slums, were stymied by evidence that progress was not occurring because few people recognized or acted upon their own best interests. When the first generation of compulsorily educated, politically enfranchised adults went to the polls, they demonstrated that education and the vote were necessary for democracy, but certainly not sufficient. The erosion of liberal values, usually associated with totalitarianism and depression in the 1930s, actually began in the early 1870s, when swelling urban populations responded to the old techniques of mass agitation with new political power. A semiliterate then, unlike his counterpart in a free-trade mob of 1845, could translate his confused anger and disappointment into a decisive political act. Throughout the nineteenth century there were popular demonstrations, riots, and threats of rebellion; but this sporadic activity had a random effect, at best, upon decision-making processes. Even after the wide extension of suffrage in the mid-1880s spasmodic violence continued to recur as a form of political protest. In 1884 the Junior Carlton Club was bombed, and there were threatening encounters between the unemployed and the police throughout the next decade. Accelerating labor "unrest," the arming of Ulster and immanently approaching civil war, and suffragette guerrilla fighting subsided only with the unifying diversion of World War I.

The idea of progress had been an essential part of liberalism throughout the nineteenth century, but not all liberals agreed that democracy was necessarily a progressive step in the history of liberalism. Whenever nineteenth-century liberals debated the desirability of democracy, they divided along either elitist or egalitarian lines. When egalitarian arguments floundered on the illiberality of democratic behavior, the elitist persuasion was strengthened. The traditional elitist position, reasserted in W. E. H. Lecky's much-read *Democracy and Liberty* (1896), was that liberty was incompatible with democracy and equality.[1] Those liberals supporting this contention—and they were an ineffectual minority within the liberal tradition—urged typically that it was a "sacred duty" of the Liberal party to "come to the rescue of the unthinking mob, whose instincts and passions are strong but whose brains are weak, and which is always ready to follow but cannot walk alone."[2]

Nineteenth-century critics of mass urban democracy worried about the rights of minorities and individuals under majority rule; in the early twentieth century, both critics and defenders of democracy recognized that the "crowd" phenomenon of urban life threatened even the possibility of individuality. This new perception about the emotionally driven anonymous crowd, when applied to politics in the prewar years, resulted in the pervasive, apolitical complaint that even political parties did not represent "any reasonable set of opinions, but only a group of emotions."[3] The urban citizen was no individual but a part of a "creature" with a personality entirely different from that of its individual members. When a liberal defender of democracy like C. F. G. Masterman went to live in a London slum, he found that the "heart of the Empire" was a "sodden mass of unskilled labour," stunted physically, mentally, and spiritually by social and economic conditions resistant to educational and self-improving influences.[4] Within the larger cities people were "reared in a Crowd, labour in a Crowd, in a Crowd take their enjoyments, die in a Crowd, and in a Crowd are buried at the end."[5] Instead of the traditional escape into religion, politics, or even drink, the urban dweller disappeared into the irresponsible anonymity of the "crowd."

Unlike the elitists, who feared the potential violence and volatility of urban populations, Masterman and other democrats saw more clearly that the true characteristics of the crowd were inarticulateness and apathy.[6] Thomas Carlyle's acute analysis, in the 1840s, of crowd psychology in the Chartist movement was echoed in Masterman's description of the "inevitable loneliness" of competing units in the "monstrous and chaotic aggregation."[7] But despite Masterman's rhetorical resemblance to the Chelsea sage, he understood that the twentieth-century urban worker might be indifferent to those middle-class values so attractive to the self-helping Chartists who thought that political reform would bring them social and economic progress. The newer danger was no longer physical poverty, which could be alleviated; but more subtly, the pauperization of intellect and will. The liberal opponents of benevolently managed democracy feared most that the great majority of the population would become either what the speculative political economists abstractly described as "the Economic Man, weighed by the gross, estimated by the million, . . ." or the Tory Democrat's ideal workingman passing "from the great deep to the great deep, industrious, vacant, cheerful, untroubled by envy, aspirations, or desire."[8]

While elitist and democratic liberals were both concerned with the unpredictable behavior of the new democracy, they diverged diametrically on what to do about it. The central question was, as Beatrice Webb put it: "Are men to be governed by emotion or by reason . . . in harmony with the desires of the bulk of the citizens or according to the fervent aspirations of a militant minority, in defiance of the will of the majority?"[9] The Fabians were such a minority. In 1896, Sidney Webb's six lectures on democracy suggested a variety of techniques for getting around decisions made at the polls, while Shaw's plays and Wells's novels justified extraordinary power for specialists on the basis of their expert knowledge. Both the elitists and the egalitarians recognized that direction within a democracy depends initially and ultimately upon the success of particular individuals, groups, or interests in creating at least a tacit base of public tolerance. But elitists denied any need for a psychology of free choice, whether for social or selfish reasons. They never considered that if choices are made for the individual, either by others acting for him or by external compulsions, then government may fall into the hands of those whose only real commitment is to the successful retention of power.

The egalitarian position, on the contrary, is only tenable if the individual members of a society feel self-confident and self-reliant; it is not politically viable unless objective conditions support those feelings. But in the three decades before the war, English life was scarred by a new decline in real wages, and by wrenching unemployment and deplorable working and living conditions. Social and economic statistics are neither precise nor adequate for those years, and the unsurveyed areas were probably the grimmest. Census figures show a growth in English population, from 29 million in 1891 to 41 million a decade later, and that this new population lived in the cities. As late as 1911 the official figure for the "occupied" portion was only 16.4 million, but this does not tell us how many were actually seeking work.[10] Consistently through the nineteenth century, *Punch* caricatured the working man as lazy, ignorant, sly, and cunning. But in the new century, the tone changed from patronizing amusement to uneasy anxiety.[11] Fear of this unknown "new city race," in Masterman's phrase, was not an unusual phobia confined to *Punch*. When Charles Booth, Seebohm Rowntree, and the recruiting examiners during the Boer War revealed the widespread poverty and physical disabilities that afflicted an alarming proportion of the population, the "condition of England" question was given a broader, more imperative form. Under these circumstances, the workingman's apparent ignorance of his own interests, demonstrated in local and national elections, became more intelligible to democratic liberals who had expected so much more from him.

Even so, the most sanguine democratic liberals were deeply disappointed by the lost and dissipated opportunities for self-help, by the new voter's indifference to his political potential, by his receptivity to the transitory excitement of sensational journalism and, after 1899, by his acquiescence to imperialism.[12] The Municipal Corporations Act of 1882, the Corrupt Practices Act of 1883, the Local Government Acts of 1884, 1888, and 1894 had provided real opportunities for ordinary people to participate in politics. Beginning in 1885 working people would have been a majority in nearly every constituency, if only they had voted. Of those who did go to the polls, between one-third and one-half voted as Conservatives in the election of 1885, as they had done in 1874. Ostensibly "popular" issues, such as Lloyd George's "Peoples' Budget" of 1909, excited greater interest in the House of Lords than in the slums. Especially after the Boer War, more candidates were elected by appealing to the elector's viscera than to his interests. When there was a clear issue, such as the contest between free trade and protection in 1905, it had little to do with the new elector's immediate social and economic problems.

Although certain options were available to the new voter, they were much less tangible than they appeared. Despite attempts by working-class leaders and by young middle-class liberals to persuade the new voter to act, policy in local as well as national government continued to be formulated by a small group at the top who did not actively encourage those at the bottom to have independent opinions, let alone express them politically. This discrepancy between the promise of possibilities and the actuality of controlled politics explains in part the indifference and apathy in working-class districts toward efforts to register new voters by promising them effective political roles.[13] Opinion was cleverly manufactured for "the advantage, not of those who vote, but of those who pay."[14] Wealthy and energetic men, responsible for raising the individual's standard of living in the great cities, were also responsible for exploiting him at the polls. As the defenders of democracy saw, a new industry of political manipulation had been developed to organize passions not only in the slums but among those who had "passed through elementary schools and live in hundreds of miles of new, healthy, indistinguishable suburban streets."[15]

The most effective manipulative instrument in early twentieth-century democracy was the sensational press. Despite enormous and unprecedented circulation figures, few critics understood exactly how effective it was. An experienced journalist like J. L. Garvin was convinced that Alfred Charles William Harmsworth's *Daily News* had no influence in proportion to its circulation, because it was without an "intellectual and moral system."[16] The editor of the liberal *Nation*, H. W. Massingham, was almost alone in seeing, more correctly, that the twentieth century would be dominated by precisely the kind of sensationalism Garvin discounted.[17]

As a remedy against any exploitive control of democratic processes, liberal reformers looked to local agencies to establish patterns of self-government within communities. When the London

County Council was created in 1888, the reformers exulted: "Now we have the machinery of social democracy."[18] At the victory celebration of the election of the "liberal forces" to the first London County Council, Wallas shared the general elation that "at last when London had the opportunity of electing for her general work by a simple process which everyone could understand, after the campaign which appealed to everybody" democratic processes were vindicated. Eight years later, after his own sobering experience in London's county government, Wallas had learned that "people in general are very ignorant and indifferent. . . . We are under absolutely no illusion on that point. Therefore we understand that any election is not the mere mechanical and spontaneous expression of an already popular will, but a long and painful process of education by which the knowledge from which alone will can result, is slowly matured."[19] Wallas and the other liberals, known in the County Council as the Progressives, tried to provide London with optimal conditions for training the new democracy by providing municipal socialism and a comprehensive educational system. Then, in 1907, the conservative opposition, a minority since 1889, changed their names from the Moderates to the Municipal Reformers to fight a "virulent" election.[20] Cartoons and posters attacking the "extravagance," of the Progressives flooded newspapers and billboards, while trucks perambulated the streets with dioramas of "Progressive" steamers sinking into the Thames. Fifty-five percent of the electorate, the highest percentage to vote in a municipal election until then, returned seventy-nine Municipal Reformers to the Progressives' thirty-eight.[21] Wallas, then a Progressive candidate for reelection, watched the canvassers of both parties in a poor district round up the confused, drunk, and semiconscious in a last-hour effort to capture their votes. Disgusted, Wallas could not accept this "as even a decently satisfactory method of creating a government for a city of five million inhabitants."[22] In the remaining prewar elections, commercial advertising, a manipulative sensational press, and aggressive nationalism combined to sustain public irrationality on the periphery of mass hysteria.[23]

There were two conventional responses among liberals to the

discrepancy they recognized between liberal values and democratic practices. Both responses were riddled with inconsistent sets of assumptions and non sequitur conclusions; and neither satisfied those liberals who wanted to see reform result from the new elector's genuine participation in political decisions affecting the quality of his life. The first, most pervasive group, tacitly accepted nineteenth-century rationalist psychology, but its members differed in their interpretation of the meaning of apparently irrational political behavior. Most of them treated the behavior of the new democracy as a temporary aberration, while some insisted that such behavior actually concealed calculated planning. Still others, although much less influential than either of the rationalist conciliators of ideals and conduct, gave up liberalism altogether because it predicted the eventual dominance of a rationality they dismissed as artificial and undesirable. Instead, these few peripheral thinkers valued the more immediate satisfaction of spontaneous emotion.

When John Maynard Keynes, one of the most distinguished products of Cambridge rationalism, looked back upon those prewar days he admitted that "we completely misunderstood human nature, including our own. The rationality which we attributed to it led to a superficiality not only of judgment, but also of feeling."[24] Keynes's generation at Cambridge was governed by Sidgwick, Marshall, and the philosophers G. E. Moore and Bertrand Russell; while at Oxford, T. H. Green's influence resulted too in absolute reliance upon rational thinking. Outside the universities, rationalism was perpetuated by popular writers and journalists despite overwhelming evidence of its inability to account for actual experience. In analyses of political thought, the English could still read in 1900 that the average radical and the average conservative were "equally careful of their own interests" besides being "actuated by general feelings of humanity."[25]

The tenacity of the rationalist tradition was evident among the major liberal spokesmen in journalism, social criticism, and legal and political theory. Even so sharp an observer as the journalist John Alfred Spender shared these rationalist illusions. Although genuinely startled by the "vehemence and spontaneity of the war sentiment" in 1902, an understated description of "mafficking," he managed still to find behind that sentiment a reasoned "sense of discipline."[26] As late as 1920 even Viscount Bryce continued to describe human nature as the one "constant" in politics through which "reason has become so far the guide of [men's] conduct that sequences in their action can be established and their behavior . . . can to some extent be foretold."[27] Bryce's own lengthy career in parliament, his membership in Gladstone's last cabinet, his ambassadorship to Washington from 1907 to 1913, and his historical and legal studies should have taught him more than they did.

Not even a heretical social critic like J. A. Hobson would admit the reality of irrational compulsion, and he explained the existence of the irrational "mob" by attributing their behavior to inadequate opportunities for "sober reflection and judgment." Until World War I began, he continued to believe in rationality without knowing exactly where to find it.[28] While badly shaken by the horrors of the war, his faith remained strong. As late as 1931 he affirmed that "Man is not a very reasonable animal, but (barring such temporary outbursts as the Great War), he becomes consciously more reasonable."[29] Hobson even found economic evolution inherently rational in its development towards industrial cooperation.[30] And his famous explanation of imperialism assumes that financiers always think that they are acting in their own interest.[31]

In his treatment of politics, Hobson set rational limits for potential individual irrationality by subordinating individual decision to a greater "social will" or "will of the people," an instinctive "craving for self-realization" that was a "collective as well as an individual feeling." Wallas distrusted Hobson's "easy-going optimism," for which there was no evidence, because it absolved people from thinking for themselves. As a practicing politician, Wallas was not about to tell "eight million voters or eight hundred officials that there exists an 'instinctive wisdom of the people.' "[32] Hobson's rejoinder was axiomatic: that collectivity he called the people, "knows what it wants." Although denying that a collective mind was the repository of virtue and reason, Hobson continued inconsistently to describe society as a "moral rational organism" with a "common psychic life, character and purpose which are not to be resolved into the life, character and purpose of its individual members." While most liberals dreaded what Wilfred Trotter labeled "the herd instinct," Hobson found in the "Herd" the "true spirit of society," with a "single unity of purpose in the common unity. . . ."[33] Hobson was a dogmatic rationalist, but he distrusted the reliability of individual reasoning. To protect progress from individual vagaries, he called upon superior leaders who, through the creation of benevolent and progressive impulses, would convert a democratic people's ignorance, dullness, and capriciousness into sober judgment on issues, political leaders, and public policy.[34] Despite his assurances that popular will was inherently rational, Hobson relied more on the anipulative skills of supposedly rational leaders: he trusted popular will only when it was controled.

But Hobson could not always find evidence of rationality among leaders. When he explained their irrational behavior as a strategm serving wholly rational purposes, he bridged both camps of rationalist apologists. His tortuous justification by faith was tenable because, in some conspicuous cases, irrationality was contrived to serve reasoned ends. Emmeline Pankhurst, who told her suffragette followers on February 16, 1912, that the "argument of the broken window pane is the most valuable argument in modern politics," led a movement relying upon the calculated use of irrational violence.[35] Irish Home Rulers justified activities ranging from parliamentary obstruction to indiscriminate terrorism in terms of the eminent reasonableness of their ends. Indifference to the morality of particular means so long as they concluded in ultimately moral ends was characteristic of this confusion between tactics and purposes.

Engaged activists, concerned only with their ends, received some measure of endorsement from that species of academic analysis that treated random, and often irrational, phenomena as if they were the result of clever forethought and contrivance. The most important example of an academic analysis that explained away clandestine organization, machine politics, and bureaucracy as inevitable consequences of universal suffrage, was Moisei Ostrogorski's *Democracy and the Organization of Political Parties* (1902). Ostrogorski was a Russian liberal, educated in France during his late twenties, who spent his scholarly life studying English and American politics in the 1880s and 1890s. Political parties, he explained, worked by organizing campaigns and voters through a political machine that staged deliberately emotional appeals.[36] Ostrogorski's attitude was symptomatic of a "liberal" effort to curtail democratic choices through carefully managed politics.

The second response to irrational behavior as a rejection of rationalism belongs essentially to a persistent, if minor romantic tradition that found contemporary roots in naive admiration for syndicalist methodology and for Bergson's *élan vital*. One of the most characteristic English representatives of this muddled retreat from reason was Stephen Reynolds. Especially in *A Poor Man's House* (1909), Reynolds's stay with a Devonshire fishing family persuaded him that genuine happiness depended upon a spontaneous folk wisdom denied to the educated, stilted, prosaic, and hopelessly rational middle classes.[37] This young middle-class author's effort to find personal identity within an urban society in which individuals were increasingly absorbed into large amorphous groups made his criticism, no matter how simplistic, different from the romanticism cultivated from Sir Walter Scott through G. K. Chesterton. Scott and his intellectual heirs idealized an organic, hierarchical society in which people performed traditional functions appropriate to their social places. Reynolds, on the contrary, glorified the uniqueness of the individual and the necessity of his freedom from all social restraints. When Wallas considered the social criticism offered by Reynolds and other syndicalists, he concluded that they must be taken seriously because their complaints against the "unreality" of a political life that denied a "primeval need for self-expression and individuality" were just.[38] But syndicalism did not encourage disillusioned middle-class intellectuals to think critically; it led them to scorn any kind of thinking.

Democratic problems could not be solved by calling irrational things rational or by a withdrawal from reason. During the last two decades of the nineteenth century, a confident and aggressive attack upon social, economic, and political inequality came rather from that idealistic generation that devoted their lives to "progressive" ends. These people agreed that systematic reform could not succeed without a clear understanding of the nature, contents, and limits of progress. The traditional idea of progress, only vaguely ideological and never dogmatic, had been insulated against criticism during the nineteenth century by its imprecision. But above all, the idea was compelling because technological triumphs demonstrated irrefutably that material progress, at least, had occurred. Behind the Victorians' pride in their successes — and these were formidable considering the novelty and extent of the burdens inherited from the first part of the century — lay a trust in the continuing, cumulative growth of mind and "character." Inventiveness and determination were expected to find their reward in an accruing quantity of very good luck. When, by the end of the century, events eroded evidence of either individual or social progress, the idea of progress had already achieved the status of a scientific interpretation of history. Bishop Mandell Creighton's introduction to the monumental *Cambridge Modern History* (1902) declared unequivocally that "we are bound to assume as a scientific hypothesis on which history is to be written, a progress in human affairs."[39] Similar testimonials resounded in other cooperative historical ventures. Henry Duff Traill's vast *Social England* (1893-1898) was subtitled *A Record of the Progress of the People in Religion, Laws, Learning, Arts, Industry, Commerce, Science, Literature and Manners*. Until the war this theme was echoed loudly in historical scholarship that collected data to demonstrate the steady and consistent improvement of man and his circumstances.[40] And, J. P. Bury had already begun his classic study of the origins of the belief in progress.

Few thinkers disputed the progress evident throughout the nineteenth century in industry, public health, living standards, education, and government. But many worried either that the changes accomplished were more superficial than fundamental or that moral progress did not occur consistently but irregularly and rarely. A major premise for the consistent emphasis upon the classics in the Literae Humaniores or Greats School dominant at Oxford was that there was relatively little visible change in man, society, and the world. But no matter how dubious, few people were willing to argue that specific limits could be assigned either to human or social development. A static reading of past events never entirely precluded expectations of a more progressive future. For someone like Walter Bagehot progress was possible but extremely rare: "a stationary state is by far the most frequent condition of man."[41] This skeptical view of progress coincided with the elitist interpretation of liberalism. In contrast the "libertarian-progressivists" expected ordinary people to progress by voting their own interest. In the 1880s this optimistic expectation was modified by the emergence of a "new liberalism" among young liberals dissatisfied with the essentially negative content of Gladstone's Liberal party in the 1860s and 1870s. Instead of assuming that progress was a logical consequence of religious and political liberty, the new liberals argued that without improved social and economic conditions, working people could not make free or rational political decisions.

By the turn of the century, progressive expectations had been confounded; but there were few alternative views as attractive to most liberals as the idea of progress. Cyclical interpretations of history denied the values of reason, democracy, and sometimes humanity, by endorsing authoritarian solutions to crises to avoid cyclical deterioration. Another alternative, to find history without patterns or determined or ideological directions, implied not just a neutral process, but a fundamental unintelligibility in human affairs. If this were so, then the individual was left either to advocate despair futilely or to accept mystification helplessly.[42] Still another contemporary option was to find in inevitable and ruthless struggle the biological progress of the fit over the unfit. But cyclical, random, and social Darwinist readings of history all denied the rationality and goodwill inherent in the Victorian idea of progress. In order for turn-of-the century intellectuals to retain progress as a goal, they had to purge the concept of the nineteenth-century progressives imposition of an idealized description of society upon less than ideal social conditions.

Above all, the progressives were reformers who thought that increasing scientific sophistication about the gathering and interpretation of information would permit them to introduce changes that would be demonstrably progressive. But how would progress, regress, and a stationary state be distinguished from one another? How could anyone be certain that what was "progressive" would also be "good"?

On the one hand, progressives recognized the coercion of social phenomena such as the urban concentration of futile poverty, but on the other, they refused to accept their inevitability. The only thing they really feared was "stupidly wasting the power over nature which might make the world infinitely better."[43] But they knew that their own judgment was hampered by considerable inexperience as social reformers. What they wanted was some sort of promise that the reformist efforts of novices could succeed in spite of overwhelming social problems. That promise was extracted from their religious and educational training. They found the unquestioned values of will and discipline first in a religious sense of social obligation enforced by the late nineteenth-century church and chapel. Then the religious lesson was reenforced by the classical humanism that spilled out of Rugby into the public schools and universities. But they realized that within a democratic society, those values had to be sufficiently pervasive so that ordinary people could be helped to help themselves.[44]

The twentieth-century belief in progress which continued the eighteenth- and nineteenth-century voluntarist-rationalist tradition, was no longer a revelation of order in which individuals only accelerated inherently progressive tendencies. Instead, the new idea of progress attempted to discover a method for imposing temporary, admittedly arbitrary, form upon fluctuating, otherwise meaningless, events. The novelty of the twentieth-century concept was its recognition that random and irrational forces could be understood and limited by constantly meeting problems and solving them. T. H. Huxley's famous Romanes lecture of

1893 defined social progress as the "checking of the cosmic process at every step by the substitution of another which may be
called the ethical process."[45] Three decades later, his grandson
could argue still that the idea of progress had established the
importance of mind and values in evolution by introducing the
"normative idea of right direction into the blind automatic processes of the universe" to give us the "possibility of establishing certain external criteria of rightness or progress in human affairs."[46]

The new democratic progressivism found its fullest expression
in the Liberal victory of 1905 which ushered in the welfare state.
But the energetic effort to promote a progressive "new liberalism"
had already begun in organizations created in the 1880s. Two
strong ties connected these late nineteenth-century groups. First,
their members came from a common, overlapping roster of
serious activists eager to use any available forum for the discussion and dissemination of their "progressive" ideas. And second,
they all placed moral considerations above judgments about utility, necessity, stability, or tradition. Whether their ends were
political, educational, or religious, they defended the moralist-
rationalist-voluntarist interpretation of human nature against the
challenges of instinctual, mechanistic, and deterministic
theories. Among the most seminal, most influential, of these progressive reform groups were the Eighty Club, the Russell Club,
the Fellowship of the New Life, the new "Oxford Movement," the
"ethical societies," the Social Science Club, the Christian Social
Union, and the Rainbow Circle.

Each of these reforming groups was "new liberal" in its politics,
because their members believed that the "amelioration of mankind and the progress of civilization is the result of the striving of
individuals, of every person who sets out to participate actively in
politics."[47] Neither Conservatives nor Liberal Imperialists was
willing or able to give these reformers a warm reception. The fos-
ter home of the progressive new liberalism was the Eighty Club,
founded after the Liberal victory of 1880 to provide missionaries
who would spread the gospel of social reform all over the country.
Hundreds of young intellectuals, lawyers, and political novices
took part in this propagation of an activist liberalism meant to

give the party unity through purpose. H. H. Asquith was among the future Liberal statesmen who launched their political careers by a speech at the club.[48] In the Liberal sweep of 1905, 164 members of the elected House came from Eighty Club people. When the new president of the Board of Education, Augustine Birrell, himself an Eighty man, reminded his fellow Liberals that the club "is the nursing parent of the present House of Commons . . . and the last General Election was the triumph and the reward of years of their labour, energy, zeal, and organisation," he was not exaggerating the club's importance.[49]

At Oxford during 1880, Eighty Club members began the Russell Club as a local organization to promote "Liberal and Progressive Principles." The content of the "new liberalism" was shaped in the Russell Club debates.[50] In 1895 the Russell Club was affiliated to the Eighty Club because its members shared John Morley's conviction that the "natural energy of liberal, progressive, and rational forces is really half independent of you and me. The important thing is, when the great chance comes of using those forces of energy for rational progress, that the chance shall find us ready to seize the moment and to put it to a profitable and fruitful use."[51] These enthusiastic liberals thought of a political party as the most effective entity in the modern state. Until they read Wallas's *Human Nature in Politics* (1908), they did not understand that parties existed only as symbols in the memories and emotions of electors, quite independently of the opinions and desires of leaders like themselves.

Less political and more educational in its goals, the Fellowship of the New Life began in 1882 at Chelsea under the Scottish philosopher Thomas Davidson. Perhaps the most important achievement of the Fellowship was its offspring, the Fabian Society. But despite a limited effect, the Fellowship was characteristic of the late nineteenth-century reformist attempt to cultivate "character." After the Fabians left to form a more political group in 1884, the group called itself the "New Fellowship," and in the 1890s they experimented with such character-forming agencies as kindergartens, communes, and "moral" lectures.[52]

More influential, theoretically and practically, an "Oxford

movement" began in the 1880s as a "new faith with Professor Green as its founder, Arnold Toynbee for its martyr, and various societies for its propaganda."[52] Originally, the idea of progress had been a secular reading of the Christian epic of redemption. When T. H. Green justified "active citizenship" as a description of faith through good works, he was reconciling the activities of "good" individuals with an inherently progressive universal order. Sincere young Oxford men, trained and encouraged by Oxford Idealists, were sent out to staff urban settlement houses and to man work projects. In places like Toynbee Hall they acted out Green's creed: the improvement of social conditions was the essential requirement for any improvement in individual character, including one's own. To avoid the mistakes made by even the best and brightest people, the Idealists invoked sanctions transcending individual propensity to error. Corrective qualities were built into the universal scheme:

> The large-scale patterns of history and civilisation are not to be found within any single finite consciousness. The definite continuity and correlation of particular intelligent activities, on which human life ultimately depends — the "ways of providence" — are a fact on the whole of the same order as the development of the solar system or the appearance of life upon the surface of the earth.[54]

Oxford Idealism was partly responsible for another kind of organization, the ethical societies, dedicated, too, to the reform of character. These societies were copies from an American original which had sprung up to protect morality along with traditional religious faith from erosion. In part the English movement owed its origin to the ethical and political theories of Green and Edward Caird, and its earliest supporters included the Oxford Idealists, J. H. Muirhead, R. B. Haldane, and Bernard Bosanquet. But there were other equally active members who were not Idealists. The membership of the ethical societies was drawn from that same persistent circle of reforming intellectuals who joined every progressive society before the war.[55] Until 1896,

when a Union of Ethical Societies occurred, these bodies were
local community fellowships, among which the most important in
London were the London Ethical Society and the old South Place
Unitarian Congregation, renamed the South Place Ethical
Society in 1887. Other societies existed all over the country, although the most active of the provincial groups was in Cambridge.

In September 1886 the London Ethical Society started the mar-
velously ambitious project of defining, endorsing, and propagat-
ing the idea of progress. Their prospectus represented the general
goal of the ethical movement. There was a present great need,
they wrote, "(a) for the exposition of the actual principles of
social morality, generally acknowledged though imperfectly
analysed in current language, (b) for presentation of the ideal of
human progress, and (c) for the teaching of a reasoned-out doctrine on the whole subject."[56] At the end of its first year, the London Ethical Society reiterated its general intention of studying the
"basis of morality, with a view to elevate and purify social life,"
while setting out, in particular, to satisfy a need felt by those "to
whom the breaking up of older modes of thought and feeling, as
to the grounds of moral obligation seem to have gone far to de-
stroy the obligation itself." The ethical societies intended to arm
reformers with a "rational conception of human good" and with
the one test for desirability, the "development of good character
among the citizens."[57] Above all, the ethical societies taught that
modern life required a moral base.[58]

At South Place, Dr. Stanton Coit's group tried to give moral
lessons a pleasant and convivial setting. In addition to its own
chapel at Finsbury, the group offered Sunday concerts, monthly
soirées, courses in politics, ethics, education, and society, and
prizes for papers. Members were attracted too by a choral society
and a lending library. The popular Sunday School characteristically taught children about scientific and natural subjects.[59] It
is hardly surprising that Hobson, Patrick Geddes, and Wallas lectured there. Hobson coedited with Coit their journal, *The Ethical
World,* from April 1889 to March 1890, to rally the radical left in

a party of "Ethical Democracy." The list of contributors includes the names that recur so consistently throughout this period in every reformist venture.[60]

Hobson was at home in South Place as he could never be in the traditional corridors of academe. He began with a concern for an ethical basis for economic judgments, as did Marshall and the Cambridge economists, but only Hobson came to the radical conclusion that economic justice demanded a more equitable distribution of wealth as an essential prerequisite of democracy.[61] Even Hobson's explanation of imperialism may be interpreted as a description of the economic obstacles preventing such distribution. But Marshall, who belonged to the Cambridge Ethical Society, did share with Hobson the motto: "Give your life a moral purpose."[62]

The Cambridge group met independently from March 7, 1888, until May 1896 when it joined the new Union of Ethical Societies. Besides the Marshalls, the Sidgwicks, the James Wards, the Francis Darwins, J. H. Keynes, T. E. McTaggart, Stout, and Wilfred Trotter were among its most active members. Typically, Sidgwick was hardly "sanguine" about successfully promoting "the interests of practical morality" through discussion. But he made a minor career of writing cautionary "The Scope and Limits . . ." essays about every effort at substantial reform. But no intellectual can resist good discussion, and Sidgwick's most endearing quality was a willingness to suspend skepticism before that inclination, so powerful to his peers, to know and do good.

It was not until the ascendency of G. E. Moore at Cambridge after 1903 that the ethics of social responsibility was challenged by the narrower doctrine that one must live so as to realize the greatest good in one's own life and, within that, of a special circle of intimates. The effect of Moore's thought led to a sharp separation between "those people who were means to good (i.e., *did* good) from those who were good as ends (i.e., *were* good)." Young men at Cambridge, like Hugh Dalton, had "no intense admiration" for the states of mind of do-gooders because they saw their activity as a diversion from the more essential development of inherent goodness.[63] It simply never occurred to Sidgwick or to anyone else of his generation that a person who *was* good would not *do* good.

But people like Sidgwick and Marshall were unable to find absolute or even imperative grounds for moral obligation. Sidgwick worked within the ethical movement to promote "practical ethics" through state-aided emigration, recreative education, the suppression of sweated industry, the provision of open spaces, and the encouragement of private philanthropic efforts. But he was no more sympathetic to the attempts of the societies to discover the first principles of ethics than he was to sociologists or economists who were searching for social and economic laws.[64] By 1893, however, when Sidgwick was elected president of the London Ethical Society, his recurring ambivalence about the need for certainty led him toward a "theory or 'Science of Right'"; and he encouraged an explanation of the "mental and social origins" of moral distinctions so as to "connect them in a logical system." But while other members searched for a "scientific methodology" to solve inconsistencies between theories of obligation and actual behavior, Sidgwick increasingly relied more upon altruism than upon science.[65] Sidgwick found the effective motive for individual responsibility in the general good, but he could never account for selfless motives or for the reason they should succeed. His best explanation, and he knew it was no good, was that "aspirations after the best life" were themselves a "chief source and spring" of ethically desirable change.[66]

Adequate or not, most of the new progressives believed with Sidgwick that goodwill resulted in good works. When the Union of Ethical Societies, to better promote theoretical and practical attempts at "right being," issued their "General Object" in 1906, they resolved the conflict between selfish and social goals by defining it out of existence: the love of goodness and of man were the motives for "right" conduct because society required both self-reliance and cooperation. To overcome difficulties about how we know "right," they found in Lamarckian evolutionary theory the explanation that moral knowledge has evolved progressively through human experience. Those ethical obligations that had been generally accepted by the most civilized communities were to mark the beginning for a progressive ideal of personal and social obligation. This evolutionary explanation of the progress of moral standards and behavior was held by all the new progressives on the basis of "scientific" studies of society. The sociologists Westermarck and Hobhouse at the London School of Economics, and anthropologists like E. B. Tylor and A. C. Haddon were providing evidence of a progressive moral march from the Borneo primitive to the sophisticated ruler of an empire on which the sun still rose.

Serious reformers worked from the 1880s to give democracy a moral foundation in responsible individual choice, and they did not want such choice to be confounded by regressive, random, or irrational patterns in history. The Ethical Union summarized reformist expectations when it left to the individual's "own conscientious and reasoned judgment" the discrimination between right and wrong. But the individual's judgment was to be supported not only by progressive historical trends but by rigorous scientific study of the requirements for a moral life. Any externally imposed or ultimate criteria of right were simply not acceptable.[67] None of the late nineteenth- and early twentieth-century reformers were ever self-satisfied moralists. They did try to live according to the ideals they professed, and when conflicts occurred between their own interests and what they thought to be right, they tried to choose what was right. Careers of people like Sidgwick, Wallas, and Herbert Samuel amply demonstrate a pattern of commitment and self-sacrifice.

Still another Oxford reforming group, organized and sustained principally by Samuel, started in March 1891 as the Society for the Study of Social Ethics. By 1896 the society had changed its name to the Social Science Club and, in the early twentieth century, it was affiliated with the Sociological Society of London. Of all the progressive collective efforts, this one most clearly revealed the reformers' trust in "science" as the source of both reforming inspiration and social remedies. It is characteristic of the organization that nowhere in its eleven-page "Purpose of the Social Science Club" does any statement of a particular "purpose" appear.

This organization, like the other "progressive" groups, believed
that realistic ends could not be formulated until more complete
descriptions of social problems were available for study and assessment. The practical work of the members lay in their accumulation of social data. Through research and informed discussion,
they hoped to arrive at immediate and long-range programs. The
papers presented to the club included such topics as "Overcrowd-
ing of Towns" (1891); "Existence and Causes of Overpopulation"
(1891); "Past, Present and Future Industrial Co-operation"
(1899); "Housing of the Working Classes" (1901); and, "The Unemployed" (1904).[68]

At the same time that essentially secular impulses moved the
Eighty Club, the Russell Club, the Fellowship of the New Life,
the Oxford social reformers, the ethical societies, and the Social
Science Club, strong religious sentiments inspired similar progressive reform movements. This was most evident in the Anglican Christian Social Union.[69] At the century's end, few Church of
England leaders still believed in original sin and its corollary of
inescapable guilt. Although continuing to recognize a fixed universe governed by natural law, they wanted human affairs to progress autonomously through free will. Vigorously led by Charles
Gore, then principal of Pusey House, Oxford, and later bishop
successively of Worcester, Birmingham, and Oxford, and by
Canon Henry Scott Holland, the Christian Social Union was
founded in 1889 to persuade Anglican clergy and laymen that the
church must minister to the physical needs of the great majority
who suffered from social and economic injustice. Aside from two
influential books, both edited by Gore, *Lux Mundi: A Series of
Studies in the Religion of the Incarnation* (1899), and *Property:
Its Rights and Duties* (1913), the C.S.U. ran three journals widely
respected and read beyond the church: *The Economic Review,
Goodwill,* and the *Commonwealth.* All these publications supported the efforts of the C.S.U. to make the church an effective
reforming force, especially in urban slums. Unless the church
assumed an active social role, the C.S.U. leaders argued, it would
not survive.[70]

Whatever the private motives of progressive reformers, their acceptance of democracy meant that eventually they had to consider the organization of political life. In 1893 the Rainbow Circle attempted to "provide a rational and comprehensive view of progress" and "a consistent body of political and economic doctrine" that could be formulated ultimately in a practical program, and "in that form provide a rallying point for social reformers so much needed in the present chaotic state of opinion." This "new politics" would rest upon ethical, economic, and political foundations sufficient to permit reformers to understand and solve new problems.[71] To reach reformers, the Circle began a monthly *Progressive Review* with William Clarke as editor.[72] In February 1895 the first and sole issue of the year appeared with only one page and the single sentence: "The Rainbow Club meets every month to discuss politics, and cannot agree." There is no better testimony anywhere to the seriousness of progressivism. Launched again in October 1896, the *Review* set out to provide "coherent form and rational purpose to a progressive party" that would supplant the disintegrating Liberal Party. At no time, Clarke wrote, "has so large a body of thoughtful opinion scattered over the length and breadth of the land, been so powerfully impressed by the need for a genuine policy of drastic reform in the social, economic, and moral conditions of life."

Reformers often convince themselves that they stand at the head of a burgeoning movement, but in the 1890s there were a conspicuous number of influential people who agreed enough with Clark's analysis to immerse themselves in every available reform effort. And most remarkable of all, they succeeded in an unprecedented way in achieving a revolutionary range of reforms in thinking, method, and practical policy. Each of these reform groups, despite varying programs, was inspired by a general "feeling of contradiction between life as it is and life as it ought to be." They all believed that the "pace and character of popular progress" are not measured by the blind unconscious efforts of the past but by "conscious purpose." These reformers expected a reformist social science to supply efficient methods and programs for ordinary people whose "growing capacity" to "absorb and apply ideas" would result in the reasonable working out of progress "as the moral foundation of democracy."[73] A "new liberalism" that would assume these democratic moral and social responsibilities was first identified by Haldane in the *Progressive Review*.[74]

At the core of the "new liberalism" that grew logically out of progressivism, there was an agreement that irrational conditions limited and often prevented an individual from thinking and choosing reasonably. The explanation for this was that democracy had not gone far enough. Herbert Samuel, one of the four directors of the *Progressive Review*, provided new liberalism with a working manifesto in 1902 on the basis of two lessons learned as a history student at Oxford: a "People only obtains justice when it has in its own hands the power of exacting it"; and, if Liberals hoped to lead, they would have to regard "men's lives and happiness of higher importance than the rights of property."[75] Samuel's *Liberalism* (1902) attempted to unify dissident Liberals and recall radicals who had left the party. Sidney Webb had told Samuel that he only wished "the party weaker" until he knew "*what* the Liberal leaders *mean* . . . what reforms they really have at heart, and in what direction their intellectual convictions impel them to lead."[76] Samuel's book answered with the resounding assertion that the "trunk of the tree of liberalism" is "rooted in the soil of ethics." There was nothing evasive in Samuel's or in the other new liberals' promise to tailor reforms to fit ethical requirements. They meant the state to provide the "fullest possible opportunity to lead the best life." State interference in the private sector was no political expedient to revive the Liberal party; it was rather a necessary derivation from moral law.[77] Two years later, Samuel translated moral prescription into practical, detailed measures: workmen's accident compensation; unemployment relief; the extension of agricultural small holdings; an eight-hours bill for miners; early shop closing; higher land taxes; suppression of drunkenness; slum clearance and reconstruction; restoration of trade-union rights; poor-law reform; the extension of education; and regulation of working conditions in mines, workshops, government establishments, ships, factories, and railways. Samuel's transcription of moral progressivism into legislative proposals outlined the actual steps toward the welfare state which culminated in Lord Beveridge's famous *Report* (1942).[78] Increasingly, after the turn of the century, reformers spelled out their programs in rigorous detail with provisions for immediate implementation and administration.[79] By World War I the notion that the "social system must have an ethical basis" had become liberal dogma.[80]

9.

Graham Wallas and a Liberal Political Science

When the radical progressivism of the new liberals was directed toward specific reform measures, the Liberal Party found a positive social program to replace the essentially political goals already fulfilled by the 1880s. But few new liberals anticipated that the major problems of democracy would come from a growing erosion of the possibility of independent choice. Graham Wallas was the first Englishman to ask precise questions about the boundaries between individual good and public good, and between "good," stability, and security. Wallas's answers were neither definitive nor conclusive. First of all, there are really no answers that could satisfy all the complex and often conflicting interests within a mass urban democracy. And second, all of Wallas's questions assumed the most basic of all liberal values, the essential individuality of every person. The way in which a problem is perceived always predetermines its solution: Wallas could not believe that people could be made sufficiently alike to behave in the same way, even through eugenics.[1]

No one could deny that by the early twentieth century institutions, practices, and attitudes had changed dramatically, but it was certainly not clear that those changes had occurred in the most desirable directions. Practical men had been enthusiastic about technology because they expected industrial growth to result in a progressively superior quality of life for the entire population. This enthusiasm, shared, encouraged, and rationalized by many intellectuals, succumbed in the prewar years to corrosive anxiety about whether material prosperity was sufficient to achieve a harmonious society. New liberals continued to understand progress as an evolution of economic opportunities, of responsive social and political institutions, and of responsible character. The test for progress lay in the resolution of conflicts between individuals, various groups, and social, economic, and political interests. Wallas transcended this tradition by arguing that qualitative change depended as much upon psychological dispositions as upon surroundings or options. To Wallas progress was measured by the growth of knowledge and by the way in which individuals used new information to improve whatever was given, including their own natures. Liberal emphasis on education as the prerequisite for citizenship was extended by Wallas to include study of those internal and external compulsions preventing efficient self-government. As an experienced political campaigner and student of contemporary political thought and conduct, Wallas saw clearly that democracy had not succeeded in any democratic country.

Wallas's science of politics was an attempt to understand the irrational confounding of democratic processes. Together with the other new social scientists, he believed that progress meant meeting and surmounting scientifically identified obstacles; unlike them, he recognized irrational impulses and their effects as the most serious of these obstacles. To ignore the existence of unreasonable psychological motives was, in effect, to give them an absolute reign. From James, Wallas took the doctrine that harmony between instincts and environment was essential to the free will upon which all progress depended. James's "rationalist fallacy" became Wallas's "intellectualist assumption," a misguided trust in reason as the exclusive source of all thinking, institutions, and acts. Although the American psychologist was never really interested in political motives or behavior, his theory of the uniqueness of individual personality, needs, potentials, and experience lent itself to the support of a pluralistic democratic society. Critics of democracy condemned ordinary people either for their passivity and acquiescence or for their latent violence. In Jamesian psychology neither inertness nor aggressiveness was necessarily a determining factor in human behavior. Wallas carried

James's perception further by examining the complex relations among individuals in a variety of social situations. While crowd psychologists found men individually "thoughtful and temperate," but collectively "blind and ferocious," Wallas explained private and social behavior by James's account of emotional and intellectual evolution from primitive origins.[2] The crux of the matter was not whether people acted rationally when alone and irrationally collectively but, as James argued, that they had not yet learned either to adjust their instincts to their environment or to change their surroundings so as to accommodate their faculties.[3]

Jamesian psychology, reenforced by the work of G. F. Stout, C. L. Morgan, and C. S. Myers, assumed that instinctive evolutionary impulses could be modified by habit, memory, and thought. Wallas accepted their recognition of instinctual compulsion, their reaffirmation of the controlling power of reason, and their theory that instinctual as well as intellectual behavior involved an awareness of ends. Exclusively instinctual descriptions of human nature assumed either that social explosions were unavoidable or that they could be prevented only by some form of coercive management. Neither was acceptable to Wallas, and he worried that an inability to explain instinctual forces and social pressures might either paralyze reflective individuals, drive them to irrational sanctuaries, or persuade them of the morality of manipulation.[4] Instead, Wallas advocated a psychologically rooted science of politics that would study how best to adjust a vast, impersonal industrial society to individual scale.

Wallas's political science began in defense of the individualist tradition of Aristotle, Bentham, and Mill. Like James, Wallas rejected the Idealism taught at Oxford as incompatible with a view of progress as dependent upon individual will. If, he wrote a "super-brain is thinking for us," then the "necessity of undertaking the intolerable toil of thought for ourselves" seems "less urgent."[5] What Masterman called "the blasphemy of optimism" —that palliative habit of finding progress where none existed— could only be overcome, the reformers believed, by intense individual effort.[6] Wallas accepted the Idealist criticism that Bentha-

mite rationalist psychology relied exclusively upon hedonistic calculations, but he could not agree with the Idealist's metaphysical
transcendence of problems that demanded responses at the mundane but imperative level of ordinary experience.

Twentieth-century reformers learned from Wallas to suspect
any psychological, political, social, economic, or metaphysical
simplification of motives and conduct. Instead, they approached
the individual as a "social" being whose psychic, moral, and
material well-being dictated the priority of particular reforms
over others. But until individuals understand their own natures,
free will is only an attractive ideal. Before the shattering effect of
the Great War, Wallas taught progressives that every remedial
change must weigh the unpredictable, the irrational, and the
incalculable, or fail entirely. At the same time, he encouraged reforming ideals by emphasizing the power of individual reason,
will, and dedication. The more rational, better trained, and so,
more perceptive the reformer, the greater his ability to move
away from the scarcities, psychological as well as material, willed
by the past. The progressive theory that Wallas justified assumed
that a rationally grounded ethic would discriminate between
competing means and ends in a process without a priori origins or
final terminals. This progressivist faith maintained that an ethical system must value the future more than either the past or the
present — unless progressing, society was "dying or dead."[7] Wallas's moral theory belonged to an explicitly liberal tradition in
English ethics that dominated nineteenth- and early twentieth-
century thought. On the other hand, a moral theory drawn from
organic roots and maturing in conservative politics attracted the
revisionist social psychologists. But their interpretation of the
controlled social context necessary for ethical life exercised a relatively minor influence upon English intellectuals.

An emotionally convincing sense of justice and injustice has
always inspired reforming rhetoric whether of the right, center,
or left. The argument that politics is subordinate to ethics, because human relationships of any kind necessarily create moral
rights and duties, was coopted by both liberals and conservatives
— the difference between them lay in their interpretation of the

origin and exercise of privileges and obligations. Throughout the three decades before the war, liberal progressives tried to moralize democracy. When they took the "high note" as the "right note" in politics, they were applying "ethical principles" to democratic political processes.[8] A formidable strength of Marshallian economics was its conclusion in Marshall's ethical imperative, his "standard of comfort," that is necessary for a good life.[9] None of the new social scientists, including Marshall, were prepared to accept even the most functional criteria over ethical ones, and they were unwilling to postpone moral judgments about their own programs and activities. Methods, like ends, were tested by whether or not they prepared individuals to devise and carry out the qualitative improvement of their lives.[10]

While there was considerable disagreement about the origin and justification of ethics, there was a surprising consensus about the criteria of ethical behavior. Kantian imperatives prevailed even among those hostile to German Idealism and its anglicized variants. T. H. Green's ideal of the reformer reconciling self-interest and altruism by sacrificing himself was transcended and denied; but his concept of "active citizenship" was very compelling. At Oxford, Green's theories continued the mid-nineteenth-century creed of "civic responsibility" emphasized by Benjamin Jowett. The Master of Balliol had required Oxford men to take a "First in Life" by preparing for politics through "knowledge, reticence, self-control, freedom from personal feelings."[11]

Despite Wallas's moral disapproval of Idealism, he continued the Oxford tradition that bright, able young people should take "public work" as their "profession."[12] This lesson was reinforced by his own practical experience in politics, in which things got done only "by a steady and severe effort of will."[13] James and Marshall both did public and philanthropic work outside their universities, but only Wallas participated actively in at least four simultaneous full-time careers of public service including teaching, administration, political science, and politics. James clung tenaciously to his theory of will because he needed it to get through a neurotic life; Wallas needed will simply to get through a normal day whose demands always exceeded his time and energy. It was consistent with Wallas's commitment to decisive action that he resigned a comfortable teaching position at Highgate School rather than participate in a communion service that urged the individual to abandon his own will and trust wholly to the strength and guidance of God.[14]

Wallas shared the optimism of his generation, despite his skepticism; but his political expectations were not naïve in the context of striking reforming success in the three decades before the war. New progressivism was fed by tangible achievement, not by the psychology of failure. Self-helping adult education, and the creation and remarkable performance of the London County Council, the London School Board, and the London School of Economics and Political Science, provided satisfying proof that dedicated, informed reformers could achieve their ends. No problem appeared hopeless before a genuinely "scientific" explication of motives, conduct, and institutions. Wallas's most important book, *Human Nature in Politics* (1908), analyzed those conditions responsible for human nature and behavior so that everyone could understand themselves and the influences acting upon them. Wallas had no more illusions about democracy than the Webbs or Shaw, but he did believe, on pragmatic grounds, that it was the best political expression of moral possibilities. Like the other progressive reformers, he wanted the political order to conform to ethical ideals of what is just, and no other form of government existed able to maintain justice as well as democracy. Sidney Webb patiently explained to Wallas that in politics "nothing is either so good or so bad as it seems: and one must always be prepared to admit that the other side may be right after all."[15] None of the new social scientists, all of them progressivists, were willing to accept the Webbs's tactical distinction between means and ends or to concede that good and evil were relative qualities.

Progressives could not have planned so seriously for the future without the promises of the new social sciences. Certainly Wallas's *Human Nature in Politics* found a receptive and sympathetic audience convinced that politics was becoming an increasingly accurate science based upon actual research and no longer upon hypothetical abstraction. To people reaching middle age in 1908,

the introduction of "science" into any discussion secured a verdict
in advance: "Science" had replaced "Godliness" as the password
admitting to all right-minded circles.[16] But after a war in which
science contributed to unprecedented destruction, trust in scientific social reform seemed far less plausible. Many survivors of
those years looked back disapprovingly on their own past, as Beatrice Webb did, because the "most original and vigorous minds"
had believed so naïvely that by "Science, and by Science alone . . .
all human misery would be ultimately swept away."[17] But, from
the distance of the 1920s, she had forgotten how faith in science
acted as a genuine catalyst for prewar reformers.

But prewar social science was no talismanic faith. It was a
methodical effort to unite theory and practice in the service of
reformers who needed accurate and comprehensive data, arrived
at through precise techniques, in order to deal with overwhelming social and economic problems. The social sciences promised
to provide not only the data and a methodology for treating it but
a conceptual scheme of interpretation as well.

Wallas's experience in preparing the London Reform Union
Report of 1908 and his earlier research on the history of social
administration and legislation taught him that data, even when
collected from the widest and most diverse sources, was useless
until explained within some kind of theoretical structure. Wallas
saw that while the Poor Law commissioners of 1834 had gathered
their statistics through deductive methods that served their a
priori assumptions about the causes of poverty, the 1905 commissioners were forced to adopt inductive procedures by the overwhelming mass of dissimilar evidence before them. Unlike their
predecessors, the early twentieth-century commissioners tabu-
lated and weighed enormous quantities of figures based upon
observations of the actual behavior of the poor and of the potential poor.[18] Then, when Wallas worked on the Fabian-inspired
London Reform Union Report, the extensive statistical data
gathered, unlike the undigested figures about poverty accumulated by Charles Booth in London and Seebohm Rowntree in
York, were carefully ordered and their meaning was explicitly
argued.[19]

From Marshall's use of statistics, Wallas learned to avoid the "false simplicity" of generalizing behavior and to treat every individual instance as different from every other so that any effect would be understood as a function of complex variable causes. Quantification was no more than a method of collection and comparison; the material collected and ordered then had to be assessed by qualitative standards. Wallas admired Karl Pearson's development of statistical methods and his argument that the man "who has accustomed himself to marshal facts, to examine their complex mutual relations, and predict upon the result of this examination their . . . sequences" will use scientific method to solve social problems.[20] Pearson's pre-Boer War writings did fulfill criteria for the social scientist qua reformer, but his later religion of eugenics was a great disappointment to Wallas. Progressive reformers were entirely in sympathy with Pearson's dictum in 1885 that since social stability depended upon individual morality and that in turn depended upon education, it was a "primary function of society to educate its members."[21] But his post-Boer War rejection of nurture for a theory of the determinism of nature directly contradicted everything that reformers believed. In part, Pearson's zealotry for eugenics as an escape from biological necessity came from an essentially religious feeling, made even stronger by his agnostic break with the Church of England, that wherever error existed it must be corrected.

Unlike Pearson, Wallas expected inductive, experimental science to contribute toward a humane social science. Through experiment with a variety of successively refined methods, "as many relevant and measurable facts about human nature as possible" would become "serviceable in political reasoning."[22] Wallas saw himself as a middleman, bringing the accumulating data of psychological laboratories "into touch with the actual problems of present civilized life." He wrote *The Great Society* (1914) expressly as a bridge between science and politics.[23]

A confident reliance upon the objectivity of "facts" was common to nearly every prewar writer, conservative, liberal, and reformer. Again, Hobson stood outside the intellectual community by anticipating that a quantitative reduction of political problems could result in a "political mechanics" that judged the importance of events through statistical relationships that would allegedly be objective and, therefore, value free.[24] Within the community, the new social scientists shared Annie Besant's judgment that reform suffered because reformers, while "really good people," were insufficiently scientific.[25] Not even Wallas suspected that selection, omission, arrangement, and emphasis determined the objectivity of any particular datum. When congenial facts were challenged by contrary evidence, reformers suspected, not the facts themselves, but rather their opponents' insufficiently rigorous application of scientific method. Reforming social scientists belonged to the gentle tradition that expected anyone using scientific procedures to be searching for truth. Intellectual duplicity, self-deception, or dishonesty could not be compatible with scientific method.

The reliability of method was the central focus of most prewar ideological debates. Not everyone accepted the assertion of the Cambridge professor of biology in 1912 that the civilized world had awakened "to the fact that the knowledge needed for the right direction of social progress must be gained by biological observation and experiment," but they did recognize some relation between biology and social problems.[26] What exactly was that relation? What kinds of observations, experiments, and methods would reveal most precisely and accurately the nature of conflicts and their remedies? Then, as now, methodology was tied to convictions about psychology and society, and when science conflicted with convictions, science suffered the most.

A social thinker's position in the prewar methodological debates depended generally on his assumptions about the relative influence of instinct, genetics, and environment upon behavior. Some instinctualists were reluctant to abandon the idea of progress. They reconciled their belief in biological determinism with their meliorist desires by viewing society as an evolving organism managed by a rational elite, as the body is managed by the mind. But it was the eugenicists who were the missionaries of a biologically justified elitism that trusted "public opinion" only when guided by "the sense of what serves the interest of society as a whole."[27] The obvious political corollary of either instinctualism or genetic determinism was outright rejection of democracy or a program for its covert manipulation. In its most extreme form, biological determinism became a reading of evolution in which hidden forces worked to eliminate the unfit in a salutary struggle for survival. Benjamin Kidd's classic statement in *Social Evolution* (1894) reassured those who wanted to believe that their inability to explain or anticipate events was a deficiency in nature rather than in themselves. By 1908 Kidd portrayed an increasingly organic society in which "natural selection" and social pressures would act upon the individual's instinctual inheritance so as to create an organic or "social" man who would discard inefficient democratic institutions.[28] Kidd's Social Darwinism was supported by William Bateson, a genuinely able geneticist, who studied individual inheritance through painstaking experiments. But in his social thinking, a desire for stability led him to an eccentric view of socialism that justified class distinction as analogous to biological differentiation. When he concluded that a proper socialist community would have "but one mind," unlike the "uncoordinated resultant of individual minds" which was the mistaken democratic ideal, he was arguing, in effect, that democracy was biologically false.[29] All the biological determinists thought they discovered a corrective for instinctual compulsions in coercive social pressures. The revolutionary social scientists, on the other hand, relied on environmental opportunities to cultivate the individual reason capable of overcoming compulsions, whether biological or social. Among them, only Wallas understood how formidable such compulsions could be. James had urged individuals to shape their mental as well as physical conditions; Wallas saw how difficult it would be to detect, let alone direct, these concealed forces.

Wallas never underestimated the instinctual, prerational origin of evolutionary impulses as other reformers did in their desire to find that reason does prevail over emotion, especially in political decisions. What actually happens, Wallas suggested, was that feeling provides not only the motive for political thought and conduct but even the scale of values used in political judgment. For the revisionist social psychologist William McDougall, instincts were prime movers in every human activity, and the intellect was only the means for reaching instinctually determined ends. Despite Wallas's recognition of the primacy and strength of irrational compulsions, he denied McDougall's mechanistic description of thought as an apparatus moved only by instinct. We are born, Wallas maintained, "with a tendency, under appropriate conditions, to think, which is as original and independent as our tendency, under appropriate conditions, to run away." Jamesian psychology provided Wallas with the argument that although thought was a passion, it was not governed by "any lower instinct." Physiological and instinctive dispositions might be more compelling than rational ones, but in man they were also amenable to rational direction. Wallas's position rested upon the demonstration that even in lower animals instincts served intelligent purposes, and he used the teleological psychology of James, Stout, and Morgan to assert that both instinctive and intelligent behavior involved a conscious awareness of ends and a constant willingness to use effort and experience.[30]

Wallas conceded that instincts were controlled culturally, but this did not lead him to conservative elitism. Every writer on instinct thought of habit as the means of channeling impulses into socially desirable behavior; but they differed over which habits should be encouraged and about the method of enforcement. Wallas maintained that our own intelligence, as much as someone else's, could impose upon us a process of "habit-education" to inhibit or stimulate our instincts.[31] Admitting that habit was an important source of social cohesion, Wallas never confused cohesion and control as the social psychologists did. Any society depending entirely upon habitual behavior, he predicted, would either decay from within or be overthrown from without. Wallas distrusted any kind of habitual behavior as essentially rigid and repressive, and he urged individuals to work for a society where informed choice governed conduct.

Wallas's own political experience made him acknowledge the accuracy of the social psychologist's description of crowd behavior, but he would not admit their interpretations of its meaning. Social psychologists expected behavior to become increasingly irrational in proportion to the density of population growth. Wallas believed that modern urban communities were no more susceptible to suggestion than their rural ancestors; but "the defects and limitations of all human consciousness" were much "better understood and more cleverly exploited in the city."[32] The anti-intellectualism of social psychology was as serious a fallacy to Wallas as the persistence of uncritical nineteenth-century intellectualism. His political science tried to counter both these politically untenable tendencies through a *via media* that recognized the whole man with his thoughts and feelings going on simultaneously. Instinct and passion were susceptible to conscious direction only through methodical study and planning.

Wallas never suggested that people can control their own thoughts and emotions completely. The primary process of thought is unconscious and often surprising to us in its results; but we can control our "mental attitudes" sufficiently to influence the way in which we think and feel. The effective range of control is proportionate to three conditions: the individual's material surroundings; the state of his knowledge about himself and his circumstances; and his powers of analysis. Wallas recognized a "subconscious" self, but he insisted that an individual's understanding of impulses and their effect would protect him from exploitation even at the subconscious level. Anyone familiar with the political phenomenon of "spellbinding" would, at least half-consciously, see through attempts to play upon his emotions. But Wallas recognized that political tricks were developing more rapidly than the individual's perception of them, especially since individuals, deprived of traditional religious and ethical systems, were susceptible to alternative claims of authority. To prevent the identification of authority with power, Wallas urged the development of new ideals of thought and conduct from moral and intellectual entities such as the concept of "science." Once we better understand the origins of political impulses and the conditions of valid political reasoning, then both the "ideals of political conduct" and the structure of political institutions will change.[33]

Wallas's presumption that politics would improve was no more successful than his plea for the integration of reason and emotion.

A major theme in prewar thought in England, on the continent, and in the United States was that a civilized future depended upon a stable balance between instincts and culture. Wallas found life unendurable without the hope that men would eventually produce an environment that neither frustrates their emotions nor subordinates their intellects. But in the weighing of instinct and reason, Wallas had to tip the scale toward reason. Thought might be "late in evolution," he wrote and "deplorably weak in driving power," but without it, no one can find a "safe path amid the vast impersonal complexities of the universe as we have learnt to see it."[34] Some of the reviewers of *Human Nature* interpreted it as an anti-intellectualist brief for instinctualism. This misreading troubled Wallas deeply because he saw the political consequences of instinctualism as an authoritarian society governed by a few who would claim independence from the biological imperatives that moved ordinary men. Wallas's political science set out to end conflict between thought and instinct, mind and body, understanding and action, and political theory and politics. This attempt at reconciliation of outstanding dichotomies was also the distinguishing characteristic of Marshall's economics and James's psychology. And, like the other reforming social scientists, Wallas too turned to biology for methods and models.

In the Darwinian view of man as a product of evolution, Wallas found a systematic theory for explaining the "social motives which are the fulcrum of social change."[35] Wallas saw Darwin's *Origin* as revolutionary in its revelation of the absurdity of describing psychology and conduct through a few simple explanatory principles. Moreover, he could not find anything in Darwinian theory incompatible with either free will or social reform. All that evolution implied for society was that as the scale of social organization became more intricate, instinctual and habitual guidance became increasingly less reliable.

While evolutionary theory liberated method, it did not explain how and within what limits instincts affected political decisions and behavior. But from an analysis of the primary, clear-cut instincts that move animals and children, Wallas detected the four major "political impulses" of affection, fear, laughter, and a desire for property. These tendencies, often weakened through evolution and still more often transferred to other uses, always appeared in complex combination and interaction with each other. Each impulse could be cultivated by politicians to achieve fairly predictable political behavior.[36] Wallas's catalog of instincts was nearly identical to the lists compiled independently by McDougall and by Trotter, but he interpreted them differently. Although prepared to admit that human nature was relatively fixed, he maintained that the indeterminacy of a developing environment created new habits of thought and feeling as well as new entities about which we think and feel. Despite the rigidity of genetic inheritance, there were infinite possibilities for improvement.

Among prewar thinkers, Wallas was the first serious and dispassionate assessor of "how instinct and emotion directed and determined political activities."[37] Politics was no virgin subject in England, but it remained largely academic and abstract until Wallas combined political experience, the new psychology, and quantitative methods in an analysis of democratic processes and institutions. Political science became a professional subject in England when Wallas was appointed the first university teacher of the field he created. All the liberal progressivists, including the new social scientists, were teachers above all. Wallas was no exception. Their moralistic commitment to the reformation of character would not accept external coercion or punitive techniques; this meant that self-improvement had to depend entirely on education. All Wallas's activities were directed toward training ordinary people to recognize and resist any efforts to deprive them of opportunities for self-knowledge and development. This program first led Wallas to Fabianism in 1888, but in 1895 he resigned from the executive and, in 1904, from the society itself, because he found it more manipulative than educational.[38]

Before publishing *Human Nature,* Wallas spent twenty-five

full years in teaching and in public administration, especially of schools. Just out of Oxford in the 1880s, he began a series of university extension lectures to teach people to guard against imagined and actual political futility. His novel courses in active citizenship were organized on the premise that people are best prepared to act when they understand the mistakes of the past. Wallas's topics included the origins, development, and problems of towns; municipal government; public health; factory legislation; poor laws; the civil service; and education. When elected to the new London School Board in 1890, he took a decisive part in the massive program of public education that went beyond mere literacy to teach intellectual concepts and practical skills. In 1904, when the school board was absorbed into the London County Council, Wallas became a successful Progressive council member until losing his seat in the Municipal Reformers' victorious sweep of 1907. Wallas used his public offices to repudiate "class" government by replacing "class" education with a broad curriculum of intellectual, artistic, and practical subjects taught by professional teachers. As part of his program, he helped plan the London School of Economics and Political Science and taught political science there from 1895 to 1928.[39] Finally, as a Royal Commissioner investigating the civil service from 1912 to 1914, Wallas tried unsuccessfully to provide those outside the public schools and ancient universities with access to the highest levels of the Civil Service.

Until Wallas lectured on "English Institutions" for the London University Extension Society in 1891, England had no regular instruction of any kind in political science.[40] Even before Wallas's books gave his ideas wide publicity, serious students came to him to learn how to use politics for immediate reform.[41] Wallas's critique and synthesis of current work on political and social psychology as well as his analytical and historical examination of the adequacy of existing political concepts, institutions, and purposes were not available anywhere else. In great part, Wallas's success was due not only to the content of his lectures but to his incorporation of the Oxford tutorial dialogue and the Litterae Humaniores Honors papers as integral parts of his pedagogical style.[42]

Wallas thought of the Litterae Humaniores course as a character-forming program in method, even more than in content. Respect for this typically Oxford training was widespread. When the University Extension Guild was established in 1903 to "promote the extension of University teaching among all classes and at times convenient to all," the Guild set out to do what Wallas had already done. The Guild dedicated its efforts to bringing to great numbers what Litterae Humaniores brought to Oxford, not only "something stimulating" but also "some firm upholding of mental Character."[43]

Wallas adopted Oxford teaching devices, but he rejected most of what he had actually learned at Oxford. It was after he had left Oxford that he began the intensive study of theoretical and practical sciences: demography, local and national history, anthropology, comparative sociology, the new social sciences, ethics, and what we now call semiotics. As a result, he found that there was no constant or absolute definition of human nature. Moreover, social and political theory must not depend upon such abstractions as final causes, natural rights, rationalism, or utilitarian psychology, but must be grounded in experience. When reading the Utilitarians, he was struck most by their willingness to trust the formation of character to reason and intellectual freedom.[44] The Utilitarian believed that if only "the whole population were taught to read, if all sorts of opinions were allowed to be addressed to them by word and in writing, and if by means of the suffrage they could nominate a legislature to give effect to the opinions they adopted," then all the necessary conditions for progress would be satisfied.[45] But any teacher knows that the ability to read should not be confused with the capacity to think. Literacy was not enough; Wallas wanted everyone to understand politics through active participation. In the classics he read at Oxford, and especially in Aristotle, he discovered that the purpose of every inquiry was "not mere knowledge but action."[46] When a person was adequately informed about issues that touched him, then he could "get up the social question for himself" so that he could do something about it.[47]

It is difficult to gauge the size of a self-helping audience, eager to learn so that they could alter influences acting upon them, but it was significant enough to persuade Norgate to publish their commercially successful Home University Library series in 1911 under such editors as Gilbert Murray and H. A. L. Fisher. In university extension courses and in the books directed at these new readers, the most popular topics came from the new social sciences. In Wallas's early lectures at the London School of Economics, he found the familiar civil servants and teachers; men and women who wanted to broaden their education, or who were active in particular reform projects; and, most conspicuous by their small numbers, workingmen. But while working people had neither the time nor money for L.S.E., some did attend university extension and adult education classes all over the country. These courses proliferated and the numbers attending them grew steadily, and often dramatically, from the 1870s until the war.

The first successful effort to bring university courses to working people began in the autumn of 1873 in a University Extension Movement directed by Cambridge.[48] By 1886, after the movement had spread nationally, Cambridge adopted an "Affiliation Scheme" which accepted three years of course work at any Affiliated University Extension Centre in lieu of one year's residence and the passing of the first university examinations.[49] In 1878 Oxford's extension program began haltingly, to be abandoned until 1885, when it was vigorously revived. In an experimental series of 2,271 lectures on science and technology in 1891-1892, Oxford extension lecturers taught "upwards of 10,000 persons." Ninety percent of them passed their examinations, forty percent with distinction.[50] Within Oxford, Ruskin Hall, created in 1899 to provide a residential college for workingmen, was incorporated in 1901 as Ruskin College. Students there, unlike those at the older colleges, heard lectures on sociology, evolution, psychology, political and social problems, industrial history, and local government as well as such "useful" subjects as English grammar, phonetics, and public speaking.[51]

Oxford and Cambridge extension touched that small segment of the working classes who were nearly middle class in their ambitions for leadership, status, respectability, and mobility. But there were other important self-helping ventures in adult higher education, such as the Workers' Educational Association and the Working Men's College, that succeeded in attracting impressive numbers of men and women from a variety of working-class backgrounds. Oxford worked closely with the most effective of these groups, the W.E.A., founded in 1903 by Albert Mansbridge, a clerk in the cooperative movement, as "An Association for Promoting Higher Learning Amongst Working People." The name was changed to the W.E.A. in 1906 and the following year Oxford set up a "Joint Committee" consisting equally of university and working people to plan and begin what became enormously successful tutorial classes. The association came to see itself as a "missionary organisation," and by 1912 it governed 1,879 organizations *"including 648 Trade Unions, 299 Adult Schools and Classes, 16 University bodies, 18 Men's Clubs and Institutes, 161 Educational and Literary Societies and 210 Various societies mainly of workpeople,"* besides 7,011 individual members not affiliated with any group. Among the principal officers were Mansbridge, William Temple, Bishop Gore, Alfred Zimmern, R. H. Tawney, and John Stuart Mackenzie. In their 1912 General Report, the W.E.A. council estimated that 2,700 lectures had been delivered that year by its members apart from the ordinary work of the branches.[52]

Both Oxford and Cambridge professors were associated closely with the Working Men's College, created by Frederick Denison Maurice, Tom Hughes, and Charles Kingsley in 1854. Among the most distinguished principals at the end of the century were the versatile Sir John Lubbock, a banker and entymologist among other things, and the jurist A. V. Dicey. Although never a large body, the number of students grew steadily from 549 in 1883 to 1,428 in 1911. The working-class students had the great advantage of hearing Dicey on law, the constitution, and the rights of English citizens, and G. M. Trevelyan on history.[53]

Wallas's energies were poured lavishly into extension work, but from his first public lecture in 1886, he urged that a comprehensive national system of education must begin with a child of five. Until the age of eighteen, each person, he insisted, must be trained technically and taught to think critically and independently in science, in the arts, and through an understanding of the origin and role of "great ideas."[54] At least since the eighteenth century, English education was designed to prepare various social groups for their respective rights and obligations: it was not until the Education Act of 1944 that Wallas's concept of equal, meliorative education was accepted, at least in principle, as every individual's right and as a national obligation. When the 1944 Act instructed local authorities to contribute toward the "spiritual, moral, mental, and physical development of the community," a first attempt was finally made to fulfill the aspirations that had inspired the reforming social scientists half a century earlier.[55]

Wallas wanted political science to train the leaders of democracy, as well as its citizens. A conservative form of covert management was unacceptable to Wallas, but he believed that democratic survival depends upon leaders with a "sufficiently reliable and continuous" desire for the "good of others."[56] Wallas's altruistic model came from the reformist activities of the community in which he was so conspicuously, selflessly active. Marshall, too, derived his ideal from the kind of life he and his friends led, but he never learned, as Wallas did, that even the best-intentioned, most highly trained individuals faced decreasing opportunities to effect desirable social change. Wallas agreed with the other reforming social scientists that altruism had its roots in instinct, but he knew enough about instincts to distrust them.[57]

The only practical resolution of selfish and social motives and the most effective check against the ascendancy of "an uninstructed and unstable body of politicians and a selfish and pedantic bureaucracy" lay, Wallas thought, in the individual's participation in local democratic institutions such as the parish.[58] But by 1914, Wallas's experience on the London School Board and on the London County Council had taught him that most political decisions, at every level, were made consistently by a small, inner core of officials instead of through any species of democratic dialectic. Occasionally, when an independent and genuinely democratic candidate was elected, he too faced the temptation of viewing his constituents eventually as "purely irrational creatures of feeling and opinion, and himself as purely a rational 'overman' who controls them."[59] Coercion for the best of ends was incompatible with democracy because it denied individuals their right to become independent moral beings. Each of the new social scientists insisted that all individuals must have every opportunity to develop into responsible persons. When a man was led for his own good, he could never work out that good for himself.

If neither men nor institutions were effective guardians of democracy, than what was left? Wallas's answer was "organization." Advocates of order as a means to ultimately liberating ends often lose sight of the purposes for which their ordering methods were conceived. Hobhouse warned that organization, efficiency, and elitism were the slogans of a mechanistic society in which values disappeared as criteria and the only test was whether or not the machine "runs smoothly."[60] Certainly the Webbs wanted to organize society into a functional, expert bureaucracy tested essentially according to its efficiency.[61] The new social scientists warily dismissed order as a value to think of organization as a technique. But no one, not even Wallas, anticipated the rise of the apolitical organization man whose authority rested upon self-fulfilling prophecies and self-activating bureaucracies designed only to secure or advance his own position. Wallas stood on political platforms and promised to organize "to the highest and noblest point the life of a great city, without thereby creating the interests and monopolies which in the end would throttle that life."[62] Later, in reflection, he admitted to paralysis before a "material environment in which we are hardly beginning to see our way and a mass of specialized knowledge which leaves us bewildered among the ruins of philosophies." The only solution lay in the organized thinking out of "some meaning and purpose for our corporate life."[63]

The reformers' concept of organization was sustained by a biological account of integrated development from simplicity to complexity, from inferior to superior order. Through rational organization of conflicting interests and purposes, natural selection could be suspended, the species maintained, and mutual interdependence encouraged.[64] Not only did biological models support progressive desires to find increasing social harmony but, more fundamentally, led reformers to infer that form determined function. When translated into social and political concepts, this meant that an increasingly structured society would absorb individuals unless they controlled social forms by dividing them into smaller structures. Arguments for the compatibility of organization with individual freedom drew upon the successes of the smaller democratic countries. In Scandinavia and in Switzerland, effective self-government appeared to be proportional to the smallness of the numbers governed. If that were true, then the great societies had to be arranged into smaller units that allowed individuals an immediate part in political decisions.[65] Wallas wanted the vastness of the "Great Society" reduced to local communities that could actually be managed by people living within them. In the London Reform Union Report of 1908, centralization in the London County Council was justified as the simplest organization for city management. But because it was a central agency, checks upon it were recommended in the form of smaller, local committees of politicians, citizens, and civil servants who would together discuss community needs and draft legislation to satisfy them.[66]

Among the potential democratic organizations, Wallas placed his faith in a reformed civil service that would act as a second chamber for the analysis, preparation, and dissemination of information upon which reasoned political decisions depended. Elected bodies would decide purposes, while civil servants would invent the means for realizing them. If civil-service positions depended entirely on merit and performance, he reasoned, then an institution would emerge providing both immunity from political pressure and attractive careers in public service for ambitious and energetic people.

The actual personnel, power, and achievements of the early twentieth-century civil service has not yet been studied definitively, but census figures reveal an enormous growth in their numbers from 25,568 officers and clerks in 1881 to 198,187 in

1901.[67] This remarkable multiplication of bureaucrats, largely with discretionary powers, hardly escaped notice and, in 1911, a Royal Commission was set up to ascertain "precisely what is the system of appointments to the Civil Service . . . [and] how it is recruited."[68] Evidence presented to the commission from all grades of the service, from the universities, and from the public schools demonstrated conclusively that examination for the highest levels was written essentially for Oxford Litterae Humaniores graduates.[69] As a member of the commission, Wallas tried to open the most responsible positions to anyone who trained successfully in public policy fields.[70] If the influence of science upon the professions had done nothing else, it had shifted the "intellectual center of gravity" from "uninstructed opinion to instructed thought." This meant, Wallas maintained, that civil servants must study theoretical and practical political science as a prerequisite for public service.[71] Wallas wanted civil service examinations to incorporate the subjects that he and his colleagues taught at the London School of Economics and Political Science.

Wallas could not persuade the other commissioners to make the civil service either democratic or professional, but he did entirely change the teaching and comprehension of politics in England for at least a generation. Despite his influence, his biographer finds reluctantly that Wallas was "unconstructive."[72] Should the validity of the contents or effect of thought rest upon whether or not it ends in constructive solutions or comprehensive systems? Few solutions or systems have endured time and its surprises. Seminal questioners without answers may perceive a problem in a way that alters our understanding of it sufficiently to encourage a new kind of pursuit of solutions. Iconoclasts may not be as formidable as the intellectual architects, but they do wear better. The systems builder, H. G. Wells, recalled in 1934 that there was scarcely any "considerable figure among the younger generation" of political writers "who did not owe something to Wallas."[73]

Exactly what did they owe him? Wallas asked startling questions that disturbed the persistent, although unsatisfactory, consensus about human nature and political behavior. And he asked those questions to inaugurate more accurate methods of inquiry and analysis. Wallas never pretended to define what political science ought to be, but he did launch an entirely new line of research and theory to explore the relations between psychology, politics, and society. In the first two decades of the twentieth century, university students who wanted to improve the quality of democratic life came to Graham Wallas at the London School of Economics.[74] In part, they were attracted by Wallas's reputation as a thinker and a teacher; neither Oxford nor Cambridge had any systematic study of politics to offer them. From 1891 to 1925 the main textbook in politics at Cambridge continued to be Sidgwick's glaringly anachronistic *Elements of Politics* (1891). At Oxford, despite repeated attempts to convert the university into "the home, not only of classical teaching and academic studies, but of practical and technical teaching," there was no science of politics until Politics, Philosophy, and Economics was introduced as a degree course in the 1920s.[75]

After the war, Wallas applied and extended his earlier perceptions without developing them any further. Like Marshall and James, he was wholly a prewar thinker responding to the urgent uncertainties of his own generation by writing and lecturing in a deliberately popular style that spoke directly to ordinary people about themselves. Even in the last years of his life he held fast to the first principle of the new social sciences: progress in the quality of individual life depends upon applying scientific methods and perceptions to psychological, economic, and political problems. When political phenomena had been studied extensively, then political scientists could devise "patterns of social behavior which men may choose to follow rather than merely to discover laws of social behavior which they must inevitably follow."[76]

The reforming social sciences were never meant to be entirely autonomous disciplines, and their warrants for social progress were drawn initially and finally upon ethical imperatives. What really concerned Wallas, as well as the other new social scientists, was the search for "a standard of the humanly desirable."[77] Wallas's personal warmth and kindness and the generosity with which he gave of himself were returned by everyone who knew him. The aura of respect and affection in which he moved may have led him to expect that if other people had his opportunities for living responsibly, they would behave well in spite of the "imperfection of our knowledge, the weakness of our wills, and those strange facts in our nature which we can only understand when we remember our kinship with other animals."[78]

The revolutionary social sciences were never more than a tentative set of methods and intuitions, a prolegomenon to a practical study of economics, psychology, and politics to serve liberal, progressive ideals. For each of these founders, there was a point beyond which science ceased to be an adequate guide to life. As committed liberals, the revolutionary social scientists responded to the threat of an illiberal society by imposing ethical requirements upon the behavior of individuals and groups. They earnestly tried to be intellectually honest and scientifically objective — and they succeeded to an impressive degree — but they began and ended with a passionate belief that every person was entitled to opportunities for a rational and decent life.

PART V
Revisionist Social Science:
Social Psychology, Instinct, and Elitism

10.

Fear of the New Democracy:
The Setting for Social Psychology

Until 1908 the new social scientists were liberals who believed that informed reason and goodwill could overcome even the most intractable obstacles to social justice. When, in that year, the social psychologists explained human nature and society as determined generally by irrational instinct, a formidable revisionist tradition emerged in modern social science. In common with the revolutionaries, the revisionists considered the social sciences reformist disciplines with moral ends, and they explained the origins and development of human nature and society through evolution. But while the economists, psychologists, and political scientists were encouraged in their reforming activities by their reading of evolution, the social psychologists found a bleak confirmation of their a priori fears about inescapable instinctual compulsions in the biological and social history of men. These fears led the social psychologists to urge that the rational few must control the mindless many for their own good. In so doing, they fell into the traditional elitist ethical predicament of justifying dubious moral means by ultimately "good" ends. Instead of establishing a genuinely new social study, their deductive analysis of crowd behavior revived the positivistic traditions of the old social sciences.

An elitist social psychology came into being, as did a liberal political science, in reaction to the unreasonable and unpredictable behavior of the new democracy. Both were inspired by specific political preferences.[1] Wallas was a liberal critic of the new democracy, interested in its reform; the social psychologists were conservative elitists who did not believe democratic reform was

217

possible. The new liberalism that informed Wallas's studies
largely succeeded in qualifying rationalist assumptions and in
transforming nineteenth-century liberalism into a positive program.[2] New elitism, like old elitism, in concluding that the great
majority were fit only to be governed, failed to solve any of the
problems it raised. But an elitist critique of mass urban democracy was as compelling to many people as the new liberal's
defense. The most powerful elitist argument came from the
infant science of social psychology developed concurrently by the
physiologist, William McDougall and the surgeon and neurologist, Wilfred Trotter. In prewar Britain, social psychology was
the basis for a political critique of democracy presented as a scientific analysis of behavior, but behind an account of social evolution, the social psychologists concealed their plan for government by an elect of social scientists. An examination of the
thought of McDougall and Trotter, each pursuing similar arguments to entirely different conclusions, reveals the origins of
social psychology as political polemic aspiring to be social science.

From its inception, English social science always had implicit
political overtones. What was novel about the social psychologists
was not their polemical intentions but their credentials. Both
McDougall and Trotter were doctors and experimental physiologists who presented their sociology of the crowd as an objective
biological account of social evolution. Each man turned to social
psychology only after establishing considerable reputations as
natural scientists.

McDougall had studied at Cambridge with W. H. R. Rivers,
the experimental psychologist who did important work in the
physiology of the senses, and with Charles Scott Sherrington, the
distinguished holistic physiologist.[3] In 1897 McDougall was
elected a Fellow of St. Johns, and the following year he and C. S.
Myers joined Rivers in the physiological team of A. C. Haddon's
Torres Straits anthropological expedition of 1898-1899. In the
Murray Islands, McDougall conducted experiments on cutaneous
sensations, muscular sense, and variations in blood pressure.[4] His
early career followed Rivers's, and in 1900 he succeeded him as
reader in experimental psychology at University College, Lon-

don.[5] From 1902 to 1908, McDougall, Rivers, and Meyers participated in the study of personality traits conducted by the Anthropometric Committee of the British Association; and in 1903, when Galton set up a project to develop and make standard tests of intelligence and specific abilities in the schools, McDougall was put in charge.[6] When G. F. Stout left Oxford for St. Andrews, McDougall replaced him as Wilde reader in mental philosophy in 1905.

F. C. S. Schiller, William James's most enthusiastic English disciple, complained that the Idealist Edward Caird and the logician John Cook Wilson secured McDougall's appointment to get psychology out of Litterae Humaniores where Schiller, as an examiner, set explicitly Jamesian questions. Admitting that McDougall was "a very good man in his line," Schiller saw him as "a physiologist and medicine man, who will want a lab . . . and [will] leave the traditional philosopher alone."[7] It was typical of Schiller to be both right and wrong simultaneously, and his judgment of McDougall was no exception. McDougall did want a laboratory, but his major work and influence were to be in social psychology which dealt deductively with the philosopher's oldest problem: the relation of mind and body. In 1908, when his *Introduction to Social Psychology* appeared, McDougall had behind him over twenty studies in physiology, including an original theory of muscular contraction that came from his Torres Straits' experiments.[8] But by 1906 he had become convinced of the importance of inborn instinct. From this increasingly consuming conviction his social psychology developed before the war, in *Social Psychology,* in *Body and Mind* (1911), in *Psychology: The Study of Behavior* (1912), and in "The Will of the People" (1912).[9] After 1906 McDougall's premises, arguments, and conclusions no longer came out of any laboratory.

Wilfred Trotter worked independently and he was motivated differently, but he too published his interpretation of crowd behavior in 1908. After qualifying at University College Hospital in 1896, Trotter became a surgical registrar in neurology in 1900, a Harley Street consultant in 1905, and by 1906, a permanent staff surgeon at his hospital. Before his work on social psychology appeared, he had published five neurological papers; and in 1909, when his second essay on herd instinct came out, he also did outstanding experimental research on the sensory nerves of the skin.[10] Trotter became interested in psychology after reading a British neurologist's review of Freud's *Studies in Hysteria* and his interest was encouraged and sustained by a close friendship with his brother-in-law, Ernest Jones, the first English Freudian.[11]

Despite a failure to study crowd phenomena objectively, let alone methodically, the prestige of social psychology rested firmly upon the reputations of McDougall and Trotter as scientists. But how could anyone trained in the rigorous and precise methods of inductive, experimental medicine and physiology write such deductive, impressionistic social psychology? Were they consistent in their understanding of what constituted science and its application? The answer to both questions is that they changed hats when they changed subjects. McDougall became an essentially deductive thinker when he became interested in crowd behavior. But Trotter, while writing equally deductive social theory, hoped that his theory would eventually be confirmed empirically.

There was, moreover, no reason for either man to doubt the soundness of a deductive approach to any inquiry. Certainly their professional training was entirely compatible with a belief in synthetic order. Even an ostensibly experimental science like physiology was under the sway of older positivistic expectations of underlying order from which explanatory principles were to be deduced. The results of laboratory processes were often, though not always, evidences of the overriding belief in first principles which dominated natural as well as physical sciences, despite challenges to its sway. This was especially conspicuous in psychophysics, which continued the ordered, mechanistic assumptions of associationist psychology well into the twentieth century.[12]

When, however, researchers studied cutaneous sensations and sensory nerves, they were generally too immersed in their isolated experiment to think about the order of things unrelated to that particular experiment. They were compelled to think about the meaning of science and scientific method only when they attempted to create a broadly applicable social science. When

McDougall and Trotter turned to social psychology, they deliberately abandoned the narrow experimental science they had practiced in the laboratory. Toward the end of his life, McDougall admitted that the experimental method had failed, during fifty years, to bring us "appreciably nearer to a socially useful psychology."[13] A recent historian of psychology has suggested that in "spite of his prolonged scientific education, McDougall was never at heart a scientist." Instead, he constantly tried "to provide the answers to problems before the factual data needed even for provisional answers were available. . . . Even when he turned out to be right his methodology in arriving at his conclusions was often unscientific." It was true that McDougall "had nearly all the makings of a scientist except the scientific attitude."[14]

Trotter, too, believed that social psychology had to be based upon deductive methods. But, unlike McDougall, he expected that deductive speculation would be tested later by "those methods of measurement and coordination upon which all true science is based.[15] McDougall never looked back, but Trotter continued to be a brilliant scientist who changed the surgery of the brain and spinal cord and the study of malignant disease. His legendary acumen in medicine was conspicuous in his social psychology as well. Science always remained "measurement" to Trotter, but he saw deduction as a method that might "indicate those things which can be most profitably measured."[16]

When nineteenth-century writers called for a social science, they were demanding a form of knowledge that surpassed empirical limits. Empiricism approved commonsense and inductive, descriptive procedures for acquiring and using information. But traditional nineteenth-century social scientists tried to avoid the tentative and hypothetical implications of empiricism by deducing social and psychological laws from their axiomatic belief in a rational and predictable universe. During the last two decades of the nineteenth century, the revolutionary social scientists denied the restrictions that "natural" social laws placed on the individual's ability to improve his character and circumstances. Instead of discovering universal relations among social phenomena, economists, psychologists, and political scientists searched for unique methods of dealing immediately with individual disabilities. If social psychology had responded to the practical demand for reform characteristic of the prewar decades, it might have developed as a study of social forces and their interaction. But neither Trotter nor McDougall were prepared to relinquish the comprehensive comfort of absolute laws.

McDougall and Trotter were not unique in their justification of elitist political theory as a remedy against biological forces, nor were they the first to write about crowd psychology. But they did bring these two critiques of democracy together in a pioneering attempt to explain mass behavior through a systematic physiological sociology. A plea for the special management of democracy on the grounds of mass biological incompetence had been made blatantly by Benjamin Kidd, William Bateson and, above all, by Francis Galton, Karl Pearson, and the eugenicist camp at the University of London. These biological determinists challenged not only democracy but also its liberal past.

A similar challenge came from an entirely different kind of critic, the liberal who continued the earlier nineteenth-century elitist strain in liberalism. These elitist liberals saw democracy as a threat to the further development of personal liberty and they wrote about the dangers of crowd behavior beginning at least as far back as the 1890s. Unlike the biological determinists, their elitist remedies were not derived from a reading of evolution but rather from the moral conviction that public and private good was served best by an especially equipped few. The Webbs, Shaw, and Wells contributed to this tradition, but their interest lay in the collectivization of individuals rather than in collective behavior. Although the Fabians never idealized predemocratic liberalism, there were minor elitist liberals whose common perception of the "crowd" led them to yearn for liberalism as they thought it had been before its late-nineteenth-century culmination in democracy. None of them approached the subject "scientifically" or even systematically, nor did their views prevail. But they are important because they represented a distinct type of reaction to the new democracy that occurred among many people. Perhaps their only lasting effect was to make national readers familiar with a new and frightening subject that touched everyone. In so doing they prepared an audience for McDougall's and Trotter's systematic efforts to solve the intellectual's disappointment in democracy through the therapeutic agency of science.

These liberal elitist writers were either marginal observers, whose careers and major writings had nothing to do with social psychology, or they were peripheral commentators, read then but subsequently forgotten. The most distinguished among these occasional writers was Sir Martin Conway, the famous mountaineer and Slade Professor of Fine Arts at Cambridge. Two of the most characteristic of the minor liberal elitists were Arnold White, the religious writer, and Marcus R. P. Dorman, who attempted ambitious psychological studies of popular thought. White, Dorman, and Conway emphasized the three major elements in elitist liberalism: an idealistic reliance upon altruistic leaders; the role of the elite in educating the masses; and, an aversion to centralized power.

Writing in 1895, Arnold White saw democracy imperiled both by socialism and a selfish bureaucracy; his panacea lay in social reform checked by "the union of Christ and democracy." Despite the impracticality of his solution, he did provide an early and accurate analysis of the new methods used by the press and politicians to manipulate the new voter. The constant thread running through liberal-elitist complaints against democracy was that it deprived responsible, moral leaders of the opportunity to devote themselves to public service. White admitted readily that aristocratic and middle-class government in the past had not often been distinguished for public altruism, but he feared that democracy would mean even greater degeneration from the ideal of disinterested leadership. In particular, he wrote against the proposed payment of M.P.'s as a mistaken opening of government to completely unscrupulous adventurers. The effect, he concluded, would be to downgrade the civil service and to lower, still further, the "tone" of the House. White thought of his critique of democracy and his model of good government as originating in Burke, a continuing inspiration to liberal critics of democracy throughout the nineteenth and twentieth centuries. These critics idealized the liberal representative, eulogized by Burke in his famous address to the sheriffs of Bristol in 1780, as independent of his constituency and owing allegiance only to God and his own good judgment.[17] The political naïveté of supposing that an M.P. elected in 1895 could be entirely indifferent to the particular interests of the electorate that sent him to Parliament entirely vitiated White's already weak position.

Unlike White, Dorman's explanation of both the causes of mass ignorance and the national "mind" relied upon psychological and not social, economic, or religious factors. But his efforts were limited by an a priori commitment to the natural wisdom of altruistic leaders, and by the old liberal belief in the educational maturation of the childlike masses. Dorman argued that although the thinking workingman was eager to learn and anxious to "raise himself and his children to the grade above in the social scale," he too was moved chiefly by sentiment and feeling. But working-class desires for self-improvement were thwarted by an impatience to "apply schemes of reform which will not bear the criticism of cool reason, and which consequently fail." This was compounded by a "suggestibility" to "plausible words" and an inability "either to suggest or follow a chain of reasoning." Dorman's justification for controlling democracy was drawn from astronomical rather than biological analogies: just as "there must be stars of various degrees of magnitude, planets of various sizes and moons circulating about them, so there must be dull, dark, inert mental masses revolving in an orb of mechanical stupidity, ever passively attracted by the gravity of faith to their more noble brethren." These inert masses could be raised only through "moral education."[18] In Dorman's history of the national mind, he found leaders, ready to act in the public interest, among radicals and conservatives alike. These men, he wrote confidently, were not moved by self-interest but by general feelings of "humanity."[19] Dorman's political analysis was trite, but he did call attention to suggestibility and its political effect a decade before McDougall and Trotter analyzed it more closely.

Martin Conway wrote three essays on the crowd for *Nineteenth*

Century in the three years before McDougall and Trotter published their work. In 1895 Conway had been knighted and elected to the Athenaeum, and by 1906 he had already published eighteen books on art history, travel, and mountaineering. Whatever interest he may have had in politics was certainly episodic and never sustained. Identifying himself as a radical in 1893, Conway was adopted as the Liberal candidate for Bath in 1895. After failing to win this election, he had no further involvement with politics until 1919 when he succeeded as a Conservative supporter of the coalition government from one of the new combined university seats.[20]

What compelled Conway, whose consuming interests were climbing expeditions, photography, collecting, and art history, to write about crowd psychology? It may be that his rugged independence and his triumphs over mountains led him to euologize great men as those able to climb above democratic irrationality. Like Masterman, Wallas, and Trotter, he described the crowd and its effect upon individuals with great accuracy, but he did not suggest remedies for the dilemmas he exposed. Whenever crowds pressed upon him, he turned his back upon them and escaped to the aloof perspective of the highest peaks.

In 1905 Conway's first essay on mass psychology described the crowd not as "mere assemblages of individuals, but as a kind of creature." The "opinion of a crowd" is "not either the greatest common measure or the least common denominator of the individuals composing it, but something altogether different" that compels people to act and feel differently from the way they do as individuals. Conway saw that instead of one homogenous undifferentiated entity, there were a great number of crowds to which every person belonged at some level. These communities determined their member's sentiments, thoughts, and actions.[21] In an analysis much like that of James, Wallas, and Trotter, Conway defined the greatest contemporary predicament as the internal struggle between nongregarious and gregarious impulses. Every individual was "crowd-assailed at any hour and in all places,"[22] and voluntarily or involuntarily, people joined different groups whose collective opinions "infected" their members without any intervening process of intellectual scrutiny or conviction.[23] Only the wisest men refused to give up their individuality and, while belonging to many crowds, they yielded themselves "to none."[24] The retention of independence was Conway's essential criterion for leadership.

The conflict between gregariousness and individuality was external as well as internal. In urban, heavily populated areas, gregariousness dominated, while in sparsely populated rural areas, it lay dormant. Neither urban congestion nor rural isolation fulfilled genuine individual and social needs. Although the individual, representing the reasoning force within society, needed to be protected from the tyranny of "crowddom," it was only through collective social forces that the emotional reservoir necessary for individual inspiration was preserved. Urging that an equilibrium be maintained between the intrinsically hostile claims of individual freedom and public liberty, Conway gave no indication in his writing of how such a balance would be achieved. He had no apparent interest in institutions, organizations, or any of the actual agencies through which government is carried out.

Conway's only means for reconciling private and public good lay in the "crowd-compeller" who would force the public "to adopt his opinion" and make it "public opinion." But since the crowd is inherently irrational, how will a crowd-compeller compel them to follow his rational direction? Although indifferent to methods, Conway was a typical liberal critic of democracy in his fear of central authority, organization, and discipline. Crowds, he warned, can be welded into an organic entity by public officials under authority granted them by "the people," so that no freedom whatever would be left to the "individual."[25] Society would then suffer, because only the independent individual can create those concepts that propel the crowd forward. What passes as "public opinion" is actually "imposed upon the public by a succession of thinkers." Whenever public opinion is irrational or ill considered, it is the fault, not of the crowd but of the leaders that control it. Democracy is no better or worse than its managers.

But he who rises to a position of public confidence is not a desirable leader if he is no more than a "crowd-exponent" who feels by "sympathetic insight and mere sensitiveness...as the crowd feels or is going to feel, and who expresses in clear language the emotion of the dumb organism." Conway's examples of the most influential of crowd exponents were Gladstone and Lloyd George. Although not necessarily demagogues, such exponents never had the new ideas of the compeller, and they were typically ambitious men seeking only the approval of the crowd.[26] The trouble with Conway's distinction is that it permits us to applaud those who reflect our own opinions as "compellers," while dismissing those with whom we disagree as mere "exponents."

Conway was concerned about the formulation of public opinion because he recognized it as the only effective moralizing force within a democratic society. In an argument similar to Trotter's, he observed that although individuals invented ideals, those ideals would be without influence unless incorporated into the community. Rail against the crowd as we may "for its intolerance, its fickleness, its lack of measure, and all the other shortcomings," upon "crowds our spiritual life depends...from them we draw our enthusiasms." When an ideal is accepted by the crowd, it goes on trial; when it is retained, it becomes part of "humanity as a whole." The total of these "tried and established ideals form what we call 'the moral law' which is binding upon all crowds and all individuals alike."[27] Conway's account of the origin of ethical obligation does not explain why the crowd rejects certain ideals and retains others. Since he has characterized the crowd as mindless, how can we expect it to exercise any kind of discrimination?

Even more seriously, he confuses success with worth. Morality by consensus would never have passed any of the new social scientists as an index of goodness, desirability, or obligation. Conway tried to avoid equating morality with success by arguing that concepts of right and wrong are given to the crowd by exceptional individuals.[28] But this introduces still another confusion, since we are not told the qualifications for "exceptionality" nor why we should expect outstanding people to be good, too. Conway's explanation went no further than the observation that since the crowd is mindless, those with minds must "strive to mitigate the disadvantages of an inevitable situation."[29] Democracy's thinking had to be done for it so that the results of the poll would be transformed, through a mysterious alchemy, from an "average of foolish opinions" into an "integration of popular aspirations."[30] This was not terribly helpful to anyone looking for practical political advice.

Social psychology, as defined by McDougall and Trotter, was not explicitly elitist. Neither author claimed to be a systematic political thinker concerned with the form or content of political institutions. Never aggressive, the elitism of social psychology made no partisan appeals and endorsed no political program. Apparently free of vested interest and ideological motive, social psychology appealed to a lay audience as a scientific exposition that even nonspecialists could understand. Other prominent elitists, such as Karl Pearson, explicitly argued the conservative bias by adopting biological metaphors and evolutionary vocabulary to strengthen their arguments. But the social psychologists believed themselves to be disinterested scientists methodically analyzing the psychology of man in society.

The effect of social psychology in England before the war is ironic in that it accomplished one of Wallas's major goals for the social sciences. Until then, sociologists discussed the origins of institutions and the comparison of societies, or they collected the data necessary to investigate special social problems. Social psychology introduced a new content into sociology by insisting, as Wallas did, that a comprehensive study of society must include an explanation of the psychological forces affecting thinking and behavior.

Unlike some earlier elitists, McDougall's and Trotter's ends were exclusively moral, and their elitism was derived from a fear that mass urban democracy would obliterate moral distinctions. Both writers accepted, though on different grounds, Huxley's contention that since the evolutionary process was nonmoral, social progress depended upon moral factors.[31] Elitism became their means for concentrating those factors so that they could be used most efficiently to raise the rational and moral level of human nature. As a matter of procedure they subordinated their means to their ends. The effect of justifying manipulation — an inherently immoral means which robs people of their choice — by moral ends made the social psychologists appear suspiciously like traditional elitists appealing for special privilege. But their new elitism, unlike the older elitism characteristic of writers like Lecky, was not concerned to demonstrate that democracy and equality were destructive to liberty, but that democracy, equality, and liberty were all incompatible with human nature and its instinctual crowd propensity. Democratic critics in search of authoritarian sanction could turn to the evidence presented in social psychology.

In addition, both social psychologists were articular members of that close-knit intellectual community that met at the frontiers of the new sciences and the new politics for the purpose of reforming the immediate present. These were men to whom the social psychologists spoke directly and their success in introducing social psychology to this community may be measured by its acceptance at tradition-bound Oxford, by the numerous editions of McDougall's works, and by the influential character of Trotter's audience.[32]

McDougall and Trotter were widely read because, in the early twentieth century, the new democracy's irrational political behavior could no longer be explained through any variety of rationalist psychology. To many middle-class observers, the new voter appeared to prefer large political units to his individual political independence. The myth of the reasonable individual, idealized by nineteenth-century political reformers, disappeared with the growth of increasingly collective groups that dictated their members' behavior. Few contemporaries among the older propertied classes confused the new voter's relative quiescence with impotence. The unprecedented and spontaneous popular celebrations at the relief of Mafeking in 1900, lasting from May 18 to May 23, brought home forcefully the frightening prospect of a "vast concourse demonstrating, apparently unchecked and uncontrolled, with such fervour."[33] As Masterman watched the ebullient demonstrators, he knew that they could just as easily be hostile.[34] The unorganized crowd, more conspicuous than any organized group and politically more powerful, emerged in the early twentieth century as an unpredictable and antidemocratic entity.

Democracy is a theory of choice which assumes, first, that people will choose whatever helps themselves or those for whom they care and, second, that they recognize, approximately, what their interest is. The social psychologists tried to refute democratic theory by repudiating choice and its rational context. They substituted instinctual motivation, a deterministic "gregarious" or "herd" instinct, compelling all individuals to think and act in conformity to crowd opinion. McDougall threw out the rationalist-voluntarist tradition and its revival by Green, Sidgwick, and James because he believed that men were "moved by a variety of impulses whose nature had been determined through long ages of evolutionary process."[35] These "impulses," or instincts, were supplemented by the master instinct, the "gregarious impulse," a "mere uneasiness in isolation and satisfaction in being one of a herd."[36] Trotter, too attributed responsibility to gregariousness for an "important group of instinctive impulses."[37] The "herd instinct" had the "characteristic that it exercises a controlling power upon the individual from without."[38]

Unlike the social psychologists, Karl Pearson had used the concept of herd instinct in 1900 to prove that altruism was a natural and instinctive product of gregariousness. And, Westermarck, the Finnish sociologist at L.S.E., found gregariousness to be a positive, altruistic, and even affectionate instinct in his chart of human development from savagery to civilization. In an ambitious account of gregariousness appearing in 1906, Westermarck explained the differences among people as stages in a uniform process: instinctual behavior belonged to an earlier stage of precivilized history and could still be found among primitive peoples. And as late as 1909, Hobson eulogized the "herd" as the true repository of social unity.[39]

The social psychologists, however, saw instinctual behavior as the defining characteristic of their own time. The savage was not "without," in darkest Africa, but within every twentieth-century Englishman. There was no difference in kind in the behavior of individuals when alone or when part of a crowd, because in both cases individuals respond only to emotional stimuli. Directed by animal instinct, the primitive and random mob could not be treated as if it were a temporary assembly of reasonable, well-informed individuals each taking his own counsel. In their attempt to correct the facile individualist psychology that underlay democratic theory, the social psychologists swung to the other extreme to find the source of all behavior in the homogeneous crowd that dominated its individual parts.[40]

Both McDougall and Trotter found the explanatory key to society in the disappearance of the individual into the crowd. Herbert Spencer had argued that as society developed, the individual grew increasingly independent and self-reliant, and the influence of environment upon him decreased.[41] Social psychology turned Spencerian evolutionary theory inside out by maintaining that as society developed, the individual's dependence upon his environment increased. While the social psychologists were not unique in perceiving this phenomenon of mass urban life, they did offer a "scientific" explanation for "suggestibility." McDougall formulated his notion of "suggestibility" in an investigation of size-weight illusions when he was in the Torres Strait.[42] When applied to social phenomena, it meant that any concept suggested by an accepted source of authority led the individual to act upon it without questioning its origin or validity: human nature and democracy were inherently incompatible. McDougall found susceptibility to suggestion proportional to crowd or stress conditions. More perceptive than McDougall, Trotter analyzed suggestibility as a basic psychological fact, a defensive adaptation of the human organism to every situation, private as well as public.[43] But both agreed that suggestion stimulated only emotional or passive responses that were unsuited to the informed and rational foresight necessary for free political choice.

If it was suggestibility that united men in society, then the revolutionary social scientists' understanding of rationality as the most cohesive of social forces could hardly be correct. In contrast to the economists, psychologists, and political scientists, the social psychologists argued that what really held people together was their common fear of change, difference, and originality. This argument meant that any justification of political democracy on the basis of group consensus was absurd, since that consensus was initially irrational and ultimately conservative of past decisions, whether or not they were appropriate to the present.

The new elector's reluctance to use his potential political power in his own interest provided both social psychologists with evidence that political democracy was a mass commitment to the status quo in which people showed a constant and increasing tendency to acquiesce to authoritarian demands. Every elitist critic could challenge democratic theory by pointing to the willingness among the first adult beneficiaries of compulsory education to be guided by a sensational press into support of a South African war and away from pursuit of their own pressing social and economic needs. Even the tools of political freedom — secret ballots, frequent elections, literacy, and publicity of public questions — had not encouraged the new citizen to declare his psychological independence from authority that led him to repress dissent indiscriminately.

The social psychologists went beyond apparent democratic failures to question the ameliorative expectations of liberal democrats on the basis of psychological reality. Rejecting associationist psychology and the Jamesian account of the subordination of instinct to reasoned will, they saw the mind as filled still with precivilized instincts that, under the "crowded" conditions of urban democracy, intensified social conflict. Traditionally social conflict had been understood as the product of irreconcilable individual and social interests or, more abstractly, as an ideological incompatibility between the values of freedom and order. Nineteenth-century thinkers were unable to find acceptable compromises between private and public good and they left the problem, unresolved, as a troublesome legacy to the next century.

A new dimension was added to this old problem when the social psychologists defined social conflict as the psychological tension between the individual's crowd instinct and society's need for reasoned and consistent direction. McDougall believed that this social conflict could be resolved by raising the rational competence of the crowd. But Trotter, generally more farsighted than McDougall, realized that the novel dilemma of the individual in twentieth-century society was that he would perpetually be torn between need for group support and an equally strong abhorrence of groups.[44]

It is undeniable that the social psychologists succeeded in exposing the irrational motivations that influence mass urban behavior, but their attempt to document their perceptions with scientific argument never went beyond pseudobiology and contrived psychology. Most writers in the new century rejected grossly deterministic theories of social development, but many retained the biological model of natural selection which they interpreted in various ways. Trotter and McDougall used natural selection to explain how contemporary man's nature and development is formed in response to continuing instinctual needs. To demonstrate the existence of a social instinct, they constructed a biological history of man in society from primitive origins in group security to its conclusion in a crowd culture persisting beyond its evolutionary time. Listing biological examples, phsyiological analogies, and inferences, neither social psychologist succeeded in making his account of behavior scientifically or logically compelling. Both men based the evolution of social relationships upon the development of the nervous system. On the one hand, McDougall maintained that an "instinctive action . . . implies some enduring nervous basis whose organization is inherited . . . which, anatomically regarded, probably has the form of a compound system of sensor-motor arcs." On the other hand, Trotter suggested that natural selection effected a neurological transition from the "unicellular to the multicellular" by the same evolutionary mechanism that changed men from "the solitary to the social."[45] But neither conclusion about crowd behavior was derived from physiological evidence; instead, they were inspired by a hostile view of the new democracy enforced by very limited impressions of democratic processes.

11.
Social Psychology as a Solution:
McDougall, Trotter, and the Elitist Refuge

Social psychology was explicitly deductive in its method; but decked out in physiological trappings, the new discipline appealed to reformers as another revolutionary social science responding to their demand for a separation of social fact from positivistic theory. Both McDougall and Trotter promised to separate actual from speculative origins of behavior in their evolutionary explanations of men-in-society. Although sincerely given, that promise could hardly be fulfilled in writing limited to the preparation of a theoretical foundation upon which an applied social science might eventually be built. Still, each author could insist that his work was "scientific" because he held an essentially positivistic view of the methods of social science. McDougall introduced social psychology as the "positive science of the mind in all its aspects and modes of functioning...[and] of conduct or behavior...an evolutionary natural history of the mind." Trotter saw his subject as a "body of knowledge derived from experience of its material...man in society or associated man."[1] But both of them relied upon a deductive theory that combined Herbert Spencer's social statics and social dynamics in an evolutionary treatment of human nature in relation to social functions. But no analysis of social structure, no inquiry into the nature of social relations, underlay what was largely an a priori insight into instinctual origins of conduct. Even though neither social psychologist really based his axioms upon experience, each perceived, almost intuitively, the crucial importance of gregarious instincts in behavior.

In their creation of a social science that assumed psychological and historical laws from which unavoidable political consequences were deduced, McDougall and Trotter revised nineteenth-century positivism. Each writer's social science was a gloss upon his preconceived notions of social good. Using social evolution as a historical background, both social psychologists tried to predict the future.[2] Although they did not use evolution to discover specific laws, they did use it to isolate processes or trends which had the causal character of laws.

The great aspiration of nineteenth-century positivist science had been to solve complex problems through the application of a few relatively simple laws of human nature and society. This program was continued into the twentieth century by the social psychologists, but they realized that such laws, especially those defining human nature, were less simple and less accessible. While the proper purposes and methods of social science were clear enough to nineteenth-century positivists, they became a subject of chronic and divisive controversy in the twentieth century. It was the inductive and experimental method advocated by Marshall, James, and Wallas that was generally accepted as the method of the social sciences until the 1920s.[3] When applied to social and political problems, induction produced more practical results, in terms of concrete, reliable reform, than the kind of deductive speculation pursued by Trotter and McDougall.[4]

The major innovation in nineteenth-century social science, Spencer's assimilation of evolutionary methods and metaphors into an a priori social theory, was carried further by the social psychologists. Spencer had believed that the march of progress was clear; the revisionist social psychologists were more like the revolutionaries in their refusal to find the existing state of society satisfactory. But while accepting Spencer's view of biological process as a movement toward increasing levels of complexity and organization,[5] they found the source of contemporary problems in undesirable instinctual forces which had become unimaginably complex and organized. Furthermore, the new elitism of McDougall and Trotter rejected two major tenets of older varieties of evolutionary elitist theory: first, an assumption about the uniqueness of individual personality; and second, the progressive judgment that society had improved rationally. Instead, the social psychologists explained personality through absolutely uniform instincts; and, they condemned the institutions and customs inherited by the twentieth century as biological anachronisms based still upon instinctual needs.[6]

But, like other social evolutionists, the social psychologists could not give up the idea of progress even though it contradicted their analysis of human nature in society. In order to reconcile their essentially progressive view of society with a fundamentally irrational view of mass behavior, they transcended the older social scientists' superficially progressive interpretations by a more analytical effort to explain the underlying causes of change. Trotter restored progress to evolution by making it depend upon especially trained, morally superior free agents. McDougall, who relied initially upon agents, tried to guarantee absolute progress by imposing a rational and moral teleology upon evolution.

In agreement upon the basic pattern of social evolution, Trotter and McDougall differed fundamentally in interpreting its direction and ends. The contradictions implicit in trusting an elite to achieve progress in spite of the fundamental irrationality characteristic of all human nature, led McDougall eventually to a belief in an organic community somehow more rational and moral than its individual components. McDougall believed that progress was obstructed by "individualism," because it was a deluded faith in the eventual rational and moral maturity of each man. Trotter, in contrast, insisted that a few extraordinary individuals could free themselves from both their own instinctual limitations and the compulsions of social pressure.[7] Hobhouse had already attempted a sociology that promised to reconcile individualism and organicism by fulfilling the individual's claims to a unique personality "and the duties of a common life" through political democracy as the mediating process between the extremes of individualism and organicism.[8] But Hobhouse had no disciples until after the war. The eventual ideological conflict over whether society should promote individual or collective ends controlled McDougall's and Trotter's social analysis and it pre-

figured the controversy characteristic of the subsequent development of social psychology.[9] It is interesting that an almost identical model of social development should have led the two social
psychologists to such diametrically opposed conclusions.

McDougall arrived at his ideal of an organically harmonious
society because of his unalterable conviction in the stability of the
group and the instability of the individual. To justify his belief,
he suggested a secret evolutionary purpose that compelled society
to move toward an entirely organic, morally higher form of social
organization. Evolutionary cunning, the irresistible mover of
human affairs, progressed through transitory stages which included the self-interested individualism accepted as a virtue by
democratic theory.

In evolution, McDougall believed that he found irrefutable
evidence of the individual's dependence upon the moral support
of the group. The collective life of well-organized society, he
wrote, "attains a higher level both intellectually and morally than
could be attained by its average members, and raises those who
participate in it to much higher levels of thought and action."[10]
Society was a life form moving at an undetermined rate from selfish individualism toward the maturity and altruism of collective
ends. Assuming further that personal ends must always be selfish,
he argued that altruism, the attribute of maturity, lay at the end
of the evolutionary process in the moral collectivization of thought
and conduct. His "scientific" conclusion, put more succinctly,
was that true morality required individual interests to be subordinated to collective goals which alone "enrich our emotional life
and raise our emotions and conduct to an over-individualized
plane."[11]

McDougall rejected individualism as a regrettable deviation
from a collective and ordered good. To check erratic individualism and its divisive consequences, he invented a corrective hand
hidden in evolution. On the basis of an evolutionary pattern that
reflected only his desire for social stability, he predicted an immanent social synthesis greater than and superseding its individual
members. He concluded, as he had begun, with a conservative's
essential distrust of the ordinary man's ability to improve his con-

dition. Individual conflicts within a mass urban democracy were explained away by dismissing individualism as a biological pause in the human race's march to collective consciousness. Social growth, part of the natural movement of evolution, would culminate, eventually, in a national personality that would solve individual and social conflicts by completely incorporating the individual into his society.[12] Since the individual was never the best judge of is own interests, majority rule could have only mythological merit. McDougall's version of national personality was an elitist form of the theory of general will.

After 1908 McDougall used social psychology increasingly to explain and justify the group mind as a lofty national entity. His yearning for "some guarantee of stability and some prospect for the continued progress of mind and culture" inspired his social psychology and set its conclusions in advance.[13] As he understood psychology, its purpose was clearly an "understanding of, and power of control over, the behavior of men."[14]

Equally aware of the collective impetus of forces within the new democracy, Trotter differed from McDougall in his conviction that such forces must be resisted. While Trotter's psychology, like McDougall's, began with a deterministic or instinctual view of human nature, its main contention was that while evolution described the past, it had no absolute bearing on the future.[15] Social evolution was nothing more than a blind, amoral force that had indeed affected social direction, but entirely at random. Trotter could find no covert direction in evolution which required individuals to be sacrificed to a social good different from individual good. On the contrary, he believed that social purposes were always forced upon the morally neutral or purposeless direction of social processes by intelligent individuals concerned with achieving human ends. Trotter's end was a rapport between individuals and the collective groups within society for the sake of individualism. Society existed for Trotter only as an organized system of goods and services to enable creative indivduals to pursue the good life.

Trotter's construction of evolutionary history was intended to show that instinct controlled men because they allowed it to do so, and he wanted informed individuals to rebel against the historical determinism of instinct. Through expert direction of evolutionary tendencies, herd instinct, man's "abiding sense of incompleteness," could be transformed into a progressive social asset.[16] Trotter's psychology was explicitly didactic, even Jamesian, in insisting that either men thought through and controlled their directions, or they abandoned themselves to evolution to become one more of "nature's failures."[17]

Trotter wanted to believe that even within the compulsions of powerful herd instincts, human nature and society could be changed for the better. Like McDougall, he admitted the unavoidable pressures exerted by prevalent traditions and values upon even extraordinary individuals. He recognized too that the most serious dilemma of mass urban life was not simply the play of coercive forces, but the individual's inherited affinity for a herd life which was bound to make him wretched. With prophetic insight he predicted that the most thoughtful and sensitive individuals would be torn chronically between their individual needs and a public opinion that demanded conformity to standards contradicting those needs. If the individual resisted, he was censured and isolated; if he conformed, he violated his pragmatic experience and feeling.[18]

Trotter's sympathy for the individual's predicament led him to analyze psychological reactions to conflicting and irreconcilable demands. To explain how individuals were still able to act, given their paradoxical evolutionary heritage, Trotter invented "rationalization," a concept that Ernest Jones was to incorporate into the emerging framework of Freudian psychology on the continent.[19] The individual, although conforming to public opinion, convinced himself that he was critical of herd suggestion by rationalizing that suggestion so that it seemed to be the result of his independent thought. In this way an individual fulfilled his craving for certainty, a cardinal psychological need, and he retained the illusion of independence as well. Unfortunately, the cost of rationalization was intellectual and emotional paralysis which deprived the individual of any opportunity for moral conduct. From the unsatisfactory self-deception of rationalization, individuals were forced into the conditions of "resistiveness on the one hand" and "mental instability on the other" that led inevitably to the unbearable "isolation of the individual."[20] When individuals capable of imaginative leadership were penalized in these ways, psychological and social development reverted to natural or purposeless activity.

Another major problem in McDougall and Trotter's social psychology, which they never solved, was the paradox of innately irrational men achieving a rational and moral society. When McDougall and Trotter established the irrationality of human nature, they created an apparently irreconcilable antagonism between what man is and what they wanted him to be. This problem, the dichotomy between the real and the ideal, lay at the heart of contemporary social and moral theory. At the end of the nineteenth century the intellectual community to which McDougall and Trotter belonged demanded a view of the world that was "rational, progressive and secular."[21] Even though both social psychologists found the real world dominated by irrational, regressive forces, they were driven, as much as other progressive theorists, to make reality rational and progressive. But unlike Marshall, James, and Wallas, McDougall and Trotter could not trust ordinary reason because they found reason an "unnatural" or acquired attribute. At the same time, their belief in human progress compelled them to attempt to discover progressive tendencies in their biological history of human nature in society.

In biology, the social psychologists uncovered natural laws governing human development. But while admitting that human nature had been subject to instinctual laws in the past, they wanted higher moral forces to overcome and supersede such causality in the future. During the nineteenth century moral philosophers often assigned the moral and physical worlds to different causal systems to reserve freedom for the area of conduct. But in the twentieth century, some philosophers have suggested that it is misleading to use distinct causal explanations for different types of phenomena because the establishment of causal laws is ultimately only a tool for correlating different elements of our experience.[22] McDougall and Trotter did assign the mental and physical worlds to the same causal system in which instinctualism lay behind and determined experience. As progressivists, the social psychologists could only justify faith in progress by overcoming their instinctual definition of human nature. When, on the eve of the First World War, A. J. Balfour wrote that a belief in progress assumed belief in permanent values, he was expressing one of the most pervasive convictions of his time.[23] For the social psychologists this conviction created a serious dilemma: How could men, with so fallible a psychological inheritance and with institutions arising from irrational conditions, sustain permanent values? To solve this dilemma, McDougall and Trotter had to find ethical development as an outcome of irrational evolutionary processes.

Neither social psychologist could ignore the amoral consequences that flowed logically from their irrationalist interpretation of human nature and history because it was important to them to explain not only how men did act but how they ought to act. Within their critique of mass urban democracy lay the prevailing moralist's impulse to make human nature less natural, more disciplined, and reasonable. Other elitists criticized contemporary political democracy as inefficient; the elitist social psychologists found it immoral. McDougall and Trotter tried to do what T. H. Huxley had urged in his famous Romanes Lecture of 1893: neither social psychologist was willing to admit a view of social process which was not morally significant.[24]

When the social psychologists thought about the instinctualist-moralist dilemma they had created, they recognized only two alternative means of escape. On the one hand, they could be mistaken in their failure to find any moral purpose in social processes; or, on the other, if those processes were neutral, then they had to be made moral through a heroic act of personal will. Since their social psychology was founded on the biological history of instinct, the first alternative was dismissed initially by both men, to be revived eventually by McDougall. At first, both sought to control evolution through a technocratic elite of social scientists with an aptitude for reforming human nature. Neither writer argued for a permanent institutional elite. Instead, they called for an expert application of social science to social problems. Scientific expertise and social conscience were to be the credentials for election in a new society where social choices required special psychological knowledge. If their analysis of human nature was correct, then it followed logically that the future of the new mass urban society depended entirely upon the qualifications of its management.

Agreeing that moral progress was related intimately to an increase in the rationality of all men, McDougall and Trotter were bound to reject elitism eventually because it assumed a continuing gulf between rational leaders and irrational followers. The privileged morality of the elite minority could not serve general moral progress because it did not affect the great majority of men.

To the social psychologists, elitism was merely a means without inherent value or superiority, but it is significant that theorists concerned with moral ends should be so indifferent to the morality of their means. Despite their final goals, their greatest emphasis fell upon elitism as the most efficient instrument for turning social development from a disastrous to a progressive course. Even a casual reader of social psychology could not miss the emphasis upon "management" which ennobled the manager by contrasting him to those requiring management. But neither McDougall nor Trotter wanted special advantage for an elite whose temporary existence would be dedicated exclusively to public service.

Wallas, unlike the social psychologists, repudiated elitism as an avoidable corruption of democratic government; he criticized Ostrogorki's *Democracy and the Organization of Political Parties* explicitly for its conclusion that bureaucratic management was inevitable. Wallas proposed "organization" as a genuinely democratic counterfoil to the manipulative and politically irresponsible managers elevated by the social psychologists into guardians of public intelligence and purpose. As a fundamental part of the functioning democratic process, Wallas wanted participatory government to begin with the political dialogues of local government and to proceed through more general levels of political organization to Parliament. An individual's only protection against the monolithic, impersonal government of a great society lay in his access to self-governing organizations within his community. Wallas was no political simpleton and he had seen that local political groups, voluntary or elected, were filled only by those with strong interests and ambitions. But he hoped that a more sophisticated political education would encourage every citizen to enter democratic forums in pursuit of his own needs and interests. There is a considerable difference between providing opportunities for participation, whether they are used or not, and urging that organization be equivalent to a controlling bureaucracy functioning as society's general staff. Any resemblance between Wallas's conception of the civil service and the social psychologist's specialized managers is entirely superficial.

The civil service, as Wallas tried to arrange it, would have been responsible for accumulating and presenting the complex social information each individual required before he chose among competing alternatives. Wallas's civil servants were experts, not managers. Their activities were to be reviewed and restricted by the actual governing done within participatory bodies, locally and nationally, that considered and discussed all matters affecting them. What Wallas never imagined is that experts in the process of translating large quantities of specialized information into the simpler and more condensed form meant for popular consumption, may easily persuade cabinets, members of parliaments, and even substantial portions of the electorate that only one conceivable course of action follows from their "objective" data.

Within the English elitist tradition in which McDougall and Trotter fell, private benefits were inseparable from public duties.[25] The new social scientist whom they evoked was to be a superior man, able to overcome not only his own lower nature but social pressures too.[26] Their view of personality as torn between "higher" and "lower," rational and irrational elements was closer to continental developments in psychology than to the Jamesian idea of a unified personality. When J. S. Mill tried to revise the foundations of Benthamite morality, he had rejected the notion that pleasure or happiness could be assessed by quantitative tests and substituted a qualitative distinction between "higher" and "lower" pleasures. But he could not identify the contents of either category, because he recognized them as essentially matters of moral choice. James went beyond Mill in his definition of higher behavior as responsible rational activity, but his definition carried no clear social or political implications. While McDougall saw the highest elements in personality as those that tended to the greatest social order, Trotter was closer to James in valuing those that contributed to the greatest sensitivity of the unusual individual. But both social psychologists conjured up an ideal social scientist, able to marshal the highest aspects of his personality and willing to use his science paternally and didactically for the benefit of the great majority of men permanently restricted by their lower natures.

McDougall and Trotter tried to avoid explaining the source of the social scientist's altruism by describing his role as sociologically and biologically assigned, rather than as personally chosen. This invocation of biological coercion sprang from the social psychologists' distrust of ordinary men and their preference for the specialist. But they had difficulty in justifying such trust. To make their elitism compelling within their own system of analysis, they had to show that their scientific elite was not only technically but morally superior. In attempting this, Trotter and McDougall became entangled in the traditional contradictions inherent in elitist apologetics. When they tried to resolve those contradictions they failed, just as elitists before and after have failed.

The first, most obvious difficulty was how to reconcile an instinctual reading of human nature with the rational behavior expected of the elite.[27] If rationality was only an acquired characteristic, then what guarantee was there that even the most apparently rational men would not revert under stress to instinctive behavior? The social psychologists' answer was that the elite, unlike other men, would understand human nature well enough to recognize and discipline their own irrational impulses. Both McDougall and Trotter had gone to great and detailed length to describe the inherently irrational and unpredictable nature of all men. Then, unhappy with their success, they tried to make man into something contrary to the nature they had given him.

The social psychologists' mechanistic instinctualism and their zeal for ameliorative change led them to search for rational and ethical development in spite of irrational and immoral evolutionary processes. Nineteenth-century progressive theorists had recourse to rational social laws or to rational psychology as a source of prediction and, eventually, of control over social forces. For this absolute rationality McDougall and Trotter substituted an absolute instinctuality that confounded their reforming aspirations. To overcome instinctuality, each found an escape clause in evolution through which reason and morality could emerge. McDougall came to rely upon a predetermined progressive thrust beneath the surface of evolutionary events, while Trotter, in keeping with his individualism, turned to an idealization of free will. McDougall combined Huxley's "ethical" and "cosmic" processes by finding a moral teleology animating both, while Trotter set them far apart in a deep and perpetual conflict waged by a few in the interests of all.

Trotter and McDougall made instinct and progress compatible by relegating instinctual determinism to the historical past and by finding rational control in the present and future. For both social psychologists freedom and compulsion were complementary aspects of a true description of reality. McDougall's elite were agents through which greater or inevitable forces were realized. Their free will could do no more than accelerate or delay arrival at this predetermined end. Trotter, admitting the force of irrational compulsion, found an area for voluntary influence lying within the greater area of instinctual restraint.

McDougall's initial premise was that the compelling power of instinct was qualitatively alike for everyone without exception. To explain the emergence of morality as socially responsible reason, he found evidence of "group selection" acting in evolution to produce reason. Then he assumed that social conscience was a complementary facet of intelligence, and in the evolutionary history of reason he found a corollary development of prudence and altruism.[28] In spite of his elaborate evolutionary history of reason, McDougall continued to be troubled by the fear that instinct would always resist progressive change. He could not even convince himself that intelligence was naturally sufficient for morality.

When evolutionary theory did not help McDougall to resolve the irrationalist-rationalist conflict, he abandoned suppositious science and turned instead to a mystical collective wisdom. This led him to discard his theory of acquired rationality as a means of justifying the special individual. Eventually his distrust of individuals led to the decision that the elitist stage of social development could be bypassed. Doubting the ability of even the wisest and most altruistic leaders to remain wise and altruistic, McDougall subordinated them to a "nation," in which each person existed to serve the life of the "race."[29] By 1912 he was convinced that genuine social progress toward moral ends depended upon a supracollective, biologically superior mind, structured to defeat the unpredictable impulses latent in all individuals. Although never defining moral ends, he expected to find them at the end of the collective metamorphosis of human nature into the "nation," an organic entity, expressing the "will of the people" fully because it was "far more than the sum of the individuals in which its life is embodied."[30] Through "group-sentiments" everyone would rise above selfish levels of behavior to become "capable of steady labor for and enthusiastic devotion to the common ends of society."[31] Ultimately, then, individuals would follow a larger historical impulse driving them forward for the sake of a greater social good.

Why was a deterministic interpretation of history so appealing to McDougall? The new liberal's idea of progress rejected underlying determinants in history to emphasize instead an open future. Explicit within this rejection is the expectation that expanding knowledge will solve problems previously insoluble. Confidence was abundant in the early twentieth century when, before two tragic world wars, people still believed that technology was inherently beneficent. McDougall's reliance upon a moral teleology with deterministic power superior to the lesser determinism

of instinct, was his security against leaving decision of the future
with the new democracy. To thwart democratic or crowd behavior (the terms were synonymous for McDougall), he invested absolute control in an evolutionary movement toward corporate
national ends.

Wilfred Trotter began with the same biological reading of
human nature as William McDougall, and he faced the same initial problem in justifying elitism: how can irrational men be
trusted to behave rationally? Trotter replied in the tradition of
individualist or liberal elitism. Informed introspection would produce the self-knowledge to control instinct permanently. That
individual capable of abstracting critically from conflicting experiences would be mature enough to conduct his affairs with
rational consistency. Moreover, with the aid of psychological
insights, the mature individual would be able to discover and
implement the requisites for rational social conduct in general.[32]
Trotter evaded this first problem by postponing its practical solution until psychology became a genuinely experimental science.

Granted that reasonable men can exist, why should they care
for anyone else? Why should they feel social responsibility? This is
the second and more difficult conundrum in elitist social psychology. But altruistic expectations were more plausible in those
enthusiastic and undaunted Edwardian days than in these more
cynical times. In England, arguments for elitist altruism had
ancient roots in the paternalist's performance of social obligations in justification of his property and privileges. Then, in the
late nineteenth and early twentieth centuries, the tradition of
obligation, now divorced from questions of status, was strengthened and given new vitality by the expansive energies of reform
organizations that successfully affected developing British policy.

But evidence of altruistic activity does not explain why reasonable men should be interested in reforming the unreasonable. If
human nature compels men to push and shove toward destruction, why should those few who might escape bother to save the
rest? In answer, the social psychologists vacillated between a
moral imperative and simple utilitarianism. They argued, on the
one hand, that those with expert understanding of human nature

in society were morally bound to keep their brother and insisted, on the other hand, that exceptional men served their own selfish interest best by responsible social behavior. The social psychologists continued the nineteenth-century equation of reason, will, duty, and right by translating the older blend of religious and utilitarian obligation into the newer language of social psychology. Their explanation of elite motivation did not satisfy either writer.

It was easier for McDougall to explain altruistic behavior because his elite were moved by the beneficent forces of social evolution. He expected his stewards to assume power, use it for social good, and then relinquish it when the appropriate evolutionary moment arrived. But the difficulty with McDougall's expectation is that individual members of a power structure are often driven out by people or forces beyond their control, or by weariness and frustration, but they rarely leave when their programs and plans prosper. Another difficulty is that if evolution is not actually controllable, then what point can there be in winning or exercising illusory power?

Trotter had still greater trouble than McDougall in trying to account for elitist obligation to govern. He saw the superior person, by definition, as a unique individual interested in protecting his individuality. Why then should such a person become involved in social reform that would certainly compromise and impinge upon what he valued most? Since Trotter did not believe in teleological forces for good, he could scarcely use them to explain obligation as McDougall did. His explanation rested rather on a concept of morality that calculated the consequences of all acts. This meant that reasonable men must behave altruistically even when they were not motivated by altruism.

To compel an able elite to commit its ability to social good, Trotter equated self and social interest ecologically. No individual, no matter how extraordinary, can exist satisfactorily outside of society. But within society he is so restricted that eventually his survival became a matter of total cultural reform. Moreover, Trotter argued, exceptional individuals are too "sensitive" to be indifferent to other people. In "sensitivity," a sympathetic response to experience, Trotter found his best explanation for individual social commitment.[33] Ironically, his own life and career testify to the voluntary rather than the imperative nature of social commitment. Wilfred Trotter, the most perceptive social psychologist before 1914, yielded, after 1914, to Wilfred Trotter, distinguished surgeon and Fellow of the Royal Society, a skeptic who had overcome his sense of obligation.[34]

In justice to Trotter it must be noted that he meant to be iconoclastic rather than constructive. His essays on herd instinct were directed at the facile optimism of reformers acting upon a nineteenth-century understanding of human nature. Neither goodwill nor competence appeared as serious problems to Trotter. His major concern was rather the reformer's psychological ability to remain effective in the face of the unrelieved insecurity that came from the suspended and tentative judgments essential to scientific procedures. Trotter was afraid that the most capable and altruistic men might avoid the frustrations of leadership by exchanging the contemporary world and all its problems for a metaphysical certainty that reduced the conflicting demands both of experience and public opinion to relative insignificance.[35] The same fear gripped James and Wallas.

A third problem, and the one social psychologists were most confident they had solved, concerned training. How were the elite to prepare for their trusteeship? The answer was social psychology: To understand men, the social psychologist had to study mankind.[36] Through analysis of biological and psychological motivation, McDougall and Trotter expected the elite to learn how to solve the traditional problems of social organization which had always resisted solution. Since social choices relied essentially upon special knowledge, social psychology would provide a precise analysis of social behavior, and a series of new techniques, procedural and substantive, to make a practical applied social science possible for the first time. Although their introductions to social psychology were speculative and deductive, McDougall and Trotter wanted social psychology to be an empirical, critical, and autonomous study of man in society. The social scientist would succeed where previous reformers failed because his knowledge of human nature would equip him to respond to emotional problems objectively. Trotter and McDougall assumed, erroneously, that the social psychologist's ability to diagnose social ills was equally an ability to remedy them.

A fourth difficulty in elitist theory concerned the methods by which the new elite were to reach power and, once in power, were to transform human nature.[37] Neither social psychologist directly approached the problem of power and its efficient use. Instead, both argued that in a society where the great majority were manipulated for selfish purposes contrary to the public good, those who understood the strategems of manipulation should either become manipulators themselves, but for moral ends, or should expose manipulation so that it could be defeated.

The social psychologists accepted manipulation as an expedient method of affecting public purposes. They were never concerned, as was Graham Wallas, about the relation between the processes by which the manager "forms his own opinions and purposes," and that "by which he influences the opinions and purposes of others." With an active lifetime in politics and administration, Wallas knew at first hand the practical, as well as the moral, problem of deciding whether "overmen" were pursuing general or personal goods.[38] The social psychologists, like the Fabians from whom Wallas separated, expected the greatest public good to flow from especially prepared and dedicated people. McDougall wanted social scientists to devise rational and moral models to guide ordinary people. These models would be acted upon through "imitation," the "great conservative force in society . . . essential to all social progress." Trotter, too, relied upon charismatic leadership, but he warned the aspiring leader that to go beyond the crowd's understanding meant rejection and eventual suppression by natural selection, like the wolf who starved because he ignored herd impulse.[39]

Neither social psychologist saw himself as a leader of the crowd. Instead, each addressed himself to the enlightenment of the existing elite that was restricted by rationalist misconceptions about human nature in society. Just exactly how this was to lead to an innovating technocracy is never discussed by either writer. Their vague suggestions were not exactly blueprints for the acquisition, let alone exercise, of power. Although their attacks upon rationalist psychology were successful, they never understood that there is no necessarily causal connection between knowledge and remedy.

The social psychologists were sincere in their concern for the reformation of human nature, but their scientific mechanism was inadequate. Their "science" reflected only the particular ideological assumptions of each social psychologist, and their elitism contained no provision for distinguishing a social science for public good from one concerned with power. Treating manipulation as an expedient means to ultimately moral ends, the social psychologists accepted techniques that could as easily serve immoral ends. Even if social psychology could analyze human nature in society, what evidence was there that accurate knowledge results in effective prescription? Clear perception, indispensable in stating a problem, was not necessarily enough for arriving at its solution or for seeing that solution to its practical conclusion. While the elitist social psychologists recognized and described convincingly the problems of a mass urban society subjected to the strains of unprecedented growth, neither had "scientific" solutions to these problems. William McDougall and Wilfred Trotter were social critics who attempted to revive elitism by making it follow inescapably from their instinctual interpretation of human nature.

Until the 1930s the influence of the revolutionary social scientists was ascendant over the revisionist elitists. But the debate over the proportional strengths of reason and instinct, environment and heredity, causality and choice, never abated. Periodically, and especially in times of the erosion of intellectual faiths, the chronic controversy flares up again within the social sciences. Whenever policy decisions must be made, assumptions again assume the status of objective data. Only the participants change. The rhetoric, the delineation of sides, and the underlying ideological commitments appear very much as they did in the three decades before World War I when science was summoned to support ethics.

Postscript
How Successful Was the Revolution?

At the beginning of the twentieth century, Paul Vinogradoff, the Corpus Christi Professor of Jurisprudence at Oxford, described the dominant concern of his time as a "craving for a scientific treatment of the problems of social life."[1] This craving was not satisfied by social theory that tried to reduce a complex phenomena to a few simple laws. When Marshall, James, and Wallas defined specific social problems empirically, they successfully challenged an a priori scientific model accepted since the 1840s as most appropriate for all forms of scientific theory. Increasingly, the new social sciences circumscribed social theory with inductive procedures and tentative conclusions, separating economics, psychology, and political science from positivistic quests for universal truth. While nineteenth-century positivist theorists had gone beyond observable reality to postulate an essential unity of knowledge and experience, the new social scientists between 1880 and 1914 repudiated the grandiose ambitions of their predecessors and attempted instead to measure reality only as it appeared in such concrete problems as poverty, trade, and local government. Their methods and concepts introduced a behavioral social science designed for the analysis and solution of social problems. First Marshall "recast" political economy as "the Science of Social Perfectibility"; James then tried to identify the psychological state of mind essential to social progress; and Wallas combined their perceptions into a science of politics that would enable people to participate in progressive planning.

None of the enthusiastic exponents of an inductive social science, not even Wallas, believed that a social scientist would select and arrange his data to serve arbitrary assumptions leading to unwarranted conclusions. Many years earlier, Charles Kingsley, sickened by the conditions under which the majority of the population lived, had evoked "science" as the sovereign means of achieving the moral, spiritual, physical, and economic well-being of man.[2] The new social scientists clung to this same faith in the inherent "goodness" of science, except that they made its effect conditional upon a precise methodology. Their only cautionary defense against the abuse of their methodology was to hope for a reversal of Gresham's Law so that the bad currency of inadequate ideas would eventually be driven out by the good. The reforming ambitions of the new social scientists blinded them to the potential deficiencies of their method. They wanted to solve social problems by carefully measuring their component parts; but as recent social scientists have learned, the really important problems are often not measurable in the actual world as they occur. Either the components are never entirely known or, if they are taken into account, they may be so numerous as to be unmanageable. Another weakness of the new social scientists was the paucity of their data, too limited even for projects more modest than the complete reorganization of economic, social, and political institutions that they proposed. The principles of individual and social behavior they inferred from their data were often naive and inaccurate. Yet, despite these deficiencies, they understood that social theory, no matter how satisfying intellectually, had ultimately to be validated by practical experience.

There is no doubt that social science changed dramatically for Englishmen and Americans in the three decades before World War I. But to what extent did the revolutionaries set the meaning and purpose of future social science? This study of the four decades before 1914 reveals that the small community responsible for education, letters, science, religion, politics, economics, and society wanted assurance about its ability to act with responsible effectiveness. In the last decades of the nineteenth century, members of this community made strong personal commitments to work for the extension of individual opportunities for personal development and social justice. And they asked for some sort of guarantee, no longer offered by traditional religion, science, ethics, or social theory, that their reforming activities would succeed in improving the quality of life. The revolutionary social scientists replied by initiating inductive and theoretical procedures to attack social conditions that deprived individuals of opportunities. The great Liberal victory at the polls in the first decade of the twentieth century, and the dedication of scores of Samuels and Mastermans, resulted in legislation vitally concerned with the quality of life. The Liberal government's introduction of measures such as old age pensions and medical insurance was epochal in effect. But no matter how "progressive," these measures did not fulfill the late-nineteenth-century reformer's demand for an ethical reconstruction of character and conduct — a demand that lay behind his reform proposals. When social and economic opportunities increased, ordinary people's levels of expectations rose; but there was no evidence to support the reformer's expectation of a corresponding development in individual rationality or responsibility. Disappointment over the lack of demonstrable moral progress did not drive prewar moralists to resignation or despair. Instead, their systematic attempts to analyze social phenomena as a prelude to redressing social evils, resulted in a new economics, psychology, and political science and in a new social psychology. Both political science and social psychology, developed two decades after Marshallian economics and Jamesian psychology, tried to explain the ineptitude of individuals and the failure of institutions. But the purposes of the last two social sciences were diametrically opposed. The political scientist Wallas wanted to strengthen democracy by preparing ordinary people to be self-governing citizens. The social psychologists McDougall and Trotter argued instead that the supremacy of instinct over reason, particularly in a crowd-dominated society, made widespread individualism and democracy impossible.

Neither the revolutionary nor the revisionist tradition wholly succeeded or failed. Since World War I, the theories and methods of the social sciences have grown more precise, complex, sophisticated, technical, specialized, esoteric, and therefore less

assailable. The two revolutionary and revisionist traditions continue to compete still in rhetorical, ethical, and ideological terms
set in the prewar years. Despite their relatively modern dress,
each has ancient roots. The social psychologists remain the heirs
of the oldest tradition which condemned human nature as evil
and irrational and will as demonic and beyond reason. Remedy
against the characteristic violence of human behavior was sought
either in religious institutions or in an organically conceived
society that subordinated conflict through hierarchical controls.
Original sin along with its secularization were challenged in the
late seventeenth century by optimistic and rational individualism.
But reason and will continued to be antagonistic forces until the
mid-nineteenth century when the Victorians reinterpreted them
as mutual, complementary components of character that
explained past successes and made future prospects possible. An
ethic of rational, purposeful and, above all, effective activity was
held alongside deterministic readings of progress until the 1860s.
At that time, the development of biological and psychological
portraits of people as reactive machines began to threaten the
concept of even limited individual responsibility. Only toward the
end of the century did the revolutionary social scientists make a
self-conscious and empirically "scientific" effort to reclaim and
strengthen a rational, voluntaristic concept of individualism.
They triumphed over the revisionist social psychologists' biological mechanisms by promising to arm individuals with knowledge
and techniques sufficient to thwart biological impulses, random
chance, and other adverse circumstances. The social psychologists, on the other hand, also wanted to believe in the remedial
force of science, but they found the problem of evil more arrest-
ing than any proposed solution.

In postwar England, social scientists continued to search for
explanations of human nature in society compatible with ethical
reform. Far more than their prewar predecessors, they enormously influenced practical policy designed to promote opportunities for education, social and economic mobility, political
participation, and moral responsibility. Although it is undeniable
that Freudian and behavioristic psychologies challenged the effi-

cacy of individual will and reason, the social scientist qua reformer could ignore these mechanistic theories. Instead, he drew upon James's account of the rational individual able to carry out his purposes. In these interwar years, even McDougall discovered a theory of mind and behavior very much like that of James.

In the 1920s, Hobson, isolated so long from positions of influence, emerged as a respected elder statesman clothed impressively in the revolutionary social scientist's robes denied him thirty years earlier. Appearing at the newly fashionable conferences and writing "definitive" statements on the meaning and purpose of social science for the collaborative compendiums characteristic of both sides of the Atlantic in the twenties and thirties, Hobson preached the text that social science must serve ethics. With prewar rhetorical flourish, he insisted that human welfare depended on the application of "psychology to politics, economics, and ethics." Only through "more conscious social organization" would welfare ends be met.[3] Economics would be intelligibly related to ethics only when a standard of a good life was adopted as the measure of economic decisions. As a postwar spokesman, Hobson combined Wallas's reliance upon individuals organized to achieve their ends with Marshall's ethical standards of value. But while Hobson thought of his friend Wallas a a mentor, he remained contemptuous of the founder of the Cambridge school of economics who continued, until his death, to argue that industry had indeed come to recognize that its property was a moral trust. Hobson, in contrast, was delighted with the postwar transition to a welfare society that viewed the state as the only responsible "moral guardian."[4]

But though Hobson was a representative figure in the postwar expansion of the social sciences, he did not speak for every social scientist. Throughout the 1920s and 1930s, there was heated controversy about the appropriate function and purpose of social, political, and industrial organization. Despite the controversy, nearly every social study in both England and the United States was conceived "in the interest of ethical ideals and of social reconstruction."[5]

A major contention carried over by Hobson from the revolutionary social sciences was that psychology must inform the other social sciences. But although psychologists were less prolific intellectually than economists, they were even more acerbic and irreconcilable in their factitiousness. In two major surveys of the field, *Psychologies of 1925* and *Psychologies of 1930,* twenty-five different schools were represented.[6] Among them was McDougall, whose classic *Introduction to Social Psychology* had run to sixteen editions by 1925,[7] and who, interestingly enough, finally recognized that instinctual determinism, even when mitigated by the uniquely rational qualities of a caretaker elite, created too formidable an obstacle to his ethical purposes. Beginning in 1922, he dramatically recanted his prewar work and urged instead a "hormic" or "purposive" interpretation of human behavior. Purposive striving now became McDougall's fundamental psychological category and, with all the zeal of a convert, he vehemently opposed the mechanistic implications of Watsonian behaviorism.[8] One of the most influential British social psychologists had become an advocate of Jamesian psychology. James's own direct influence remained strong in England and the United States, where it was reinforced by the work of John Dewey and the Chicago School. Moreover, many social psychologists adopted James's theory of the social "self" as the product of social instincts and of those groups to which an individual belonged.[9]

With the exception of Cambridge economists and L.S.E. political scientists, many English social scientists felt that their influence was marginal both within and without their universities, especially in comparison to the well-financed and influential activity of American social science. Out of their discontent with the lack of public support and funds for research, the English stressed four new ideas. First, there was a widespread attempt to alter and expand the place of social science in British universities. Then, since few theorists or practitioners in any of the disciplines agreed on what was expected of them, questions as to the proper nature and possible effect of social studies became more introspective. A third direction led toward institutional and financial facilities for the study and implementation of interdisciplinary projects. Finally, the dominant figures within each subject concurred that in the university training of social scientists, theory was of a higher order than practice: the best minds would study theory, while data-gathering was for those with lesser ability.[10] In the study of politics generally, and especially at Oxford, theorists completely drove out "scientists" until after World War II.[11] The first three postwar goals were not realized until the 1960s. Only the idea that serious students should concentrate exclusively upon theory prevailed, and its effect was to repudiate the emphatic synthesis of the prewar revolutionaries.

The scope and ends of the social sciences were devised in England, but the revolution's most spectacular effect was in the United States. Americans in the 1920s contributed a grand scale of organization and enormous sums of money to create interdisciplinary establishments governed by the most prolific, articulate, inventive, and influential people in each of the member disciplines.[12] Voluntary groups like the Social Science Research Council, government organs like the National Bureau of Economics, and professional societies all worked to carry out the revolutionary social scientist's dream of bringing together specialists for cooperative research that would culminate in policy innovation. Their aspirations were encouraged by powerful interests; government, business, and the universities all invested heavily in the burgeoning social science enterprise, and they expected a return for their money. Investors and beneficiaries were bound to each other by the revolutionaries' principle that science should serve policymakers in the private and public sectors by formulating and studying clearly defined problems of "human behavior which could be attacked by cooperative effort with good prospects of achievement."[13]

The dichotomy of nature versus nurture, embodied in the conflict between the revisionist and revolutionary social sciences, was to be reconciled in America.[14] Geneticist and environmentalist, psychologist, anthropologist, biologist, and sociologist would bring their various perspectives to the fundamental social problems "in which they are all concerned and which cannot be effectively solved without their joint consideration."[15] In the twenties, the solution to the old dichotomies was still Wallas's: there are formidable instinctual compulsions governing behavior, but trained reason could provide an environment capable of redirecting those compulsions to ends that would benefit the individual and society.[16] A growing, general impatience with all monistic interpretations of human nature and behavior as well as a concerted effort to subject policy proposals to specialized but interdisciplinary studies were the most conspicuous evidences of the postwar success of the prewar revolutionaries. Within the postwar social sciences in England and in America the revolutionary tradition continued to strive for organization and endowment, for the reconciliation of opposing methods and interpretations by treating each as a different part of a greater whole, and for progress in the quality of character and life.[17]

When social science became largely an American activity in the 1920s, it was governed by the values and purposes set by the prewar revolutionaries. But this tradition was seriously undermined both by economic depression and by the advent of fascism in the mid-1930s. Although the S.S.R.C. remained the center of a flourishing research industry in America, social scientists and their sponsors were increasingly disturbed by the lack of practical results and by the multiplication of divisive factions within each discipline. Confident anticipation of future success gave way to a closer examination of the limits of social science as science and as a guide to policy.[18] A new concentration upon methodology led eventually to a strong conviction that problems of value were extraneous and must be excluded. But today there appears to be a vital renaissance of the one prewar conviction resolutely held by revolutionaries and revisionists alike: in matters that really interest us, moral neutrality is impossible.

Notes

Introduction

1. Although Stuart Hughes brilliantly discusses the European contribution to the "fund of ideas . . . most characteristic of our time," he has not really considered the English contribution. H. S. Hughes, *Consciousness and Society: The Reorientation of European Thought, 1890-1930* (New York, 1965), p. 13. And while J. W. Burrow has provided a remarkable interpretation of Victorian social thought in his *Evolution and Society. A Study in Victorian Social Theory* (Cambridge, 1966), his conclusion that "England made no distinctive contribution to the rethinking of the fundamental concepts of social thought at the turn of the century" (p. 260), does not recognize the revolution occurring within economics, psychology, and political science.

1. Deductive Science and Positivist Social Theory in the Nineteenth Century

1. Herbert Spencer, *Social Statics* (London, 1851), p. 42; Noel Annan, *Leslie Stephen* (London, 1951), p. 144. An older, but less important "scientific" tradition during the nineteenth century (developed by Charles Babbage, inventor of the calculating engine, Lucasian Professor of Mathematics at Cambridge from 1828 to 1839, and a founder of the Statistical Society in 1834), argued that physical laws were no more than statements of probability. Boole and Jevons belong in this tradition. But nineteenth-century social scientists found the absolute implications of demonstrative laws more persuasive. Henry Thomas Buckle approved Mill's *Political Economy* as a "branch of political knowledge which is not empirical . . . the only one raised to a science." Buckle to Miss Shireff, July 5, 1855, quoted in A. H. Huth, *The Life and Writings of H. T. Buckle* (New York, 1880), p. 89.

2. William Stanley Jevons, *Principles of Science: A Treatise on Logic and Scientific Method,* 3d ed. (London, 1879), p. 592. Arthur James Balfour's *Theism and Humanism* (London, 1915) was to be based upon a similar psychology of doubt.

3. *Lectures on Education, delivered at the Royal Institution of Great Britain* (London, 1855), p. 6.

4. Lord Kelvin never completely accepted Clerk Maxwell's brilliant mathematical model for describing electromagnetism, but he could not help admiring its "beauty." William Thomson Kelvin, "Presidential Address to the Royal Society, November 30, 1893," in *Popular Lectures and Addresses* (London, 1894), II, 547.

5. George Boole, *Investigation of the Laws of Thought* (London, 1854), p. 4. Boole made a distinction between the essentially probabilistic character of natural laws and the absolutely certain laws of logic and mathematics (p. 11).

6. Paul R. Heyl, *Fundamental Concepts of Physics in the Light of Modern Discovery* (Baltimore, 1926), p. 28; Florian Cajori, *A History of Physics in its Elementary Branches (through 1925)* rev. ed. (New York, 1962), p. 142.

7. W. S. Fowler, *The Development of Scientific Method* (Oxford, 1962), p. 101. See also Max Planck, *The Philosophy of Physics,* trans. W. H. Johnston, in his *The New Science* (New York, 1959), p. 286.

8. John Tyndall, "On the Importance of the Study of Physics as a Branch of Education for All Classes," in *Lectures on Education,* p. 210. Tyndall was one of the most important popularizers of nineteenth-century science.

9. Michael Faraday, "Observations on Mental Education," in ibid., pp. 71-72.

10. L. Pearce Williams's definitive biography, *Michael Faraday* (London, 1967), pp. 89-105, 106, 335-336, uses Faraday's letters, lectures, and private papers extensively to demonstrate his skepticism. Faraday was an elder in the Sandemanian Church, a sect that taught that God moved the heart beyond the powers of science or logic, ibid., p. 106. See also comments by Tyndall, Faraday's successor at the Royal Institution, in his book printed in 1868, *Faraday as Discoverer* (New York, 1961), p. 180; and see *The World of the Atom,* ed. Henry A. Boorse and Lloyd Motz (New York, 1966), I, 318. Faraday doubted atomism and action-at-a-distance because neither could be proven experimentally. Faraday, "On the Absolute Quantity of Electricity Associated with the Particles or Atoms of Matter," in *The World of the Atom,* I, 321-328.

11. William Ballyntine Hodgson, "On the Importance of the Study of Economic Science as a Branch of Education for All Classes," in *Lectures on Education,* p. 264. Hodgson was an educational reformer and eventually the first professor of political economy and mercantile law at the University of Edinburgh.

12. Jevons, "Opening Address as President of Section F [Economic Science and Statistics] of the British Association for the Advancement of Science," in *Methods of Social Reform and Other Papers* (London, 1904), p. 189. By 1880, Jevons had modified his public position to argue that, while social reforms could be designed on the basis of generalized theory, "specific experience on a limited scale and in closely approximate circumstances is the only sure guide in the complex questions of social science." "Experimental Legislation and the Drink Traffic," in ibid., p. 265. But in his most serious work, *Principles of Science,*

originally published in 2 volumes in 1874, he had identified "scientific genius" as the "ability to discover the one in the many." (II, 626).

13. John Stuart Mill, *A System of Logic* (London, 1843). William James tried to reconcile this dichotomy through pragmatism as a via media between the "empirical thinker" who "stares at a fact in its entirety, and remains helpless, or gets 'stuck' and the rationalist with his a priori assumptions." *Principles*, II, 330.

14. Mill, *A System of Logic*, II, 485.

15. Ibid. (1851), II, 431.

16. Mill, "Inaugural Address at St. Andrews," in *Dissertations and Discussions* (New York, 1874), IV, 158, 197.

17. This was particularly true of the use of statistics. Philip Abrams, *Origins of British Sociology: 1839-1940* (Chicago, 1968), pp. 26-30.

18. In the first issue of the *Journal of the Statistical Society* (1838), statistics was described as a science which "neither discussed causes nor reasoned upon probable effects, but sought only to collect, arrange and compare...facts." Quoted in Abrams, *Origins of Sociology*, p. 15. But the Belgian astronomer, Quételet, the mover behind the formation of the London Statistical Society in 1834, hoped that statistics would reveal the kind of laws characteristic of astronomy. Paul Lazarsfeld, "Notes on the History of Quantification in Sociology," *Isis* LII (1961), 278; Harold M. Westergaard, *Contributions to the History of Statistics* (London, 1932), p. 174. The collection of physical and moral statistics by the British societies was hardly aimless. Quételet's a priori concept of "l'homme moyen," a social, physical, and moral ideal, was arrived at by confusing statistical averages with desirable attributes. Many statisticians set out to find a numerical warrant for this ideal type.

19. Abrams presents a perceptive analysis of the origins, development, and failure of the NAPSS in *Origins of British Sociology*, pp. 39-52.

20. Charles Booth, "Inhabitants of Town Hamlets," *Journal of the Royal Statistical Society* L (1887), 376.

21. Rowntree insisted that he wanted to "state facts rather than to suggest remedies," but he did suggest social reforms. B. Seebohm Rowntree, *Poverty: A Study of Town Life*, 2d ed. (London, 1922), p. 360.

22. Even Herbert Spencer, the most zealous advocate of positivism, modified the force of social law by individual action. See especially his "Progress: Its Laws and Cause" (1857) in *Essays: Scientific, Political, and Speculative* (London, 1858), pp. 1-54.

23. During the nineteenth century William Whewell was the most persistent and influential intuitionist, and J. S. Mill the most important of the rationalist psychologists, particularly in his desire for a social science based upon individual control of character, as well as environment. See Mill's reply to Adam Sedgwick's intuitionist argument in "Professor Sedgwick's Discourse—State of the Philosophy of England," *Westminster Review* XXX (1835), 94-135.

24. Abrams, *Origins of British Sociology*, p. 39.

25. Thomas Henry Huxley, "On the Hypothesis that Animals are Automata,"

in *Collected Essays* (New York, 1917), I, 198-250.

26. Quoted in John Passmore, *A Hundred Years of Philosophy*, 2d ed. (London, 1966), p. 36. See also Lazarsfeld, "History of Quantification in Sociology," p. 309.

27. Boole, *Investigation of the Laws of Thought*, p. 21. Boole did concede that an individual's free will was not "inconsistent with regularity in the motions of the system of which he forms a component unit," but what impressed him, and Quételet's other readers most, was that statistical records contained "the seeds of general truths" buried "amid the mass of figures" (p. 21).

28. James Clerk Maxwell, "Does the Progress of Physical Science tend to give any advantage to the Opinion of Necessity (or Determinism) over that of the Contingency of Events and the Freedom of the Will?" reprinted in Lewis Campbell and William Garnett, *The Life of James Clerk Maxwell* (London, 1882), p. 444. This paper was read to the Eranus Club, men who had been "Apostles" together from 1853 to 1857.

29. T. H. Green, *Prolegomena to Ethics*, ed. A. C. Bradley, 5th ed. (Oxford, 1907), pp. 3-12.

30. See Melvin Richter's discussion of T. H. Green's philosophical idealism in *The Politics of Conscience* (London, 1964), p. 176.

31. Francis H. Bradley's *Ethical Studies* (1876) contained a similar kind of social and ethical theory revolving around the idea of "self-realization," 2d ed. (Oxford, 1962), pp. 79-81. See also Bernard Bosanquet, *The Philosophical Theory of the State* (London, 1965), p. 310.

32. George Edward Moore, *Principia Ethica* (Cambridge, 1956), p. 188. Keynes's account of Moore's influence appears in Roy F. Harrod, *The Life of John Maynard Keynes* (London, 1951), pp. 75, 78, 80.

33. Until Lord Rayleigh took over the Cavendish Laboratory at Cambridge in 1879, Clerk Maxwell's appeal in 1871 for the encouragement of experimentation had hardly been answered. R. B. Lindsay, "Historical Introduction," in John William Strutt, Lord Rayleigh, *The Theory of Sound* (New York, 1945), I, viii. Although experimental work became essential to physics, portions of Albert Einstein's deductive system have still not been proven experimentally.

34. Passmore, *A Hundred Years of Philosophy*, p. 175. Passmore traces the agreement from Mill's associative mechanisms through T. H. Green's notion that facts are constructed by thought, F. H. Bradley's version of facts as man's distortion of reality, to James's and Henri Bergson's view that they are the mind's tools for dealing with experience.

35. Huxley, "On the Educational Value of the Natural History Sciences," in *Science and Education* (New York, 1964), p. 54. While the inductions of the mathematician had been formed and completed and he was "occupied now with nothing but deduction and verification," the biologist, "deals with a vast number of objects, and his inductions will not be completed . . . for ages to come," but when they are, biology will be as "deductive and exact" as mathe-

matics (p. 56). Huxley viewed biology as the midpoint between the physico-chemical and the social sciences.

36. Charles Gillispie argues convincingly that although not numerical in expression, Darwin's work was "quantitative" in method and matter of thought because selection determined the quantity of living things that could survive in any given set of objective circumstances. *The Edge of objectivity, An Essay in the History of Scientific Ideas* (Princeton, 1960), p. 339.

37. William James, *Human Immortality* (Boston, 1898), pp. 32 f.

38. Boole, *An Investigation of the Laws of Thought,* pp. 403, 404, 422.

39. Kurt Mendelssohn, "Probability Enters Physics," in *Turning Points in Physics* (Amsterdam, 1959), pp. 54-67.

40. Francis Galton, *Natural Inheritance* (London, 1889), p. 66.

41. Karl Pearson, "Autobiographical Sketch," in *Speeches Delivered at a Dinner Held in University College, London, in Honor of Professor Karl Pearson, 23 April 1934* (Cambridge, 1934), p. 19. Pearson began as a liberal socialist whose sympathies were moved toward an elitist and conservative position by the Boer War.

42. Raphael Meldola, "Evolution: Darwinian and Spencerian," in *Herbert Spencer Lectures at Oxford: Decennial Issue, 1905-1914* (Oxford, 1916), p. 41. A generation later, the Herbert Spencer Lecturer for 1933, Albert Einstein, affirmed that "the axiomatic basis of theoretical physics cannot be extracted from experience but must be freely invented" by "purely mathematical constructions," and that we can discover "the concepts and the laws connecting them with each other, which furnish the key to the understanding of natural phenomena." Albert Einstein, "On the Method of Theoretical Physics," in *Essays in Science* (New York, 1934), p. 17.

43. William Farr's quantitative methods of inquiry as registrar-general were extended by his successors in the 1880s and 1890s to relate health and occupation. Westergaard, *Contributions to the History of Statistics,* pp. 213, 216, 250-251.

44. For James's letters complaining of his medical studies, see Gay Wilson Allen, *William James* (New York, 1949), pp. 98, 121.

45. See Part V of this book.

46. Richard H. Shryock argues that the use of quantification in medicine, most conspicuous in public health, is as an instrument of social observation. "The History of Quantification in Medical Science," *Isis* LII (1961), 237.

47. Leonard Trelawney Hobhouse's sociology belongs in the newer or reforming tradition of social science. See his *Morals in Evolution* (New York, 1906), II, 280.

48. See Idus L. Murphee, "The Evolutionary Anthropoligists: The Progress of Mankind: The Concepts of Progress and Culture in the Thought of John Lubbock, Edward B. Tylor, and Lewis H. Morgan," *Proceedings of the American Philosophical Society* CV (1961), 265-300; George Stocking, " 'Cultural Darwin-

ism' and 'Philosophical Idealism' in E. B. Tylor," *Southwestern Journal of Anthropology* V (1965), 140-141.

49. Edward Westermarck, *The Origin and Development of the Moral Ideas* (London, 1906), II, 739-745. Edward B. Tylor saw history as progressive emancipation from irrational and primitive "survivals" from the past. *Primitive Culture,* 3d ed. (London, 1891), Vol. I, chap. 3. McDougall began his social psychology with a healthy suspicion of evolution's effects upon man's morality, but the effects of his own destructive critique led him eventually to seek security in a higher plane of evolution not unlike Westermarck's modification of utilitarian psychology by evolutionary theory.

50. See Adam Kuper, *Anthropologists and Anthropology: The British School, 1922-1972* (New York, 1973).

2. Revision, Revolution, and the New Sciences

1. All quoted in Philip Abrams, *Origins of British Sociology: 1939-1940* (Chicago, 1968), pp. 80-81, 83.

2. The crisis in the Sociological Society resulted from the conflicting purposes of the society's members. These appear in the pages of the *Sociological Review* from 1908 to 1914.

3. William McDougall, *Psychology: The Study of Behavior* (London, 1912), pp. 105, 242-243, "The Will of the People," *Sociological Review* V (1912), 99, 101.

4. Thomas S. Kuhn, *The Structure of Scientific Revolutions* (Chicago, 1962), p. 5. "Normal" is used by Kuhn to describe that activity that the particular professional "community acknowledges for a time as supplying the foundation for its further practice" (p. 10).

5. Supply and demand had been treated as functions of price by Antoine Auguste Cournot as early as 1838, but the concept was first made popular by Alfred Marshall's *Principles of Economics* (Cambridge, 1890), Joseph Spengler, "On the Progress of Quantification in Economics," *Isis* LII (1961), 267. Jevons's work, important for its use of probability theory, its definitions of marginal utility and value, and its rejection of the labor and cost of production theories (especially in his *Theory of Political Economy* [London, 1871]), was still conceived in the classical belief that "the theory of economics proves to be, in fact, the mechanics of utility and self-interest," in which the *"laissez-faire* principle properly applied is the wholesome and true one." William Stanely Jevons, "The Future of Political Economy," written in 1876, in *The Principles of Economics: A Fragment of a Treatise on the Industrial mechanism of Society, and Other Papers* (London, 1905), pp. 199, 203. To Jevons, political economy was nothing more than "the science of wealth." Jevons, *Primer of Political Economy* (London, 1878), p. 13. In technical analysis, especially price analysis, and in his view of

the interdependence of economic phenomena, Marshall went far beyond Jevons. It might be argued that John A. Hobson's economics were more "revolutionary" than Marshall's, especially his theories of "underconsumption" or the "maldistribution" of cyclical unemployment, which appeared in *The Psychology of Industry*, written with A. F. Mummery (London, 1889), *Problems of Poverty* (London, 1891), and *Problem of the Unemployed* (London, 1896). But Hobson never reached the audience that rushed to sit at Marshall's feet.

6. Jevons, *Principles of Science*, pp. 149-150. Cf. Karl Pearson, *The Grammar of Science* (London, 1892), pp. 136-180.

7. In addition to "Are We Automata?" (1879) and "The Sentiment of Rationality" (1879), William James's most important early papers — "On Some Omissions in Introspective Psychology" (1884), "What is an Emotion?" (1884), "Absolutism and Empiricism" (1884), "On the Function of Cognition" (1885), "The Perception of Belief" (1889) — all appeared in *Mind*. His central concept of the necessary relation between thought and feeling was first presented to the British "Scratch Eight," which included Edmund Gurney, Frederick Pollock, Leslie Stephen, Frederick William Maitland, Carveth Read, and Shadworth Hodgson. The other two members, G. Croom Robertson and James Sully, were not present. Although James had taught psychology at Harvard from 1875 and had signed a contract for a book on psychology, he made no significant progress on the book until he worked out the Scratch Eight paper. Gay Wilson Allen, *William James* (New York, 1949), pp. 264-267.

8. John Maynard Keynes, often credited with the "new economics" of the 1930s, attributed the significant revolution to his mentor, Marshall. J. M. Keynes, "Alfred Marshall," in *Memorials of Alfred Marshall*, ed. A. C. Pigou (Cambridge, 1956), pp. 24-27. As professor of economics at Cambridge from 1885 until the 1920s, Marshall trained such influential economists as W. H. Beveridge, Lujo Brentano, J. H. Clapham, E. R. A. Seligman, and Joseph A. Schumpeter, to mention only a few. "Address to Marshall on his Eightieth Birthday (July 26, 1922) from Members of the Royal Economic Society," in *Memorials*, pp. 497-499. Until 1929 theoretical economics in England and in the United States consisted very largely of "the discussion and interpretation" of Marshall's *Principles*. T. W. Hutchinson, *A Review of Economic Doctrines, 1870-1929* (Oxford, 1953), p. 62. See also Frank Knight, "Economics," in *On The History and Method of Economics* (Chicago, 1963), p. 21; and Joan Robinson, *Economics is a Serious Subject* (Cambridge, 1932), p. 8. Marshall contributed to the problems of his interpreters by constantly revising the *Principles* until the eighth edition in 1920. Marshall, *Principles*, annot. C. W. Guillebaud, 9th [variorum] ed. (London, 1961), II, 15-30. Increasingly after 1890, Marshall moved away from his reforming purposes of the mid-1860s through 1890 and accepted existing conditions as progressive, especially in his *Industry and Trade* (London, 1919). This book is concerned only with the younger Marshall. All citations are from the 1890 edition of the *Principles*. James was Graham Wal-

las's friend (Wallas's unpublished papers at the London School of Economics and Political Science contain some of their correspondence), and the first chapter in Wallas's *Human Nature in Politics* (London, 1908) was derived largely from James's *Principles of Psychology* (New York, 1890). Ferdinand Canning Scott Schiller's *Humanism* (London, 1903) was based upon James. John Passmore, *A Hundred Years of Philosophy*, 2d ed. (London, 1966), pp. 232-262. For a discussion of the reception of James's *Principles,* see Allen, *William James,* pp. 323-326, and Ralph Barton Perry, *The Thought and Character of William James,* briefer version (New York, 1964), p. 196.

9. Graham Wallas, *Human Nature in Politics,* 3d ed. (New York, 1921), p. 206. All subsequent references will be to this edition.

10. Christian Socialists who became economists, like the Rev. Wilfrid Richmond, trusted in the benevolence of God to further their efforts; more secular reformers like McDougall, and eventually Pearson, trusted to evolution; while even a voluntarist like Hobhouse discovered certain reassuring tendencies in historical development. Richmond, *Christian Economics* (London, 1911); McDougall, *Psychology,* and "The Will of the People"; Pearson, *National Life from the Standpoint of Science* (London, 1900), Hobhouse, *Morals in Evolution.*

11. In a recent UNESCO survey on main trends of research in the social sciences and humanities, Ludwig von Bertalanffy asserts that it was only after 1950 that psychological theory rejected the automation model to treat man "as an *active personality* system." Bertalanffy, "General Theory of Systems: Application to Psychology," in *The Social Sciences: Problems and Orientations, Selected Studies* (The Hague, 1968), p. 309. This ignores James's influential rejection of positivist-mechanist psychology.

12. James, *Principles,* I, 138, 139.

13. James, *Pragmatism, A New Name for Old Ways of Thinking* (New York, 1907), pp. 119, 120.

14. James, *Principles,* II, 576.

15. Marshall, "The Present Position of Economics," in *Memorials,* I, 171; "Social Possibilities of Economic Chivalry" (1907), in ibid., p. 324.

16. Wallas, *Human Nature in Politics,* p. 211.

17. William Kingdon Clifford, "On the Aims and Instruments of Scientific Thought," *Lectures and Essays,* ed. Leslie Stephen and Frederick Pollock (London, 1879), I, 157.

18. Pearson, *Grammar of Science,* p. 23.

19. James, "What Physical Research Has Accomplished," in *The Will to Believe, and other Essays in Popular Philosophy* (London, 1897), pp. 119-120.

20. Bertrand Russell, "Mathematics and the Metaphysicians," in *The World of Mathematics,* ed. James R. Newman (New York, 1956), III, 1578.

21. For a complete discussion of the history, content, and implications of the new mathematics, see ibid., pp. 1576-1590. In England, non-Euclidean geom-

etry was advocated enthusiastically by W. K. Clifford, the brilliant Cambridge mathematician, popularizer of science, and militant agnostic, in his important paper to the British Association in 1872, "Aims and Instruments of Scientific Thought," I, 136-141; and his *Common Sense of the Exact Sciences,* ed. Karl Pearson (New York, 1946), pp. 203-204. After Boole, and into the twentieth century, the major work in the new mathematics was done on the Continent.

22. James Clerk Maxwell became the first Professor of Experimental Physics and the head of the laboratory. Clerk Maxwell never confirmed his theoretical structure through experiment, although other physicists eventually did so. Edmund Whittaker, *A History of the Theories of Aether and Electricity. The Classical Theories* (London, 1958), pp. 240-275.

23. James, Marshall, and Wallas relied upon improvements in social and economic conditions, increased opportunity, and widespread education to produce healthy and rational men. See especially James's famous chapter on "habit," written in 1877, in his *Principles,* I, chap. 4; his *Talks to Teachers on Psychology, and to Students on Some of Life's Ideals* (New York, 1900); Marshall's *Principles,* chaps. 4, 5; his "The Future of the Working Classes" (written in 1873), "Where to House the London Poor" (1884), "A Fair Rate of Wages" (1887), "Co-operation" (1889), "Social Possibilities of Economic Chivalry" (1907), all in *Memorials;* and see Wallas, *Human Nature in Politics,* p. 305.

24. See James's 1904 review of F. C. S. Schiller's *Humaniam,* in *Collected Essays and Reviews* (London, 1920), p. 448; and his *Pragmatism,* p. 57.

25. Pearson, *Grammar of Science,* pp. 136, 392, 116.

26. Pearson, *National Life,* 2d ed. (London, 1905), pp. 26, 43-44, 46-49, 63.

27. James's review of Schiller's *Humanism,* p. 448.

28. James, *Pragmatism,* p. 218. Fowler argues that James's pragmatism took scientific method a great step forward by bridging the "dichotomy between the theory of the philosopher and the practice of the scientist." W. S. Fowler, *The Development of Scientific Method* (Oxford, 1962), p. 78.

29. Kuhn, "Measurement in Modern Physical Science," *Isis* LII (1961), 181.

30. In an appendix to ibid., Kuhn readily admits that the lack of agreement about subjects and method in contemporary social science excludes the application of his model (191-193).

31. George Edward Moore, *Principia Ethica* (Cambridge, 1956), p. vii.

32. James, "The Sentiment of Rationality," in *The Will to Believe,* p. 109.

33. Raphael Meldola, "Evolution: Darwinian and Spencerian," in *Herbert Spencer Lectures at Oxford* (Oxford, 1961), p. 38.

34. The amateur continued to be the dominant mover in British educational and professional institutions. See A. W. Coats, "The Origins and Development of the Royal Economic Society," *Economic Journal* LXXVIII (1968), 369; Beatrice Edgell, "The British Psychological Society, 1901-1941," *Bulletin of the British Psychological Society,* Suppl. (1961), 5; O. J. R. Howarth, *The British Association* (London, 1931), pp. 93, 301-304; Keynes, "Alfred Marshall," p. 54;

F. H. Lawson, *The Oxford Law School, 1830-1965* (Oxford, 1968), pp. 36-37; W. J. Reader, *Professional Men* (London, 1966); Sheldon Rothblatt, *Revolution of the Dons* (New York, 1968), pp. 248, 258; *Royal Commission on the Civil Service, Appendix to the First Report of the Commissioners and Appendix to the Second Report of the Commissioners* (London, 1912); and William R. Ward, *Victorian Oxford* (London, 1965), p. 278.

35. Although Marshall was professor of economics at Cambridge from 1885 until 1908, he did not succeed in establishing a separate tripos in economics until 1903. Keynes, "Alfred Marshall," p. 57; Marshall, *The New Cambridge Curriculum in Economics and Associated Branches of Political Science; its Purpose and Plan* (London, 1903).

36. Older scientists, such as T. H. Huxley, equally concerned to make science accessible to ordinary men, were sharply divided from the "newer" men by their rejection of value as a legitimate concern for a social science. Huxley to Thomas H. Farrer, Dec. 19, 1894, in *Life and Letters of Thomas H. Huxley,* ed. Leonard Huxley (New York, 1900), II, 407.

37. Wallas, *The Great Society, A Psychological Analysis* (New York, 1920), p. 14.

38. James, *Principles,* II, 402-430.

39. James, "Frederick Myer's Services to Psychology," *Memories and Studies* (London, 1911), p. 166.

40. James, *Principles,* I, 127.

41. Marshall to James Ward, Oct. 23, 1900, in *Memorials,* pp. 418-419.

3. *Political Economy and Economics until the 1870s*

1. Sir Rowland Hill found this "questionable assumption" dominant at the Political Economy Club after 1864. G. B. Hill, *Life of Sir Rowland Hill* (London, 1880), II, 416.

2. First paragraph of the rules adopted by the Political Economy Club in 1821. *Political Economy Club Centenary* (London, 1921), p. 375. This volume contains a comprehensive list of all members from 1821 to 1921 and the dates of their election and retirement or demise (358-372); a list of all questions debated from 1821 to 1899 (18-126); and, in the minutes of meetings from 1899 to 1920, (127-204).

3. William James Ashley, "A Survey of the Past History and Present Position of Political Economy" (August 1907), *Essays in Economic Method: Selected Papers read to Section F of the British Association for the Advancement of Science, 1860-1913,* ed. R. L. Smyth (London, 1962), p. 225.

4. Reprinted in *Political Economy Club Centenary,* p. 33.

5. This was the dominant theme, especially in Robert Lowe's address. ibid., pp. 7-21.

6. J. A. Hobson, *Confessions of an Economic Heretic* (London, 1938), p. 23.

7. See E. C. K. Gonner, "On the Condition of Economic Studies in the United Kingdom," *Report of the 64th Meeting of the British Association for the Advancement of Science,* Oxford, 1894 (London, 1894), pp. 388-391.

8. W. Cunningham, E. C. K. Gonner, F. Y. Edgeworth, H. S. Foxwell, L. L. Price, H. Higgs, and J. Shield Nicholson, "Methods of Economic Training in this and other Countries"; and Gonner, "On The Condition of Economic Studies," pp. 365-366, 387.

9. A specimen set of questions for Part I of The Cambridge Moral Science Tripos included under Political Economy I.: "Indicate the main respects in which modern conditions of industrial life have modified the conclusions of Adam Smith as to the normal rate of wages in different employment"; and "Give a definition of Money, explaining fully the grounds on which you reject certain applications of the term. By what sort of conditions is the relative amount of the different forms of instruments of exchange determined?" *Moral Science Tripos,* Part I, May 20, 1895, pp. 9-12.

10. Sir George Campbell, "Presidential Address," Transactions of the Sections, *Report of the Forty-sixth Meeting of the British Association for the Advancement of Science,* Glasgow, September 1876 (London, 1877), p. 187.

11. Henry Sidgwick, *Principles of Political Economy* (London, 1883), p. 1.

12. J. K. Ingram, "The Present Position and Prospects of Political Economy" (August 1878), *Essays on Economic Method,* pp. 41-70.

13. Bonamy Price, *Chapters on Political Economy* (London, 1878), pp. 15-16.

14. H. Sidgwick, *Methods of Ethics* (London, 1874). Cf., J. B. Schneewind, "First Principles and Common Sense Morality in Sidgwick's Ethics," *Archiv für Geschichte der Philosophie,* Band 45, Heft 2 (Berlin, 1963), pp. 148, 154.

15. H. Sidgwick, "The Scope and Method of Political Economy" (September 1885), *Essays on Method,* pp. 78, 84, 87, 74.

16. H. S. Foxwell, "The Economic Movement in England," pp. 85, 102, 95, 99.

17. Wilfrid J. Richmond, *Christian Economics* (London, 1888), p. 26 n; v. Richmond was a cleric, a tutor at Keble and an original member of the C.S.U. *The Economic Review* attracted contributors such as Sidney Webb, L. T. Hobhouse, H. Llewelyn Smith, and William Cunningham.

18. William Cunningham, "The Comtist Criticism of Economic Science" (1889), in *Essays on Method,* p. 107.

19. A. W. Coats, "The Historicist Reaction in English Political Economy, 1870-1890," *Economica,* N. S., XXI (May 1954), 145.

20. Foxwell, "The Economic Movement in England," p. 90.

21. Ibid., p. 92.

22. James Thorold Rogers, *A Manual of Political Economy for Schools and Colleges* (Oxford, 1868), p. 263.

23. Rogers, *Six Centuries of Work and Wages: The History of English Labour* (New York, 1884), pp. 524-526.

24. Ibid., pp. 523-528.

25. William James Ashley, "James E. Thorold Rogers," *Political Science Quarterly* IV (September 1889), 381-407.

26. Rogers, *The Economic Interpretation of History. Lectures at Worcester College Hall, Oxford, 1887-1888* (New York and London, 1909), pp. vi-xiii.

27. Archibald Henderson, *G. B. S., Man of the Century* (London, 1911), pp. 130, 157-159. Members of the Economic Circle included G. B. Shaw, Sidney Webb, Graham Wallas, Marshall, and William Cunningham.

28. Clara E. Collet, "Professor Foxwell and University College," *Economic Journal* XLVI (December 1936), 617. Clara Collet, Henry Higgs, G. Armitage Smith, F. Y. Edgeworth, Charles Booth, C. S. Loch, and Beatrice Potter were among the original members.

29. Cf., Melvin Richter, *The Politics of Conscience* (London, 1964), pp. 118-121. The Ethical Society of South Place, Unitarian in origin, was less interested in individualism and more concerned with radical and socialist remedies for social and economic problems. J. A. Hobson found a natural home there and he remained closely associated with them for thirty-six years. J. A. Hobson, *Confessions*, pp. 56-57. But Hobson, along with Edward Caird, William Wallace, Henry Sidgwick, Leslie Stephen, Sir John Seeley, and Graham Wallas also belonged to the London Ethical Society. See chap. 8 of this book.

30. J. A. Hobson and A. F. Mummery, *Physiology of Industry* (London, 1889); J. A. Hobson, *Problem of Poverty* (London, 1891), and *Problem of the Unemployed* (London, 1896).

31. Coats, "Sociological Aspects of British Economic Thought," p. 721. Hobson had been invited to lecture on economics to the Charity Organisation Society, but after the *Physiology* appeared the invitation was withdrawn without explanation. Hobson, *Confessions*, p. 31.

32. Hobson, *Confessions*, pp. 11, 12, 168.

33. Joseph A. Schumpeter, "Alfred Marshall's 'Principles': A Semi-Centennial Appraisal," in *Ten Great Economists* (Oxford, 1965), p. 102.

34. Hobson, *Confessions*, p. 171.

35. Hobson rejected the quantitative apparatus of Marshall's economics and of Wallas's political science because he feared that the process of quantification was inherently antithetical to humanistic ends. *Confessions*, p. 79.

36. Paul Ford, *Social Theory and Social Practice: An Exploration of Experience* (Shannon, 1968), p. 53.

37. William Stanley Jevons, *The Coal Question: An Inquiry Concerning the Progress of the Nation, and the Problem of the Probable Exhaustion of our Coal-Mines* (London, 1865).

38. Jevons, "Economic Policy," Presidential Address to the Economics and Statistics Section of the British Association for the Advancement of Science,

Liverpool, September 1870, reprinted in *Methods of Social Reform and Other Papers* (London, 1904), p. 189.

39. Jevons, *The Coal Question,* 2d ed. (London, 1866), p. 460.

40. Jevons, *Theory of Political Economy* (London, 1871), p. vii.

41. Jevons, "Economic Policy" (September 1870), in *Essays on Economic Method,* pp. 25-40.

42. Coats, "The Origins and Development of the Royal Economic Society," *Economic Journal* LXXVIII (1968), 350 n. 4.

43. Francis Galton, "Considerations Adverse to the Maintenance of Section F (Economic Science and Statistics)," *Journal of the Statistical Society* XL (September 1887), 471, 472.

44. William Farr, "'Considerations in the form of a Draft Report, submitted to Committee, favourable to the maintenance of Section F,'" *Journal of the Statistical Society* XL (September 1887), 475. Giffen and Chubb were the secretaries of the Statistical Society.

45. Jevons, *Principles of Science: A Treatise on Logic and Scientific Method,* 3d ed. (London, 1879), p. 592.

46. Arthur James Balfour, *Theism and Humanism* (London, 1915); W. Trotter, "Herd Instinct and its Bearing on the Psychology of Civilised Man," *Sociological Review* I (July 1908), 244-245.

47. Jevons, *Principles of Science,* p. 761; "Economic Policy," p. 189.

48. Jevons, *Principles of Science,* p. 120.

49. Ibid. (London, 1874), I, viii, 579, 594.

50. Ibid., p. x.

51. Ibid., 3d ed., p. 585.

52. Ibid., p. 228.

53. Ibid., pp. 594-595.

54. Ibid., p. 218.

55. Ibid., p. 626.

56. Ibid., p. 587.

57. Ibid., p. 599.

58. Ibid., p. 730.

59. Jevons, *Theory of Political Economy,* p. 3.

60. W. S. Fowler, *The Development of Scientific Method* (Oxford, 1962), p. 96.

61. Jevons, *Principles of Science,* 3d ed., p. 217.

62. Ibid., pp. 149-150, 738.

63. Jevons, "The Periodicity of Commercial Crises and its Physical Explanation" (1878), reprinted in *Investigations in Currency and Finance* (London, 1884), p. 214.

64. Jevons, unfinished introduction to *Investigations in Currency and Finance,* quoted by H. S. Foxwell, p. xxiv.

65. H. S. Foxwell, Introduction to *Investigations in Currency and Finance,*

p. xxv. Foxwell, then Fellow and Lecturer at St. John's College, Cambridge and Professor of Political Economy at University College, London, published the *Investigations* two years after Jevons's death.

66. Jevons, unfinished introduction, quoted by Foxwell, ibid., p. xxiv.

67. Jevons, "A Serious Fall in the Value of Gold Ascertained, and its Social Effects set Forth" (1862), in ibid., p. 49.

68. Ibid., p. 58.

69. Jevons, "The Variation of Prices, and the Value of the Currency since 1782" (1865) in ibid.

70. When Foxwell was editing Jevons's papers in 1883, Marshall warned him that the results of Jevons's tables of prices for is paper on "The Variation of Prices" differed considerably from those of the *Economist* for the years 1860-1865. Letter to H. S. Foxwell, January 19, 1883, in the Marshall Papers, at the Marshall Library, Cambridge, England. The Marshall Papers will be cited as *M.P.*

71. Jevons, "A Serious Fall in the Value of Gold," pp. 93-101.

72. Jevons, "Trade Societies: Their Objects and Policy" (1868), *Methods Of Social Reform and other Papers* (London, 1904), p. 107.

73. Jevons, "Married Women in Factories" (1882), ibid., p. 172.

74. Jevons, *Primer of Political Economy* (London, 1878), p. 102.

75. This concept appeared in a paper: "Notice of a General Mathematical Theory of Political Economy," read to Section F of the British Association at its Cambridge meeting in 1862.

4. *Alfred Marshall and the Revolution in Economics*

1. H. S. Foxwell, "The Economic Movement in England," *Quarterly Journal of Economics* II (1887), 92.

2. T. W. Hutchinson, *A Review of Economic Doctrines, 1870-1929* (Oxford, 1953), p. 3.

3. Alfred Marshall, *Principles of Economics*, 9th variorum ed., annotated by C. W. Guillebaud (London, 1961), p. 42 margin. All citations, unless otherwise noted, are from this two-volume edition. The first volume contains Marshall's *Principles,* and in the second are Guillebaud's notes and commentary and additional pieces by Marshall.

4. Roy Harrod, "How Can Economists Communicate?," *Times Literary Supplement,* July 24, 1969, p. 805.

5. A. W. Coats, "Sociological Aspects of British Economic Thought, 1880-1930," *Journal of Political Economy* 75 (August 1967), 715.

6. Paul Ford, *Social Theory and Social Practice: An Exploration of Experience* (Shannon, 1968), p. 86.

7. The principal homily that the overwhelming Jowett preached repeatedly to

the receptive young Marshall was the necessity of avoiding controversy because Alfred was too "sensitive," and because Jowett believed that controversy diminished an individual's influence besides lowering his character and injuring his peace of mind. Jowett to Mary Paley Marshall on William Cunningham's gratuitous attack on Marshall. October 16, 1892; January 21, 1893, The Marshall Papers of the Marshall Library, Cambridge, England. Cited as *M.P.* Whenever Marshall wrote to respond to criticism he was scrupulously courteous, but his handwriting changed into a larger and nearly illegible script.

8. Marshall, Preface to 1890 ed., *Principles,* p. v.

9. William Cunningham, "The Perversion of Economic History," *Economic Journal* II (1892), 493; A. Marshall, "A Reply (to W. Cunningham)," *Economic Journal* II (1892), 508, 519.

10. Marshall to Foxwell, July 1883, on whether he should publish the lectures on "Progress and Poverty" which he had delivered at St. Philip's Vestry Hall, Bristol, on February 19, February 26, and March 5, 1883, in *M.P.* These lectures were never published by Marshall, but the text and an account of the discussion following appeared in the *Daily Bristol Times and Mirror* and in the *Western Daily Press,* February 20, February 27, and March 6, 1883. This version, and some correspondence between Marshall and Alfred Russel Wallace, were published with an introduction and commentary by George J. Stigler as "Alfred Marshall's Lectures on Progress and Poverty," *Journal of Law and Economics* XII, 1 (April 1969), 181-226.

11. Undated fragment in *M.P.*

12. *M.P.* contains detailed, analytical accounts of Marshall's rural and industrial trips in Britain and the United States; statistical and comparative records he compiled; and his lecture notes based upon meticulous observation and extensive reading.

13. John Stuart Mill, "Inaugural Address at St. Andrews," in *Dissertations and Discussions* (New York, 1874), IV, 197.

14. Charles Booth, *Life and Labour of the People in London* I (London, 1892), 172-178.

15. B. Seebohm Rowntree, *Poverty: A Study of Town Life,* 2d ed. (London, 1922), p. 360.

16. Karl Pearson, "The Moral Basis of Socialism" (June 1887), *The Ethic of Freethought: A Selection of Essays and Lectures* (London, 1888), p. 340.

17. Pearson, "Socialism: In Theory and Practice," (February 1884), ibid., p. 362.

18. MSS notes, February 16, 1924, *M.P.*

19. In *Human Nature in Politics* (London, 1908), Graham Wallas adopted Marshall's quantitative techniques to expose successfully rationalist fallacies about political and social behavior which most theorists, including Marshall, held.

20. Marshall, *Elements of Economics of Industry,* 3d ed. (London, 1900), p.

256. Originally published in 1892, the *Elements* was essentially an abridgment of the *Principles* for junior students.

21. See Talcott H. Parsons, "Wants and Activities in Marshall," *Quarterly Journal of Economics* XLVI (November 1931), 102.

22. Marshall, "Distribution and Exchange," *Economic Journal* VIII (March 1898), 54. This article was an additional preface to the *Principles* to explain further Marshall's original contentions and to reply to his critics.

23. Marshall, "Minutes of Evidence Taken Before the Royal Commission on the Aged Poor," June 5, 1893, in Marshall, *Official Papers* (London, 1926), p. 245.

24. Marshall, discussion following, "Causes of Poverty: What are the Limits of Work and Wages?," Lecture 2 in Bristol Lectures on Progress and Poverty (1883), in Stigler, "Alfred Marshall's Lectures on Progress and Poverty," p. 198.

25. When the trade-union organizer Tom Mann visited the Marshalls, they wrote delightedly to Jowett that he was a gentleman and Jowett responded, characteristically, that "working men will never be good for much" until they are made "into gentlemen." Benjamin Jowett to Mary Paley Marshall, January 2, 1893, *M.P.*

26. Stephen Reynolds, *A Poor Man's House* (London, 1907).

27. Marshall, "The Social Possibilities of Chivalry" (1907), in *Memorials of Alfred Marshall*, ed. A. C. Pigou (New York, 1956), p. 331.

28. Marshall, "The Future of the Working Classes" (1873), and "Co-operation" (1889), ibid., pp. 117, 229.

29. Marshall, *Principles,* p. 17 n. 1. Marshall's interest in Kantian ethics was supplemented by his work with the Charity Organisation Society and with the Cambridge poor as a Poor Law Guardian. Marshall tried to live by the ethical imperatives he preached and each summer his Cambridge home, Balliol Croft, was converted into a refuge for paupers from the Women's Settlement from Southwark under the care of the Marshall's maid Sarah. Mary Paley Marshall, *What I Remember* (Cambridge, 1947), p. 41. Marshall was a pioneer in university extension directed toward working people and he kept in touch with working-class leaders to know of prevailing attitudes toward economic policies. *M.P.* contain correspondence with Tom Mann on sliding scales (March 1891), and with Thomas Burt on state-aided pensions (May 1892).

30. Marshall, "Remedies for Poverty: Is Nationalisation of the Land a Remedy?" (1883), Lecture 3 in Bristol series, in Stigler, "Lectures," p. 200.

31. Fragment in *M.P.*

32. Marshall, "The Future of the Working Classes" (1873), p. 115.

33. Marshall, "The Old Generation of Economists and the New" (1896), *Memorials*, p. 310; fragment in ibid., p. 367.

34. Marshall, *Elements*, p. 112.

35. Ibid., p. 17.

36. Marshall, "The Future of the Working Classes" (1873), pp. 111, 117.

37. Marshall, *Elements,* p. 17.

38. Marshall, "Wealth and Want: Do They Increase Together?" (1883), Lecture 1 in Bristol series, in Stigler, "Lectures," p. 190.

39. Marshall, "Causes of Poverty: What are the Limits of Work and Wages?" (1883), ibid., p. 198. Marshall wrote to J. Hilton, recalling how he recognized, while playing tennis, that the game was enjoyable without concern for its outcome; August 14, 1919, *M.P.*

40. Marshall, "Causes of Poverty," p. 198.

41. Marshall to Edward Caird, the Master of Balliol College, Oxford, October, 22, and December 5, 1897, in *Memorials,* pp. 398-399.

42. Marshall, "Co-operation" (1889), in *Memorials,* p. 243.

43. Marshall, *Principles,* p. 17 n. 1. Beginning in the fifth edition, Marshall substituted the words "satisfaction" for pleasure, and "detriment" for pain.

44. Marshall, "The Present Position of Economics" (1885), in *Memorials,* p. 174.

45. Marshall, *The New Cambridge Curriculum in Economics and Associated Branches of Political Science: Its Purpose and Plan* (London, 1903). On June 26, 1902, the Drummond Professor of Political Economy at Oxford urged his university to adopt Marshall's economics curriculum. F. Y. Edgeworth, *A Statement of the Needs of the University* (Oxford, 1902), p. 115; and earlier in January, L. L. Price had appealed to the vice-chancellor of Oxford for a "real study of economics" on Marshallian lines. *The Present Position of Economic Study in Oxford, a Letter,* January 14, 1902 (Oxford, 1902).

46. See especially, James Clerk Maxwell's inaugural lecture on experimental physics at Cambridge in October 1871, in Lewis Campbell and William Garnett, *Life of James Clerk Maxwell* (London, 1882), p. 356; and twenty years later, Albert A. Michaelson's convocation address on "Some of the Objects and Methods of Physical Science," delivered at the dedication of the Ryerson Physical Laboratory, July, 1894, in the *University of Chicago Quarterly Calendar* III (August 1894), 15.

47. J. C. Maxwell, "Does the Progress of Physical Science tend to give any advantage to the opinion of Necessity (or Determinism) over that of the Contingency of Events and the Freedom of the Will," read to the Eranus Club, Apostles, now more mature, on February 11, 1873, in Campbell and Garnett, *Life of James Clerk Maxwell,* p. 438. See too, the most frequently quoted of any of Clerk Maxwell's writing: "Discourse on Molecules," read to the British Association at Bradford, September 1873, ibid., pp. 358-361.

48. W. C. Dampier Whetham, "Science," *Encyclopedia Britannica,* 11th ed. (London, 1911), XXIV, 402.

49. Whetham, "Thomson and the Cambridge School of Experimental Physics" (November 23, 1903), reprinted in Eric Homberger, William Janeway, and Simon Schama, eds., *The Cambridge Mind: Ninety Years of the Cambridge Review* (London, 1970), p. 175. Whetham (later Lord William Cecil

Dampier) had been elected a Fellow at the Cavendish in 1891 and there worked on experiments in electricity with Thomson.

50. Whetham, "Science," p. 403. Whetham's, *The Recent Development of Physical Science* (London, 1904), went through three editions from August to December 1904, reaching a 6th and final edition in 1927.

51. Marshall estimated that in three cases out of four men became economists because of the belief that in spite of a growing command over nature, "Things are in the saddle and ride mankind." *The New Cambridge Curriculum*, p. 8.

52. *M.P.*, no date. Written probably for the Cambridge Grote Club, these are Marshall's only extant papers in psychology. While Marshall believed that traditional introspective psychology was not useful to economists, he did later urge the development of an inductive social psychology which would observe "men's notions in masses and subdivisions of masses." Letter to H. S. Foxwell, January 29, 1902, *M.P.*

53. Marshall, "Mechanical and Biological Analogies in Economics" (1898), from "Distribution and Exchange," in *Memorials*, p. 318.

54. Marshall, Preface to 5th ed. of *Principles*, in 9th ed., II, 49.

55. Marshall, "The Present Position of Economics" (1885), pp. 158, 163-168.

56. Ibid., "Some Aspects of Competition," Marshall's Presidential Address to Section F of the British Association, at Leeds, 1890, in *Memorials*, p. 291.

57. Marshall, *The New Cambridge Curriculum*, p. 25; Letter to F. Y. Edgeworth, August 28, 1902, *Memorials*, p. 437.

58. Marshall, "The Graphic Method of Statistics" (1885), in *Memorials*, pp. 175-181.

59. Marshall, *Elements*, p. 24; Appendix A, pp. 398-399.

60. See the *Times* (London), *The Pall Mall Gazette*, and *The Daily News*, July 1890, for the enthusiastic response in the popular press.

61. L. L. Price, "A Recent Economic Treatise," in *Economic Science and Practice, or Essays on the Various Aspects of the Relations of Economic Science to practical Affairs* (London, 1896), pp. 299-320.

62. J. M. Keynes, "Alfred Marshall," in *Memorials*, pp. 24-27; Frank Knight, "Economics," *Encyclopaedia Britannica* (1951), in *On The History and Method of Economics* (Chicago, 1963), pp. 19-21; Hutchinson, *A Review of Economic Doctrines*, p. 63; Lekachman, *History of Economic Ideas*, chaps. 10, 11. Marshall had begun his study of economics in 1867 and his final theories were set by 1883, but these were not available to a wider public until 1890. Charles Guillebaud, in a painstaking line by line comparison of the seven subsequent editions, had concluded that his uncle's major ideas and techniques appeared in 1890 and remained substantially unchanged thereafter. Guillebaud, "The Evolution of Marshall's "Principles of Economics," *Economic Journal* LII (December 1942), 330-349.

63. Paul T. Homan, *Contemporary Economic Thought* (New York, 1928), pp. 195, 199.

64. Joan Robinson, *Economics is a Serious Subject* (Cambridge, 1932), pp. 4, 8.

65. A complete account of the revolution at Cambridge appears in Sheldon Rothblatt's important and perceptive study, *Revolution of the Dons* (New York, 1968). See esp. pp. 179-180. Cf. Part IV of this book for a discussion of the changes in Oxford.

66. Marshall, "Minutes of Evidence... Royal Commission on the Aged Poor," p. 237.

67. In his biographical memoir of 1924, "Alfred Marshall," Keynes observed that to his pupils Marshall remained "a true sage and master outside criticism, one who was their father in the spirit and who gave them such inspiration and comfort as they drew from no other source" (p. 57).

68. Marshall founded the British Economic Association which became the Royal Economic Society in 1902 while he was President of the Economic Science and Statistics Section of the British Association. The *Economic Journal* was edited by F. Y. Edgeworth.

69. Foxwell, "The Economic Movement in England," p. 103.

70. British Economic Association, "Report of the Proceedings at the Inaugural Meeting," *Economic Journal* I (March 1891), 2. Although Marshall's powers at Cambridge were formidable, he never used them to enforce economic homogeneity. When Foxwell was unwilling to change his old lectures in February 1906, Marshall simply supplemented them and wrote to Foxwell that their differences were "an advantage" since there should be "considerable diversities of temperament among the teachers of any subject, and especially of one of which the past and the present are so meagre, and the future is so uncertain as economics." Letter to Foxwell, February 12, 1906, *M.P.*

71. A. W. Coats, "The Notion of Authority in British Economics," *Journal of Law and Economics* VII (1964), 98. In 1891 the Association had 710 members, 115 had foreign addresses and 94 were unidentified. The remaining 501 fall into these categories: accounting—16; administration—29; army—8; banking—48; business—113; civil service—44; church—16; government—12; insurance—47; journalism—16; landowners—22; law—51; medicine—14. Coats, "The Origins and Development of the Royal Economic Society," *Economic Journal* LXXVIII (1968), 370, App. I. In 1902 when the Association was incorporated by Royal Charter, the president was R. B. Haldane and the vice-presidents were Charles Booth, James Byrne, Lord Courtney, Robert Giffen, Alfred Marshall, Viscount Milner, and Viscount Morley.

72. Geoffrey Millerson, *The Qualifying Associations: A Study in Professionalization* (London, 1964), p. 10.

73. E. C. K. Gonner, "On the Condition of Economic Studies in the United Kingdom" *Report of the Sixty-fourth Meeting of the British Association for the Advancement of Science,* Oxford, 1894 (London, 1894), p. 391.

74. H. S. Foxwell taught the "Pass" section of the new degree at University

College while the Honors degree became the exclusive prerogative or the London School of Economics which had been admitted to the reorganized University of London in 1900. In the *University of London Calendar*, 1900-1901, the Honors examiners in economics were C. F. Bastable and W. A. S. Hewins, and the papers they set were Marshallian: "Consider fully the connection between descriptive and theoretical economics"; or, "To what extent are the methods of (1) experimental science (2) biology, applicable to economic investigation?"

75. W. J. Ashley, "A Survey of the Past History and Present Position of Political Economy," Address to Section F of the British Association, Leicester, August 1907, in *Essays in Economic Method: Selected Papers read to Section F of the British Association for the Advancement of Science, 1860-1913*, ed. R. L. Smyth (London, 1962), pp. 244, 243. There had been a Cobden chair of political economics at Owens College, Manchester since the 1860s, and Jevons had held a combined professorship there in Mental and Moral Philosophy and Political Economy from 1866-1876, when he resigned and was replaced by Robert Adamson as professor of Political Economy until 1882. Adamson was succeeded by J. E. C. Munro who held chairs in Political Economy and Law. But the University of Manchester, which absorbed Owens College, was not chartered until 1880 and only began to award degrees several years later. See W. H. Chaloner, "Jevons in Manchester: 1863-1876," *The Manchester School* (March 1972), pp. 73-84.

76. As early as 1871 Marshall had urged university reforms to unite theoretical and practical education in "The Previous Examination," *Cambridge University Reporter* (March 1, 1871), pp. 222-223. Part I of the new tripos in Economics and Political Science was held for the first time in 1905; Part II in 1906; and by 1908, 47 honors degrees were awarded. Fifty additional students, including ten candidates for the civil service, had attended lectures. On June 2, 1909, Marshall wrote to the Guilder's Company urging them to renew their grant to the growing Economics School which then had 24 students preparing for the Honors exam; *M.P.*

77. A. J. Balfour, then Conservative Prime Minister, to Marshall, March 23, 1901, asking Marshall to sit on the Labour Commision, *M.P.*

78. House of Commons Paper, No. 321.

79. Letter to Lujo Brentano, August 26, 1903, in McCready, "Alfred Marshall and Tariff Reform," p. 266.

80. A. J. Balfour, *Parliamentary Debates*, 4th Series (1903), p. 103; "Speech at Annual Dinner of Royal Economic Society," in *Economic Journal* XIV (September 1904), 351-354.

5. *Economic Analysis: Means and Ends*

1. Alfred Marshall, "Distribution and Exchange," *Economic Journal* VIII (March 1898), 52.

2. Francis Galton's *Natural Inheritance* (London, 1889), induced the socialist mathematician Karl Pearson to develop Galton's statistical methods, and the work strongly influenced W. F. R. Weldon, appointed in 1890 Jordell Professor of Zoology at University College, London, and the Cambridge mathematical economist F. Y. Edgeworth. Pearson, *Life, Letters and Labours of Francis Galton*, III (Cambridge, 1930), 57.

3. Harold Westergaard, *Contributions to the History of Statistics* (London, 1932), p. 141.

4. Edwin G. Boring, "The Beginning and Growth of Measurement in Psychology," *Isis* LII (1961), 252.

5. George Boole, *An Investigation of the Laws of Thought on which are Founded the Mathematical Theories of Logic and Probabilities* (London, 1854).

6. Galton, *Natural Inheritance*, p. 17.

7. Galton, *Probability, the Foundation of Eugenics: The Herbert Spencer Lecture* Delivered on June 5, 1907 (Oxford, 1907), p. 9.

8. Notice describing Lab in Pearson, *Life*, II, 357.

9. *Photographic News* XXVIII (April 17, 1885), 243-245.

10. Galton, "Generic Images," *Nineteenth Century* VI (July 1897), 162.

11. David Heron, *The Influence of Defective Physique and Unfavorable Home Environment on the Intelligence of School Children, being a Statistical Examination of the London County Council Pioneer School Survey* (London, 1911), p. 58.

12. Karl Pearson, *Darwinism, Medical progress and Eugenics*. The Cavendish Lecture, 1912 (London, 1912), p. 19.

13. Edgar Schuster, *Eugenics* (London, 1912).

14. Galton, *Probability, the Foundation of Eugenics*, p. 25.

15. Pearson and Ethel M. Elderton, *A First Study of the Influence of Parental Alcoholism on the Physique and Ability of the Offspring* (London, 1910).

16. William Bateson, *Variation and Differentiation*, printed for the author, 1903, pp. 1-11. This pamphlet was a reply to Pearson's "On the Fundamental Conceptions of Biology," *Biometrika* I (1902), 320-344. Bateson was professor of biology at Cambridge from 1908 to 1910, when he resigned to direct the newly founded John Innes Horticultural Institute at Merton.

17. *Reports to the Evolution Committee of the Royal Society*, Report I. *Experiments* Undertaken by W. Bateson, F. R. S., and Miss E. R. Saunders. (Presented to the Committee, December 17, 1901.) (London, 1910), p. 159.

18. Bateson, Preface to *Mendel's Principles of Heredity. A Defence* (Cambridge, 1902), pp. x-xiii. In 1904 and again in 1907, Pearson wrote papers about the instability of masonry dams. While "the mathematic work was excellent, the experimental work being based on models made of gelatine" was not as his son E. S. Pearson observed "altogether applicable to the engineers' problems." *Karl Pearson: An Appreciation of Some Aspects of His Life and Work* (Cambridge, 1928), p. 47. Pearson was not an experimentalist or an inductive scientist of any sort; he was a first-rate mathematician.

19. Bateson, "Presidential Address to the Zoological Section, British Association," Cambridge Meeting, 1904, in Beatrice Bateson, *William Bateson, F.R.S. Naturalist* (Cambridge, 1928), p. 259.

20. Letter to William Bateson, October 26, 1908, *M.P.* As referee of the Royal Society's Philosophical Transactions, Bateson rejected Pearson's paper on the measurement of inherited qualities and his address as president of the Zoological Section of the British Association in 1904 was directed largely against the biometric school. E. S. Pearson, *Karl Pearson*, pp. 36, 39.

21. K. Pearson, *National Life from the Standpoint of Science*, 2d ed. (London, 1905), a reprint of the 1900 ed., pp. 20-21, 28-33, 45-50, 56-59, 61-64. Before he turned to eugenics and biometrics in 1900, Pearson's career was full and varied. In 1879 he was Third Wrangler in Mathematics; in 1880, a Fellow of Kings College; and in 1881, he was called to the bar. From 1880 to 1890 he studied and taught German life and thought and became a socialist lecturing to workingmen on Lasalle and Marx. In 1885 he completed William K. Clifford's *The Common Sense of the Exact Sciences* and, in 1886 and 1896, the first and second volumes of Isaac Todhunter's *History of the Theory of Elasticity*. In 1884 he was appointed to the Chair of Applied Mathematics and Mechanics at University College, London; and in 1890 he became Gresham Lecturer in Geometry. During those years he also wrote on socialism and university reform, and taught modern geometry, geometrical drawing, and projection, dynamics, mechanics, and astronomy. E. S. Pearson, pp. 4-54.

22. Bertrand Russell, "Politics of a Biologist," *Albany Review* II (October 1907), 97.

23. At the first International Statistical Congress at Brussels in 1853, there was a successful call for a new Congress to do statistical research on the physical, moral, and intellectual progress of the lower classes. Westergaard, *Contributions to the History of Statistics*, p. 176. It was assumed, axiomatically, that such progress had in fact occurred.

24. M. R. Stoll, *Whewell's Philosophy of Induction* (Lancaster, 1929), p. 63; George Boole, *An Investigation of the Laws of Thought*, pp. 4-11, 403, 422.

25. John Tyndall, "On the Importance of the Study of Physics as a Branch of Education for all the Classes," in *Lectures on Education, delivered at the Royal Institution of Great Britain* (London, 1855), p. 210; see James Paget's, "On the Importance of Physiology," ibid., p. 259.

26. Kurt Mendelssohn, "Probability Enters Physics," in *Turning Points in Physics* (Amsterdam, 1959), p. 54.

27. Paul Lazarsfeld, "Notes on the History of Quantification in Sociology," *Isis* LII (1961), 309.

28. G. Boole, *An Investigation of the Laws of Thought*, pp. 20-21.

29. F. Galton, *Natural Inheritance*, chap 4; Pearson, "Contributions to the Mathematical Theory of Evolution. II. Skew Variations in Homogeneous Material," *Philosophical Transactions of the Royal Society* (1895), Ser. A, 186, pp. 343-414.

30. Henry Guerlac, "Quantification in Chemistry," *Isis* LII (1961), 197.

31. Marshall, "The Social Possibility of Economic Chivalry" (1907), in *Memorials of Alfred Marshall*, ed. A. C. Pigou (New York, 1956), pp. 323-324.

32. W. S. Jevons, *Theory of Political Economy* (London, 1871), p. 3.

33. Letters to Professor A. Bowley, March 2 and December 20, 1901, in *Memorials*, pp. 422, 424.

34. Graham Wallas, *Human Nature in Politics*, 3d ed. (New York, 1921), pp. 160-182.

35. This analysis is taken from Joseph Spengler's, "On the Progress of Quantitative Economics," *Isis* LII (1961), 309.

36. Joseph Schumpeter, "Alfred Marshall's 'Principles': A Semi-Centennial Appraisal," in *Ten Great Economists* (Oxford, 1965), pp. 93, 108.

37. S. S. Wilks, "Some Aspects of Quantification in Science," *Isis* LII (1961), 142.

38. Letter to Professor A. L. Bowley, February 27, 1906, in *Memorials*, p. 427.

39. Jowett had told Marshall that mathematics belonged in notes and appendixes. Letters from Jowett to Marshall, December 14 and December 25, 1884, in *M.P.* Jowett often encouraged Balliol men to read economics seriously after they took their degree, as in the case of the brilliant student of law, A. V. Dicey. Dicey to Marshall, November 7, 1893, in *M.P.*

40. Walter Bagehot, "The Preliminaries of Political Economy" (1876), in *Economic Studies*, ed. Richard Holt Huffon, 2d ed. (London, 1888), p. 77.

41. Marshall, "The Present Position of Economics" (1885), in *Memorials*, p. 172.

42. *Macmillan's Quarterly List of New Books and New Editions,* July 1890.

43. T. S. Simey, *Social Science and Social Purpose* (London, 1968), pp. 20-21.

44. Milton Friedman, "The Methodology of Positive Economics," in *Essays in Positive Economics* (Chicago, 1953), pp. 4, 16-39.

45. Jowett to Marshall, July 24, 1890, *M.P.*

46. Letter to Foxwell, January 25, 1897, *M.P.*

47. Marshall, *The New Cambridge Curriculum in Economics and Associated Branches of Political Science: Its Purpose and Plan* (London, 1903), pp. 25-26; Letter to Foxwell, August 8, 1907, *M.P.*

48. Marshall, "The Present Position of Economics," p. 164.

49. Marshall, "Distribution and Exchange," p. 54.

50. Marshall, "The Present Position of Economics," p. 164.

51. Robert Lekachman, *A History of Economic Ideas* (New York, 1959), p. 296.

52. Marshall, *Elements of Economics of Industry*, 3d ed. (London, 1900), p. 266.

53. Marshall, *Principles of Economics,* 9th variorum ed., annotated by C. W. Guillebaud (London, 1961), p. 348.

54. John Stuart Mill, *Principles of Political Economy, with some of their Applications to Social Philosophy,* ed. with introd. by W. J. Ashley (London, 1909), p. 748.

55. Marshall, *Industry and Trade* (London, 1919), p. 195.

56. Marshall, "Distribution and Exchange," pp. 40, 44, 58.

57. Marshall, *Pure Theory of Domestic Values,* pp. 20-37. This paper, published privately by Henry Sidgwick for private circulation in 1879, contains Marshall's first reference to this doctrine. In 1930 the London School of Economics and Political Science published it together with Marshall's *The Pure Theory of Foreign Trade* as the first volume in their series of reprints of scarce tracts in economics and political science. The idea of a "consumer's surplus" was developed fully in the *Principles,* chap. 6, Book III. Until the 4th edition in 1895, Marshall used the phrase "consumer's rent" to describe "consumer's surplus."

58. Marshall, *Principles,* pp. 467-470.

59. Jevons, "Economic Policy," Address to Section F of the British Association, Liverpool, September 1870, in *Essays in Economic Method; Selected Papers read to Section F of the British Association for the Advancement of Science, 1860-1913,* ed. R. L. Smyth (London, 1962), pp. 25, 30.

60. Marshall, "Minutes of Evidence Taken Before the Royal Commission on the Aged Poor, June 5, 1893, in Marshall, *Official Papers* (London, 1926), pp. 244, 249, 257-259.

61. Letter to Lord Reay, November 12, 1909, in *Memorials,* p. 462.

62. Leonard Trelawney Hobhouse saw the major conflict in the new democracy as the continuing historical clash of liberty versus order and the idea of personality in opposition to the humanitarian idea. *Morals in Evolution* (New York, 1906), I, 365-371.

63. Marshall, "A Fair Rate of Wages" (1887), in *Memorials,* pp. 218-222.

64. Marshall, Preface to L. L. Price's *Industrial Peace: Its Advantages, Methods and Differences. A Report of an Inquiry Made for the Toynbee Trustees* (London, 1887), p. xxvi. "A Fair Rate of Wages," reproduced the substance of this preface. Price was a former student of Marshall's who went to teach at Oxford.

65. Marshall described the engineers strike as an "anti-social" and regressive force, in letters to Edward Caird, October 22 and December 5, 1897, in *Memorials,* pp. 398-399.

66. Marshall, *Elements of Economics,* pp. 268-273.

67. Review of Marshall's *Principles* in the *Pall Mall Gazette,* July 1890. All reviewers, lay and academic, agreed that Marshall's *Principles* had transformed economics into a science of social reform.

68. Patrick Geddes, "A Theory of the Consumption of Wealth," *Report of the Sixtieth Meeting of the British Association for the Advancement of Science, Leeds September 1890* (London, 1891), p. 924.

69. Marshall, letter to Lujo Brentano, professor of political economy at Munich since 1892, August 18, 1903 in H. W. McCready, "Alfred Marshall and Tariff Reform, 1903: Some Unpublished Letters," *Journal of Political Economy* 63 (1955), 266.

70. Quoted in Joseph A. Schumpeter, *History of Economic Analysis,* edited from manuscript by Elizabeth Boody Schumpeter (New York, 1954), pp. 832-833. In all of Marshall's surviving correspondence there is only one harsh letter, a scathing criticism by Marshall of Beatrice Potter's *The Cooperative Movement in Great Britain* (London, 1891). Marshall found the book filled with "dogmas as sweeping and confident as those of the most doctrinaire of the old economists," because Miss Potter was not sufficiently aware of the "complexity of human affairs . . . you are constantly saying that there are only two alternatives when there seems to me to be fifty." Marshall to Beatrice Potter, July 11, 1891, *M.P.*

71. Letter to Sir William Ramsay, April 21, 1902, *M.P.* A. W. Coats argues that Marshall opposed L.S.E. because his plans to establish his own school of economics at Cambridge were upset by Hewins at the new L.S.E. Coats, "Alfred Marshall and the Early Development of the London School of Economics: Some Unpublished Letters," *Economica* XXXIV (November 1967), 408-417. Marshall's own explanation appears entirely consistent with his views and his behavior.

6. *Transitional Psychology, 1855-1890*

1. Herbert Spencer, "Review of Alexander Bain's *The Emotions and the Will* (1860)," in *Essays: Scientific, Political and Speculative* I (London, 1901), 50-55.

2. Spencer used faculty psychology from his *Social Statics* (London, 1851) until the 1873 revision of his *Principles of Psychology* (London, 1855).

3. But as Henry Sidgwick observed, Spencer's psychology remained inconsistent. "Philosophy and Physical Science: Review of Spencer's *Principles of Psychology*," 2d rev. ed., *Academy* IV (April 1, 1873), 131.

4. Spencer, *Principles of Psychology*, 3d ed. (London, 1880), II, 505n. It is revealing that Spencer called this new section "Congruities."

5. Ibid., I, 51.

6. *The Student's Guide to the University of Cambridge*, Part VIII. *Moral Sciences Tripos*, ed. Henry Sidgwick, 4th ed., rev. (Cambridge, 1881), p. 27.

7. Spencer, "Progress: Its Law and Cause" (April, 1857), in *Essays: Scientific, Political, and Speculative* (London, 1858). "Progress is not an accident, not a thing within human control, but a beneficent necessity," p. 52.

8. Carveth Read, "G. S. Lewes's Posthumous Volumes," *Mind* VI (October 1881), 485.

9. Gustav Fechner, *Elements of Psychophysics* (1860); W. Wundt, *Beiträge* (1858-1862).

10. G. Croom Robertson, "Psychology and Philosophy," *Mind* VIII (January 1883), 12, 20. Robertson was the first editor of *Mind*.

11. John Dewey, "The Psychological Standpoint," *Mind* XI (January 1886), 1-2.

12. J. A. Stewart, "Is Psychology a Science or a Method?" *Mind* I (October 1876), 445, 450-451. Stewart was White's professor of moral philosophy at Oxford from 1897-1927. In 1905 F. C. S. Schiller described him to James as a "convert to pragmatism," Schiller to James, May 21, 1905, in the *James Papers* at the Houghton Library, Harvard University. This collection will be cited as *J.P.*

13. Robert Adamson, "James Sully's Outlines of Psychology," *Mind* IX (July 1884), 434.

14. James to G. Croom Robertson, November 9, 1887, *J.P.*

15. Hughlings Jackson, influenced by Thomas Laycock's theory of reflex cerebral action and by Spencer's account of nervous evolution, repudiated faculty explanations of the brain to complete the "integration of the association psychology with sensory-motor physiology." Robert M. Young, *Mind, Brain and Adaptation in the Nineteenth Century. Cerebral Localization and its Biological Context from Gall to Ferrier* (Oxford, 1970), p. 206. In 1862 he was appointed assistant physician to the National Hospital, Queens Square, and remained there for forty-five years. Jackson began writing in 1866, but his most important work was published in 1873 as "Observations on the Localisation of Movements in the Cerebral Hemispheres, as Revealed by Cases of Convulsion, Chorea and 'Aphasia,'" *West Riding Lunatic Asylum Medical Reports* 3 (1873), 175-195; and, "On the Anatomical, Physiological, and Pathological Investigation of Epilepsies," ibid. (1873a), pp. 315-390. David Ferrier conducted experiments at the West Riding Asylum to test Jackson's theories, and the results of his corroborative research appeared in the institutions *Reports* for 1873: "Experimental Researches in Cerebral Physiology and Pathology" (1873), ibid., pp. 30-96. Ferrier's classic study was *The Functions of the Brain* (London, 1876).

16. See especially E. R. Guthrie and Gardiner Murphy, *Historical Introduction to Modern Psychology*, rev. ed. (New York, 1949).

17. Hermann von Helmholtz, "On the Conservation of Force," (July 23, 1847), read to the Physical Society of Berlin and published in an English transslation in *Scientific Memoirs, selected from the Transactions of Foreign Academies of Science and Learned Societies and from Foreign Journals.* New Series, ed. John Tyndall and W. Francis, vol. 1 (London, 1853).

18. Emil Du Bois-Reymond was the first scientist to describe the chemical and electromotor properties and changes in muscular activities. After serving as Johannes Müller's assistant at the University of Berlin, he succeeded him in the chair of physiology and in 1877 became director of the new Institute of Physiology.

19. Samuel Wilberforce, Review of *On the Origins of Species*... by Charles Darwin, *Quarterly Review* 108 (1860), 225-264. Wilberforce did not publicly admit writing this review until it was reprinted in his *Essays Contributed to the 'Quarterly Review,'* 2 vols. (London, 1874).

20. Spencer, "The Comparative Psychology of Man," *Mind* I (January 1876), 20.

21. H. Sidgwick, "The Relation of Ethics to Sociology" (1899) in *Miscellaneous Essays and Address* (London, 1904), p. 269.

22. H. Sidgwick, "The Theory of Evolution in Application to Practice," *Mind* I (January 1876), 63.

23. Frederick William Henry Myers, "Henry Sidgwick," obituary notice in *Proceedings of the Society for Psychical Research* (1900), reprinted in *Fragments of Prose and Poetry*, ed. Eveleen Myers (London, 1904), p. 103.

24. Sidgwick confided his doubts to his diary on January 28, 1887, and March 22, 1887, quoted in A. Sidgwick and E. M. Sidgwick, *Henry Sidgwick: A Memoir* (London, 1906), pp. 466-467, 471-473.

25. Frederick Pollock, "Evolution and Ethics," *Mind* I (January 1876), 337.

26. H. Sidgwick, *Moral Sciences Tripos*, p. 30.

27. The first part of the exam covered every variety of the most recent psychological work in England and the continent, while the more advanced Part II asked about current controversies, physiology, and experiment in greater detail. Psychology was optional among five subjects in the elementary exam and among six in the higher one. The schedule of subjects for examination is printed in ibid., pp. 7-13.

28. Ibid., p. 25.

29. Arthur James Balfour, "The Philosophy of Ethics," *Mind* III (January 1878), esp. 69-76.

30. H. Sidgwick, "On the Nature of the Evidence of Theism," a paper read on February 25, 1898, to the Synthetic Society. Appendix I to A, and E. M. S. Sidgwick's *Henry Sidgwick*, p. 608. The best treatment of Sidgwick, especially of his reaction against scientific naturalism, appears in Frank Miller Turner's *Between Science and Religion. The Reaction to Scientific Naturalism in Late Victorian Thought* (New Haven, 1974), chap. 3.

31. John Stuart Mill, "Inaugural Address at St. Andrews," in *Dissertations and Discussions* (New York, 1874), IV, 165.

32. Spencer, *Autobiography* (London, 1904), I, 416-418. Among absolute forms of belief Spencer included geometry, mechanical axioms, visual sensations, and pain.

33. William James, "Notes on Spencer's Chapter on 'Assumption of Metaphysics' in his *Principles*," *J.P.*

34. George Edward Moore, *Principia Ethica* (Cambridge, 1956), chap. 1.

35. Edward White Benson, Archbishop of Canterbury, 1882-1896, recalling Cambridge of the late 1860s. Benson was Sidgwick's brother-in-law and he had

been Sidgwick's teacher at Rugby. Quoted in A. and E. M. Sidgwick's *Henry Sidgwick*, p. 39.

36. See C. J. Dewey, "Cambridge Idealism: Utilitarian Revisionists in Late Nineteenth Century Cambridge," *The Historical Journal* XVII, 1 (1974), 65-78, for an able discussion of the common elements of Oxford idealism and Cambridge rationalism.

37. Thomas Henry Huxley, "Of the Hypothesis that all Animals are Automata," *Methods and Results. Essays* (New York, 1899), p. 244.

38. The revisionists of robot psychology, each developing entirely different interpretative models, include Jean Piaget, Henry Warner, Kurt Goldstein, A. H. Maslow, Gordon Allport, Pitrim Sorokin, and Eric Berne.

39. Cattell's important paper on "Mental Tests and Measurements," an inadequate though influential attempt to use sensory measurements to test intelligence, appeared in *Mind* XV (1890), 373-381. For Hall, see Dorothy Ross's impressive *G. Stanley Hall: The Psychologist as Prophet* (Chicago, 1972), especially pp. 234-236, for a discussion of the relations between Hall and James.

40. Huxley's "Of the Hypothesis that all Animals are Automata," appeared originally in *The Fortnightly Review,* new series, XVI (1874), 555-580, as did W. K. Clifford's equally controversial "Body and Mind," ibid., pp. 714-736.

41. G. Croom Robertson, "Philosophy in London," *Mind* I (January 1876), 20.

42. *Mind* published about twenty-four articles a year from professed "psychologists" and from heterogeneous contributors such as A. J. Balfour, Leslie Stephen, J. N. Keynes, J. B. Tylor, Lord Rayleigh, T. H. Green, R. B. Haldane, and Sir John Lubbock. The journal also featured "Reports" on current experimental work and summaries of the contents of every other journal published in psychology and philosophy. A section of "Notes" encouraged controversy stirred by articles in *Mind,* and correspondents debated current issues and commented on work in progress. Foreign as well as British books and articles were reviewed.

43. William K. Clifford, "Body and Mind" (1874), *Lectures and Essays,* 3d ed. (London, 1901), II, 37. Cf. Clifford, "On the Nature of Things-in-Themselves," *Mind* III (January 1878), 60-61.

44. Clifford, "On Some of the Conditions of Mental Development " (March 6, 1868) in *Lectures and Essays* I, 87; 104.

45. Clifford, "Aims and Instruments of Scientific Thought" (1872), *Lectures and Essays* I, 138.

46. Karl Pearson, *The Grammar of Science* (London, 1892); Clifford, "The Prostitution of Science" (1877), *Lectures and Essays* II, 34-39.

47. Clifford, "Body and Mind," p. 271.

48. Clifford, "The Ethics of Belief" (1877), in *Lectures and Essays* II, 363.

49. Clifford, "Body and Mind," p. 273.

50. Clifford, "Aims and Instruments of Scientific Thought," pp. 152-156.

51. Clifford, "On the Scientific Basis of Morals," *Contemporary Review* (September 1875).

7. *William James and the Revolution in Psychology*

1. James first read Renouvier in 1868, but it was not until the spring of 1870, during a period of depression, that the French philosopher's message affected him critically. On April 30, he wrote in his diary: "I think that yesterday was a crisis in my life. I finished the first part of Renouvier's second *Essais* and see no reason why his definition of free will—'the sustaining of a thought *because I choose to* when I might have other thoughts' need be the definition of an illusion. At any rate, I will assume for the present—until next year—that it is no illusion. My first act of free will shall be to believe in free will." Quoted in R. B. Perry, *The Thought and Character of William James*, Briefer Version (New York, 1964), p. 121; and in Gay Wilson Allen, *William James. A Biography* (New York, 1967), p. 168. Cf. Charles Renouvier, *Traité de Psychologie Rationelle*, 3 vols., 2d ed. (Paris, 1875), I, 399.

2. William James, *Principles of Psychology*, 2 vols. (Cambridge, 1890), II, 549, 579.

3. James, "Are We Automata?" *Mind* IV (January 1879), 15.

4. James, "Brute and Human Intellect," *Journal of Speculative Philosophy* XI (1878), 236. Cf. "Remarks on Spencer's *Definition of Mind as Correspondence*," ibid., pp. 1-18.

5. James, "What is an Emotion?" *Mind* IX (April 1884), 189.

6. James, *Principles* II, 450. This theory, developed independently by the Danish psychologist Carl Lange, was discredited shortly after it appeared, but recent experiments have demonstrated that blood pressure, heartbeat, and even brain waves can be altered and regulated by conscious effort.

7. James, "Notes on Psychology—Free-Will, pre-1870," in the James Papers, Houghton Library, Harvard University cited as *J.P.* Cf. James, "Are we Automata?" p. 131.

8. James, "The Sentiment of Rationality," *The Will to Believe, and Other Essays in Popular Philosophy* (London, 1897), pp. 64-96.

9. James, "The Psychology of Belief," *Mind* XII (April 1887), 193.

10. James, "The Perception of Space. II." Ibid.

11. James, *Principles*, II, 308.

12. James, Notebook X 1876-77, labeled: "Identity, etc.," *J.P.*

13. James, "Are we Automata?" p. 9.

14. James, "On Some Omissions of Introspective Psychology," *Mind* IX (January 1884), 11, 18.

15. James, *Principles*, I, 631.

16. James, "On the Function of Cognition," *Mind* X (January 1885), 434. This paper was originally read before the British Aristotelian Society on December 1, 1884. Cf. James, "The Psychology of Belief," p. 336.

17. James, "Are We Automata?" p. 22.

18. James, "The Sentiment of Rationality," p. 97.

19. James, "The Psychology of Belief," pp. 329-330.

20. George H. Lewes, "Consciousness and Unconsciousness," *Mind* II (April

1877). This essay was taken from *The Physical Basis of Mind* (London, 1877).

21. James Sully, "On the Definition of Instinctive Action," *Mind* VI (January 1881), 114-116. Sully was Robinson's successor as Grote Professor of Mind and Logic at University College and the founder of the British Psychological Society.

22. James, *Principles*, I, 121-122; II, 368.

23. Studies of telepathy and hypnosis led James's British friend, the psychical researcher, Edmund Gurney, to describe consciousness as a hierarchy of parts, some of which were hidden. Gurney predicted that future differences among psychologists would concern the existence and nature of these submerged facets. Edmund Gurney, "Further Problems of Hypnotism I," *Mind* II (April 1877), 42, 229-230.

24. James, *Principles* I, 288.

25. Fritsch and Hitzig were young German physicians whose epochal experiments in cortical localization in the brain were performed on a dressing table in a small house. In 1870 they published their results as "On the Electrical Excitability of the Cerebrum" in *Archiv fur Anatomie, Physiologie und Wissenschaftlich Medizin* XXVII (Leipzig, 1870), 300-332. See Robert M. Young, *Mind, Brain and Adaptation in the Nineteenth Century: Cerebral Localization and its Biological Context from Gall to Ferrier* (Oxford, 1970), chap. 7, for a discussion of their work.

26. Conway Lloyd Morgan, *Animal Life and Intelligence* (London, 1890); *Habit and Instinct* (London, 1896). L. T. Hobhouse, *Mind in Evolution* (London, 1901).

27. Cf. Morgan, "The Natural History of Experience," *The British Journal of Psychology* II (December 1909), 1-20; Hobhouse, *Morals in Evolution: A Study in Comparative Ethics*, 2 vols. (New York, 1906).

28. Alfred Binet, *The Psychic Life of Micro-Organisms. A Study in Experimental Psychology*, trans. Thomas McCormack (Chicago, 1889).

29. T. H. Huxley, "Evolution and Ethics" (Romanes Lecture, 1893) *Evolution and Ethics and Other Essays* (New York, 1899), p. 85: "I see no limit to the extent to which intelligence and will, guided by sound principles of investigation, and organized in common effort, may modify the conditions of existence. ...And much may be done to change the nature of man himself."

30. James Sully, "Comparison," *Mind* X (October 1885), 498.

31. Francis Galton, *English Men of Science* (London, 1874).

32. His introspective experiments were recorded as "Free Will Observations and Inferences," *Mind* IX (July 1884), 406-413.

33. Galton, *Inquiries into Human Faculty and its Development* (1883), 2d ed. (London, 1907), pp. 17-18.

34. Adolphe Jacques Quételet, *Man and the Development of his Faculties* (1835).

35. Galton's research team included Charles Spearman, Cyril Burt, and Wil-

liam McDougall, three young men who became dominant figures in postwar British psychology. Cf. Robert Thompson, *The Pelican History of Psychology* (London, 1968), pp. 114-115.

36. Galton, *Natural Inheritance* (London, 1889), p. 66. James, furious with this reduction of individuals to statistical common denominators, called it the "most pernicious and immoral of fatalisms." "The Importance of Individuals," *Open Court* IV (1890), in *The Will to Believe*, p. 261.

37. See chap. 5 for a discussion of William Bateson's Mendelian studies.

38. James Ward, "Psychology," the *Encyclopedia Britannica*, 9th ed. (London, 1886), p. 548. In the original 1883 article psychology had been defined less imaginatively as a science "which aims only at a scientific exposition of what can be known and verified by experience." For a perceptive account of Ward's life and thought, see Frank Miller Turner, *Between Science and Religion. The Reaction to Scientific Naturalism in Late Victorian Thought* (New Haven, 1974), chap. 8.

39. Ward, "Psychology" (1883), pp. 45-46; (1886), p. 548.

40. Ward, "Psychological Principles, I. The Standpoint of Psychology," *Mind* VIII (April 1883), 153-169.

41. Ward, "Memorandum on Psychology," *Statement of the Needs of the University*, Part I. *Literary, Dept. of Divinity, Law, Literature, Philosophy and Art*, Cambridge University Association (Cambridge, 1899), pp. 24-25. The Association was founded in 1899 as a blue-ribbon alumni organization to raise funds for expansion.

42. Ward, "Psychological Principles, II. Fundamental Facts and Conceptions," *Mind* VIII (October 1883), 465.

43. Frederick W. H. Myers, *Fragments of Inner Life. An Autobiographical Sketch.* (London, 1961), introduction. Myers printed twenty-five copies in July 1893, and distributed them among his friends, including James and Sidgwick, to be read only after his death.

44. James, "Frederick Myers's Services to Psychology," *Proceedings of the Society for Psychical Research* (1901), p. xiii.

45. Even Myers, whose loss of an idealized love led him to search desperately for evidence of an "after-life," relied entirely upon experimental, verifiable scientific methods as did the other S.P.R. members. *Fragments*, pp. 23, 42, 46-47.

46. Quoted in Alan Gould, *The Founders of Psychical Research* (London, 1968), p. 138.

47. Edmund Gurney, "The Human Ideal," *Tertium Quid. Chapters on Various Disputed Questions*, 2 vols. (London, 1887), I, 46-47.

48. Edwin Ray Lankester, "Psychology" (Presidential Address to the British Association, 1906), quoted in O.J.R. Howarth, *The British Association for the Advancement of Science: A Retrospect, 1831-1931*, Centenary, 2d ed. (London, 1931), pp. 73-74.

49. Sidgwick donated 150 books to the Society's library; he personally super-

vised all articles in the *Proceedings,* begun in January 1882, and in the *Journal,* established in February 1884, and he was president from 1892 until his death in 1901.

50. *The Phantasms of the Living,* 2 vols. (London, 1886), by Edmund Gurney, F. W. H. Myers, and Frank Podmore, was a pioneer study of hallucination based upon a random sampling of 5,000 people.

51. In 1900 the S.P.R. developed a series of questions to test attitudes toward a future life that included provisions for weighing the roles of emotion, sex, and professional bias. But this test was never applied. Schiller to James, July 7, 1900; July 21, 1900; December 22, 1900; March 6, 1901, *J.P.*

52. Benjamin Jowett to Mary Paley Marshall, July 23, 1891, *M.P.*

53. John Grote, *Exploratio Philosophica: Rough Notes on Modern Intellectual Science,* 2 vols. (Cambridge, 1865), I, 15.

54. Quoted in John Passmore, *A Hundred Years of Philosophy* (London, 1966), p. 60 n. 1. For Bradley's strongest "beliefs" see "My Station and Its Duties" (1876) in *Ethical Studies,* 2d ed. (Oxford, 1962), pp. 160-202.

55. James, "Absolutism and Empiricism," *Mind* IX (April 1884), 25.

56. James, "Notebook O, Outline of lecture at Wellesley College, 1905, Lecture V," *J.P.*

57. Bradley to James, September 21, 1897, *J.P.*

58. James, *Principles,* I, 482.

59. James, "MSS notes on Spencer's *Psychology* (1879)," *J.P.* Cf. James, "Great Men and their Environment" (1880), *The Will to Believe,* pp. 218, 232.

60. James Seth, "The Evolution of Morality," *Mind* XIV (January 1889), 34, 48.

61. James saw this explanation as the purpose of psychology. James to James Ward, November 1, 1892, *J.P.*

62. James, *Human Immortality,* The Ingersoll Lecture, 1897-1898 (Boston, 1898), p. 32.

63. James, Introduction to Boris Sidis's *The Psychology of Suggestion. A Research into the Subconscious Nature of Man and Society* (New York, 1898), p. v.

64. James to Ward, November 1, 1892, *J.P.*

65. This was done in an original and imaginative study: "Notes on the Sense of Dizziness in Deaf-Mutes," *Harvard University Bulletin* II (1881), 173. The notice was reprinted in *Mind* VI (July 1881), 4 and the results were published as "The Sense of Dizziness in Deaf-Mutes," *American Journal of Otology* IV (1882), 239-254.

66. The James Papers contain a voluminous correspondence with psychologists of every persuasion and nationality.

67. James to Theodore Flournoy, the Swiss psychologist at the University of Geneva, December 7, 1896, *J.P.*

68. James to Ward, July 31, 1904, *J.P.*

69. James, *Principles,* I, 193.

70. Edwin Ray Lankester, "Psychology," p. 74.

71. James, Preface to *Principles,* I, vii.

72. James, "The Perception of Space, II" *Mind* XII (April 1877), 187; *Principles,* I, 196-197.

73. J. S. Mill, *A System of Logic* (London, 1851), II, 431.

74. Spencer, *Principles* (1855), I, 580.

75. James, *Principles,* II, 343-384.

76. The Biometric and Galton Laboratories issued the Eugenic Laboratory Publications, divided into a Memoir and a Lecture series. The Biometric Laboratory Publications included the Biometric Series; Studies in National Deterioration; and the most polemical group, Questions of the Day and of the Fray. By 1932, there were 36 publications of Memoirs, including the famous *A First Study of the Influence of Parental Alcoholism on the Physique and Intelligence of the Offspring* by Ethel M. Elderton, assisted by Karl Pearson (London, 1910) (see chap. 2 of this book); 14 Lectures, 12 of which were by Pearson; 12 in the Biometric series, all written completely, or in major part, by Pearson; and 12 Questios of the Day, 9 of which were authored principally by Pearson. For titles see Cambridge University Press advertisement brochure (Cambridge, 1932).

77. Beatrice Edgell, "The British Psychological Society, 1901-1941," *The British Journal of Psychology. General Section* XXXVII (May 1947), 116.

78. C. S. Myers, Symposium on "Instinct and Intelligence," *British Journal of Psychology* III (October 1910), 267-268. Myers was then University Lecturer in Experimental Psychology at Cambridge. In 1914, the year after assuming the new directorship, he became sole editor of the *British Journal of Psychology.*

79. Weismann argued that "in general . . . a definitely directed progressive variation of a given part is produced by a continued selection in that definite direction." August Weismann, "Germinal Selection," *Monist* (January 1896), p. 268. Cf. Weismann, *Essays upon Heredity and Kindred Biological Problems,* authorized translation (Oxford, 1889) esp. "On Heredity," Weismann's inaugural lecture as pro-rector at the University of Freiburg in 1883 on the transmission of acquired characteristics through the "substance of germ-cells." 2d edition (Oxford, 1891), pp. 69-106.

80. G. J. Romanes, *Mental Evolution in Animals* (London, 1883), p. 48.

81. Morgan, *Habit and Instinct,* pp. 263, 265.

82. The moor hen "just lives through the palpitating situation, assimilates its teachings, and emerges from the ordeal as a new bird. As experiencer he is never again what he was before." Morgan, "The Natural History of Experience," p. 12.

83. Morgan, Symposium, pp. 220, 227. Under the more recent influence of cybernetics, we call this process "feedback."

84. H. Wildon Carr, Symposium, pp. 220-234.

85. G. F. Stout, Sumposium, p. 249.

86. Alfred Cort Haddon, Introduction to the *Reports of the Cambridge*

Anthropological Expedition to the Torres Straits (Cambridge, 1903), I, x.

87. Dr. Henry Wilde, a wealthy electrical engineer, had endowed the readership for the explicitly Lockean, nonexperimental study of mind.

88. McDougall, Symposium, p. 266.

89. Psychology began on a small but promising scale in the late 1890s at University College, London, in Cambridge and at Oxford. But despite the eminence of individual psychologists there and at the universities of Bristol (Morgan), Aberdeen and St. Andrews (Stout), Liverpool (Sherrington), and Edinburgh (George Combe), there was outspoken hostility to the new subject in every university and no fulltime chair exclusively in psychology existed until 1918, when it was established in Manchester. At Oxford, the home of Sidgwick, Ward, and Stout, the Wilde Readership, especially in McDougall's hands appeared to encourage psychology, but the sway of idealism buried both experimentalism and Jamesian psychology. Oxford was the last major university in the world to have a department of psychology. William Stephenson, "The Institute of Experimental Psychology," *Oxford Magazine* 56 (1938), 607. Only after World War II, "and considerable debate," an Honours School of Psychology, Philosophy, and Physiology was established. B. A. Farrell, "The Development of Psychological Studies at Oxford," ibid., 69 (1951), 311.

90. The British Psychological Society, founded in 1901 with ten charter members, accepted only those "who were recognized teachers in some branch of the subject" or "who had published work of recognized value." Edgell, "The British Psychological Society, 1901-1941," p. 5. At the end of the first year there were 13 members and by 1914, 79, including James and other foreign psychologists. The *British Journal of Psychology* began independently in 1904 under the joint editorship of Ward and the experimentalist, W. H. R. Rivers. The society assumed financial responsibility for its publication only in 1914.

8. *Liberal Reactions to the Failures of Democracy*

1. William Edward Hartpole Lecky, *Democracy and Liberty*, 2 vols. (London, 1896). The book was reprinted in 1898 and a new edition appeared in 1899.

2. Hattie E. Mahood, "The Liberal Party in England, A Menace to English Democracy," *Forum* XXI (July 1901), 595.

3. Martin Conway, *The Crowd in Peace and War* (London, 1915), p. 77. The Slade Professor of Fine Arts at Cambridge was merely an observer who wrote a series of articles from 1905-1908 for the *Nineteenth Century* that were later incorporated into this book. See chap. 10 of this book.

4. C. F. G. Masterman, "The Realities at Home," *The Heart of the Empire: Discussions of Problems of Modern City Life in London* by Masterman and others (London, 1902), p. 28. Masterman was a religious radical and a "new lib-

eral" social reformer whose eight years in the slums were translated into scathing journalism in the *Daily News* and into muckraking books and essays.

5. Masterman, *The Condition of England* (London, 1909), p. 118.

6. Ibid., pp. 123, 125, 128, 130; Masterman, *From the Abyss of its Inhabitants, by One of Them* (London, 1911), p. 20.

7. Thomas Carlyle, "Chartism" (1839), *Critical and Miscellaneous Essays* (Boston, 1884), IV, 61; *Past and Present* (Boston, 1884), p. 203. Masterman, "The Realities at Home," p. 28. See Eric E. Lampard, "The Urbanizing World," *Victorian Cities: Images and Realities,* ed. H. Y. Dyos and Michael Wolff (London; 1973), vol. 1.

8. Mastermann, *From the Abyss,* pp. 35-37.

9. Beatrice Webb, December 8, 1915, *Diaries, 1913-1924,* ed. M. I. Cole (London, 1952), p. 15.

10. William Ashworth, *An Economic History of England, 1870-1939* (London, 1960), p. 192.

11. "Hard to Please," *Punch,* April 4, 1906, showed labor as a dog, moving menacingly toward Henry Campbell-Bannerman after consuming the Workmen's Compensation Bill and the Merchant Shipping Bill and rejecting the Trades Dispute Bill. The caption below is: "He's had two platefuls of biscuits and isn't satisfied. Looks as if he wanted red meat."

12. Richard Price's *An Imperial War and the British Working Classes: Working-Class Attitudes and Reactions to the Boer War, 1889-1902* (Toronto, 1972) sets out to revise middle-class interpretations of working-class enthusiasm for imperialism, but concludes reluctantly: "lacking as we do any adequate direct evidence it is, in the final analysis, fruitless to try to establish that the working classes were either for or against imperialism" (p. 238). More persuasively, Gareth Stedman Jones has argued that if "the working class did not actively promote the jingoism, there can be no doubt that it passively acquiesced to it." Jones, "Working-Class Culture and Working-Class Politics in London, 1870-1900; Notes on the Remaking of a Working Class," *Journal of Social History* VII, 4 (Summer 1974), 461.

13. The London Liberal and Radical Union tried to attract the new voter away from the Conservatives who had captured the largest number of urban voters since 1867. The more democratically organized Metropolitan Radical Union, where Wallas actively worked, was equally unsuccessful. For a succinct but perceptive discussion of late-nineteenth- and early-twentieth-century politics, see Paul Thompson's superb *The Edwardians, the Remaking of British Society* (Bloomington and London, 1975), chap. 15. See Jones, ibid.

14. Graham Wallas, "The Money Power at War," (December 11, 1909), Wallas Papers at the London School of Economics and Political Science. This collection, cataloged partially by Wallas's daughter May, will be referred to as *W.P.*

15. Wallas, *Human Nature in Politics* (New York, 1921), p. 28.

16. J. L. Garvin to Northcliffe, December 1, 1906, quoted in A. M. Gollin, *"The Observer" and J. L. Garvin, 1908-14* (Oxford, 1960), p. 18.

17. H. W. Massingham was chronically fearful for the future of a democracy whose taste called "for a crime-soaked journalism, profiteering in war and brutality and will endure no other." "The Press and the People," *The Cooperative News* (June 28, July 5 and 12, 1924), in *Selections from the Writings of H. W. Massingham with Introductory Essay by J. L. Hammond and Others*, ed. H. J. Massingham (London, 1925), p. 132.

18. Annie Besant, quoted in Anne Fremantle, *This Little Band of Prophets: The British Fabians* (New York, 1960), p. 95.

19. Wallas, "History of London," lecture in the U.S., 1896, Box 16, *W.P.*

20. *The Illustrated London News*, March 9, 1907.

21. For an account of the election see G. Gibbon and R. W. Bell, *History of the London Country Council 1889-1930* (London, 1939), pp. 103-107, 677.

22. Wallas, *Human Nature in Politics*, p. 244.

23. Cornelius O'Leary, *The Elimination of Corrupt Practices in British Elections, 1868-1914* (New York, 1962).

24. Quoted in Roy Harrod, *Life of John Maynard Keynes* (London, 1951), p. 81.

25. Marcus R. P. Dorman, *The Mind of the Nation. A Study of Political Thought in the Nineteenth Century* (London, 1900), p. 451. See chap. 10 of this book.

26. John Alfred Spender, "Past and Future of the Liberal Party," *Contemporary Review* LXXXII (August 1902), 157-158.

27. James Bryce, *Modern Democracies*, 2 vols., (New York, 1924), I, 14. The research and thinking for this study was complete by 1914. From 1888, when his famous *American Commonwealth* appeared, to the 1920s, Bryce's rationalistic interpretations had not changed.

28. John Atkinson Hobson, *Confessions of an Economic Heretic* (London, 1938), p. 103.

29. Hobson, "The State as an Organ of Rationalisation," *Political Science Quarterly* II (1931), 34.

30. Hobson, *The Evolution of Modern Capitalism* (London, 1894), pp. 351-352.

31. Bernard Porter makes a good case for relating Hobson's theory of imperialism to his "restricted conception of rationalism." Porter, *Critics of Empire. British Radical Attitudes to Colonialism in Africa, 1895-1914* (London, 1968), p. 228.

32. Wallas, "The Economics of Human Welfare," *The Nation* (June 27, 1914), p. 346.

33. All the above quotes are from Hobson's *The Crisis of Liberalism: New Issues of Democracy* (London, 1909), pp. 15-16, 40, 73-74.

34. Hobson, "The Extension of Liberalism," *English Review* III (November 1909), 685.

34. The text of this speech appeared in *Votes for Women,* February 23, 1912. Pankhurst was speaking at a dinner on February 16 for Suffragettes recently released from prison.

36. M. Ostrogorski, *Democracy and the Organization of Political Parties,* vol. I: *England,* ed. and abridged Seymour Martin Lipset (New York, 1964), pp. 293-294.

37. Stephen Reynolds, *A Poor Man's House* (London, 1909), pp. 80, 83. Reynolds also wrote with Tom and Bob Wooley: *Seems So!. A Working-Class View of Politics* (London, 1913); and in 1923 he published his *Correspondence.* A similar idealization of the natural or irrational life occurs in Fabian Ware's *The Worker and the Country* (1912).

38. Wallas, "Syndicalism," *The Sociological Review* V (1912), 248-249.

39. Mandell Creighton, *The Cambridge Modern History* (Cambridge, 1902), p. 4.

40. William Stubbs, "On the Purposes and Methods of Historical Study" (1877), *Seventeen Lectures on the Study of Medieval and Modern History* (Oxford, 1886), pp. 71-92; A. F. Pollard, *The History of England. A Study in Evolution, 55 B.C.-A.D. 1911* (Oxford, 1947). This was originally published in 1912 in the Home University of Modern Knowledge series.

41. Walter Bagehot, *Physics and Politics* (1872) rev. ed. (New York, 1900), p. 131.

42. Both cyclical and random views of history were popular among turn-of-the-century German thinkers. See Georg Iggers. "The Idea of Progress in Recent Philosophies of History," *Journal of Modern History* XXX (1958), esp. 223.

43. Wallas, *The Great Society, A Psychological Analysis* (London, 1920), p. 323.

44. Wallas, Notes for lecture on "The Decay of Liberalism," at the South Place Ethical Society, October 1901, Box 6, *W.P.*

45. T. H. Huxley, "Evolution and Ethics" (1893), *Evolution and Ethics and Other Essays* (New York, 1899), p. 81.

46. Julian Huxley, "Evolution and Human Progress," *Ideas and Beliefs of the Victorians. An Historic Revaluation of the Victorian Age* (New York, 1966), p. 118.

47. Herbert Samuel, "Notebook" (1884), in the Samuel Papers in the House of Lords. This collection will be cited as *S.P.*

48. This speech brought Asquith to Gladstone's attention. Gladstone to Asquith, March 5, 1894, in the *Asquith MSS* at the Bodleian Library, pp. 9, 85. This collection will be referred to as *A.M.*

49. A. Birrell, *The Liberal Victory* (April 27, 1906) (London, 1906), p. 4.

50. The Club met four times a term. See *Rules of the Russell Club* (Oxford, 1880). Samuel, also a member of the Eighty Club, was the Club's first secretary and, in 1892-1893, president. *S.P.* A/3.

51. John Morley, *The Liberal Victory,* p. 9. Morley, Secretary of State for

India, was speaking at his installation as president of the Eighty Club.

52. Typical lecture topics were: "Moral and Social Reform" and "The Moral Basis of the New Order." W. S. Smith, *The London Heretics, 1870-1914* (London, 1967), pp. 132-139.

53. *Oxford Magazine* (November 1883), quoted in J. A. R. Pimlott, *Toynbee Hall, Fifty Years of Social Progress, 1884-1934* (London, 1935), p. 32.

54. Bernard Bosanquet, "The Meaning of Teleology," *Proceedings of the British Academy* (1905-1906) (April 1906), p. 243.

55. Sidgwick, William Clarke, and Stout were among the earliest members of the London Ethical Society.

56. First paragraph of the London Ethical Society's prospectus, in Gustav Spiller, *The Ethical Movement in Great Britain: A Documentary History* (London, 1934), p. 132. Spiller, a committed ethical culturist, was a self-educated compositor who wrote Jamesian psychology. See Gustav Spiller, *The Mind of Man: A Text-Book of Psychology* (London, 1902), esp. p. 507, and his *Autobiography, 1864-1934,* privately published by V. Spiller after Gustav Spiller's death in 1940.

57. *The London Ethical Society Report of 1886-7,* in Spiller, *The Ethical Movement.* Principles proclaimed in the *Report of 1888/9* reaffirmed the first report and went still further in a disavowal of supernatural rewards and punishments as a suitable foundation for social good. These principles remained substantially unchanged until 1920. "The General Principles of The Society" (1888-1889), in Spiller, ibid., p. 6. The society's militant secularism was best represented in the Moral Instruction League, created in 1897 to provide nonecclesiastical and nontheological moral instruction for schools in "character training, in self-control, purity, obedience, justice, courage, honesty." Quoted from John Hunter, a nonconformist minister in the Ethical movement. Ibid., p. 132.

58. The first course of L.E.S. lectures, at Toynbee Hall, December 1886-March 1887, was titled: "Morality and Modern Life." The lecturers and their topics were: J. S. Mackenzie, "Society as an Organisation"; J. S. Muirhead, "Evolution and Morality"; Mrs. Bryant, "The Union of Social and Individual Aims"; B. Bosanquet, "The Kingdom of Heaven upon Earth"; J. F. Carpenter, "Religion without God"; and C. S. Loch, "The Ethics of Charity." An Ethical Library completed between 1893 and 1910, was composed essentially of addresses before the Ethical Societies such as: Bosanquet's *The Civilisation of Christendom and Other Studies* (1893); Leslie Stephen's *Social Rights and Duties,* 2 vols. (1896); H. Sidgwick's *Practical Ethics* (1898); and the American genetic psychologist and friend of James at the University of Chicago, James Mark Baldwin's *Darwin and the Humanities* (1910).

59. A typical *Calendar of South Place Ethical Society* lists children's lectures on air, fire, and silkworkers (October 1896).

60. Among them were William Clarke, James Bryce, H. M. Hyndmann, G. B. Shaw, Ramsay MacDonald, and J. M. Robertson.

61. Hobson, *Imperialism* (1902) (Ann Arbor, 1965), p. 361.

62. This was the formal motto of the East London group which lasted from 1889 to 1912.

63. Hugh Dalton, *Call Back Yesterday: Memoirs, 1887-1931* (London, 1933), p. 34.

64. H. Sidgwick, "The Scope and Limits of the Work of an Ethical Society," address at the preliminary meeting of the Cambridge Ethical Society, May 18, 1888, *Practical Ethics: A Collection of Addresses and Essays* (London, 1898), p. 16 n. 22.

65. Sidgwick, "Aims and Methods of an Ethical Society," presidential address to the London Ethical Society, April 23, 1893, ibid., pp. 29-30. The address was published originally in the *International Journal of Ethics* (October 1893) as "My Station and its Duties."

66. Ibid., p. 51.

67. The General Object was in effect until 1920. Printed in Spiller, *The Ethical Movement,* p. 101.

68. Social Science Club Miscellaneous Papers; *Purpose of the Social Science Club,* Lent Term, 1899, Bodleian Library, Oxford. Members included J. H. Wicksteed, W. J. Braithwaite, G. Gathorne-Hardy, Rev. H. Rashdall, H. A. L. Fisher, H. W. B. Joseph, S. Ball, and C. S. Woodward.

69. The concept of "Liberal Anglican" is argued in Duncan Forbes's *The Liberal Anglican Idea of History* (Cambridge, 1952).

70. Compton MacKenzie's compelling portrait of the Anglican clergyman cum social reformer in *Sinister Street* (London, 1913) is more just and accurate than C. K. Chesterton's parody: "The Christian Social Union here was very much annoyed. It seems there is some duty, which we never should avoid. And so they sing a lot of hymns to help the unemployed. . . . [Then, Gore] said that unemployment was a horror and a blight, He said charities produced Servility and Spite, And stood upon the other leg, And said it wasn't right. . . . [Then Holland] said the human soul should be Ashamed of every sham, He said a man, should constantly Ejaculate 'I am'. . . . When he had done I went outside And got into a tram." *Autobiography* (London, 1936), pp. 167-169.

71. Quoted in Porter, *Critics,* p. 164.

72. Clarke, despite his debilitating insomnia, contributed to nearly every existing reformist group, as well as to the *Fabian Essays* (1889) and to the Fabian executive. But Clarke and the *Review's* board of Directors, Hobson, Samuel, Russeal Rea and Richard Stapley, could not quite manage the time or the financing for the venture. This difficulty was compounded by differences between Clarke and the Secretary, Ramsay MacDonald, who would not resign in spite of the Board's request for his resignation. See correspondence between Samuel, Clarke, Rea, Stapley, and MacDonald in *S.P.,* A/10, 3-25. In September 1897 the *Review* was abandoned.

73. Clark, "Introduction," *Progressive Review* I (October 1896), 1.

74. R. B. Haldane, "The New Liberal," ibid. (November 1896), pp. 133-143. Other writers for the *Review* were: William Carpenter, Scott Holland, Walter Crane, Sir Charles Dilke, Sidney and Beatrice Webb, Kier Hardie, Herbert Samuel, Havelock Ellis, Eduard Bernstein, J. M. Robertson, and W. C. MacKenzie.

75. Samuel, "Notebook," 1893-1895, *S.P.*, A/6.

76. Webb to Samuel, July 25, 1897, *S.P.*, N155.

77. Herbert Samuel, *Liberalism: An Attempt to State the Principles and Proposals of Contemporary Liberalism in England* (London, 1902), pp. 4, 6.

78. Samuel, *The Liberal View* (London, 1904), pp. 157-161; See William Beveridge, *Social Insurance and Allied Services. A Report* (New York, 1942). This edition was reproduced photographically from the English original in Her Majesty's Stationery Office.

79. See especially the detailed recommendations to the central government of *The Guildhall Conference on the Unemployed Question* (London, 1903). Called by the National Unemployment Committee, this conference was attended by 587 delegates representing 123 city and borough councils, urban and rural district councils, boards of guardians and other local officials, including the London County Council and 118 trade unions and councils and employers' associations.

80. Percy Alden, *Democratic England* (New York, 1912), p. 7. Alden had been Warden of Mansfield House in West Ham for twelve years. His experience in this chronically unemployed area led to his famous *The Unemployed* (1905) and to his influential participation in various "unemployed" committees, including the Guildhall Conference. The book is introduced by Alden's friend, Masterman.

9. Graham Wallas and a Liberal Political Science

1. Graham Wallas, *Human Nature in Politics*, 3d ed. (New York, 1921), p. 135.

2. *Human Nature in Politics* might have been called, Wallas admitted, a record of the effect on a practical politician of reading William James's *Principles of Psychology*. Preface. Cf. Wallas to James, November 12, 1908, *J.P.*, in which Wallas emphasizes his indebtedness to James.

3. Wallas, *The Great Society* (New York, 1920), p. 138.

4. The complaint that thought had "failed" was common in prewar journalism. A typical example of this attitude is: "Is Thought a Failure?" *Pall Mall Gazette*, June 23, 1914.

5. Wallas, "The Economics of Human Welfare," *The Nation* (June 27, 1914), p. 496.

6. C. F. G. Masterman, *In Peril of Change: Essays Written in Time of Tranquility* (New York, 1905), pp. 178-179.

7. Masterman, *Tennyson as a Religious Teacher* (London, 1900), pp. 108, 114.

8. Herbert Samuel, "Notebook," 1894, A/6, *S.P.* Edmund Gurney asked Wallas to lecture to Winslow and in neighboring parish councils because he always gave a moral or "high tone" to discussions of civic responsibilities. Gurney to Wallas, November 26, 1894, *W.P.*, Box 1. L. T. Hobhouse explained this feeling as the fundamental idea of democracy, the "application of ethical principles to political relations." *Democracy and Reaction* (London, 1904), p. 196.

9. Wallas thought Marshall's *Economics of Industry* was the best text available in economics in 1887, and he used it for his political economy lectures at the Working Men's College. But Wallas saw that the skill, industry, thrift, and temperance that Marshall hoped to make the general pattern of working-class behavior would reward employers more than workers. Notes for Bedford Debating Society, *W.P.*, Box 16.

10. Wallas, "Ends and Means in Democracy," lecture to the Fabian Society, October 30, 1930. Notes in *W.P.*, Box 12.

11. Benjamin Jowett to Lord Lansdowne, quoted in Melvin Richter, *The Politics of Conscience* (London, 1964), p. 66.

12. Wallas to Samuel, February 20, 1893; March 11, 1893; July 20, 1893. *S.P.* A/155. It was from Wallas that Samuel learned to think of politics as the means for creating the good life; his long and distinguished career as a public servant began with Wallas's lesson that the success of political reform depended "wholly on personal service." Samuel, *Liberalism; An Attempt to State the Principles and Proposals of Contemporary Liberalism in England* (London, 1902), p. 385.

13. Wallas, "Socialism and the Fabian Society," Review of Pease's *History of Fabian Socialism, The New Republic* (1916), in *Men and Ideas*, ed. May Wallas (London, 1940), p. 105.

14. Biographical note written by Wallas forty years later. *W.P.*

15. Webb to Wallas, September 16, 1900, *W.P.*, Box 2.

16. The *Daily Herald* reviewer of the third edition of *Human Nature in Politics* (1921), attributed Wallas's prewar influence to this pervasive receptivity to anything scientific (August 27, 1924).

17. Beatrice Webb, *My Apprenticeship* (London, 1926), pp. 112-113.

18. Wallas discusses the contrasts between the two Poor Law Commissions in *Human Nature in Politics*, pp. 166-179.

19. *London To-day and To-morrow. Proposals for the Reform of London Government prepared by a Special Committee of the London Reform Union; with a Map of Greater London and Appendices prepared for the Committee by its Chairman, M.E. Lange.* (London, 1908).

20. Karl Pearson, *The Grammar of Science* (London, 1892), p. 11, Pearson's public lectures at Gresham College, 1891, were on "The Scope and Concepts of Modern Science." Wallas read *Biometrika* and he may have attended Pearson's

Gresham College or University College lectures on statistical theory from 1894 to 1896, the first university lectures on the mathematical theory of statistics. See E. S. Pearson, *Karl Pearson: An Appreciation of Some Aspects of His Life and Work* (Cambridge, 1938), p. vii. In *Human Nature in Politics,* p. 160, Wallas attributed his use of quantitative reasoning to the economists, and cites Marshall's "Social Possibilities of Economics Chivalry," *The Journal of Economics* (March 1907), pp. 7-8.

21. Pearson, "The Enthusiasm of the Market Place and the Study" (1885), a lecture delivered at the South Place Institute and afterward published as a pamphlet, *The Ethic of Freethought: A Selection of Essays and Lectures* (London, 1888), p. 126.

22. Wallas, *Human Nature in Politics,* p. 140. See "The Future of English Education in the Light of the Past," in H. B. Binn, *A Century of Education* (London, 1908), p. 312.

23. Wallas, *The Great Society,* p. 18.

24. John A. Hobson, "The Qualitative Method," *The Sociological Review* II (July 1909), 294. This was a review of *Human Nature in Politics.*

25. Besant to Wallas, June 14, 1888, *W.P.,* Box 1.

26. William Bateson, *Biological Fact and the Structure of Society, The Herbert Spencer Lecture, Feb. 28, 1912* (Oxford, 1912), pp. 3-4.

27. Francis Galton, *Probability, the Foundations of Eugenics: The Herbert Spencer Lecture* (Oxford, 1907), p. 29.

28. Benjamin Kidd, "Individualism and After," The Herbert Spencer Lecture, 1908, *Herbert Spencer Lectures* (at Oxford), *Decennial Issue, 1905-1914* (Oxford, 1916), p. 27.

29. Bateson, *Biological Fact and the Structure of Society,* pp. 31-32.

30. Wallas, *The Great Society,* pp. 42-43 n. 1.

31. Ibid., p. 74.

32. Ibid., p. 133.

33. Wallas, *Human Nature in Politics,* pp. 200-202, 215.

34. Wallas, *The Great Society,* p. 45.

35. Wallas, "Darwinism and Social Motive" (1906), *Men and Ideas,* p. 93.

36. Wallas also recognized the importance of aggression, suspicion, curiosity, and a desire to excel; but he wanted their effects studied more carefully and completely before any conclusions were drawn. *Human Nature in Society,* chap. 1; *The Great Society,* chap. 3.

37. "Review of *Human Nature in Politics,*" *Manchester Guardian* , December 14, 1908. This judgment occurs in nearly every review.

38. Wallas joined the Fabian Society in 1886 and became a member of the executive in 1888 and a contributor to *Fabian Essays* (1889). Even after his resignation, he continued to work with the group on special and educational issues. From 1890 to 1903, Wallas sat on the London School Board; he chaired the important School Management Committee from 1890 to 1904; he served on the

Technical Education Board; and in 1907, he was appointed, for a three-year term, to the London County Council's Education Committee.

39. Wallas lectured at L.S.E. from 1895-1914 when he was appointed to the new Chair of Political Science at the University of London, which incorporated L.S.E. From 1908 to 1928 Wallas was a senator at the university.

40. Wallas, "An Historical Note," in *The Handbook of the Students' Union* (L.S.E.) October 1925, p. 21.

41. Wallas's first book, *The Life of Francis Place* (London, 1898), examined the actual life and style of a political organizer; but it was not until *Human Nature in Politics* that he reached a wide audience. In 1914 *The Great Society* appeared as a response to charges of anti-intellectualism; *Our Social Heritage* (London, 1921) examined the effect of education and learning upon personality; and, *The Art of Thought* (1926) continued this theme by analyzing the less conscious factors in thought. In May 1940 May Wallas published a collection of her father's essays as *Men and Ideas*. Besides his books, Wallas published over 100 essays, reviews, and papers.

42. Wallas's lecture on education, part of his extension series The English Towns, reveals the Oxford influence, especially in the questions he set for papers such as: (1) "Explain and comment on the following passage from Aristotle's 'Politics': 'Men come together in cities in order to live and remain together in order to live well.'" "Lecture VI: Education," *Syllabus (15)*, The American Society for the Extension of University Teaching (Philadelphia, 1897), pp. 32-33. A typical Literae Humaniores question in contemporary Oxford under the category of Ancient History and Political Philosophy was: "'All institutions ought to have for their aim the physical, intellectual and moral amelioration of the poorest and most numerous class.' What criticisms of this doctrine are suggested by the political principles laid down by Plato and Aristotle?" *Oxford University Examination Papers* (1889), p. 24.

43. *University Extension Guild. First Annual Report* (London, 1904), p. 19. The Guild was established under the auspices of the University of London's Extension Board. Lord Reay, first President of the British Academy (1902-1907) was the Guild's first president, too.

44. Wallas, *Life of Francis Place,* p. 162.

45. John Stuart Mill, *Autobiography* (1873) (New York, 1964), p. 89.

46. Aristotle, *Ethics*, I, v-viii. Wallas, Lecture Notes, 1927, *W.P.,* Box 17. Martin J. Weiner's fine biography *Between Two Worlds: The Political Thought of Graham Wallas* (Oxford, 1971), pp. 11, 103, shows the influence of the Greek classics upon Wallas.

47. Wallas, "Holiday Thoughts on the Ability to Pay," *Clare Market Review* (October 1909), p. 6. Wallas was thinking particularly of the extensive press coverage given to the Poor Law Commissioner's Report and to Lloyd George's budget.

48. The Cambridge University Extension program held 2,358 lectures be-

tween 1873-1898, attended by 221,190. Regular classes served an additional 105,369 and of these 30,000 earned certificates. R. D. Roberts, *Statement of the Needs of the University*. Part III. *Administration and External Work of the University*, vol. III. Roberts was Secretary for Lectures to the Local Exams and Lectures Syndicate.

49. Roberts, "Introduction," *University Extension Congress London, 1894. Report of the Proceedings including the Reports of the Expert Committees. Submitted to, and Adopted by the Congress* (London, 1894), pp. 7-9. Wallas sat on three of the Expert Committees as Lecturer for the Oxford Delegacy and the London Society.

50. *Report on the Peripatetic Teaching in Scientific and Technical Subjects carried on in Various Country Districts under the Supervision of the Oxford Delegates for University Extension Acting in Concert with the Technical Instruction Committee of County Councils during the Winter of 1891-1892* (Oxford, 1892), pp. 5-6. The University itself was accepting only about 800 freshmen in an average Michaelmas term. Reginald Lennard, "Oxford Through Half a Century," *Quarterly Review* 292 (January 1954), 77.

51. Ruskin College was governed by a Council representing the Trades Union Congress, the London Trades Council, the Amalgamated Society of Engineers, the Co-operative Union, and eleven public men and women "who had the confidence of the working classes." *The Story of Ruskin College* (Oxford, 1949), p. 12.

52. Italics are in the original. *The Worker's Educational Association. Ninth Annual Report* (July 1, 1912). See H. G. Crudge, *1911-1961: Fifty Years in the Life of a Voluntary Movement* (Western District, 1961), p. 4.

53. *Working Men's College Journal* VI, 83 (March 1899), 33; *Appendix to the Sixteenth Annual Report of the Working Men's College* (November 1891-31 December 1892), p. 14; *Appendix to the Thirty-fifth Annual Report of the Working Men's College, 1911-1912*. Still another working-class group, the Working Men's Club and Institution Union, although not concerned primarily with higher education, did provide their 410 affiliated clubs with a large and successful circulating library by 1892. B. T. Hall, *Our Fifty Years: The Story of the Working Men's Club and Institute Union* (London, 1912), p. 105.

54. Wallas, "Kelmscott House Lecture," Spring, 1886, *W.P.*, Box 15.

55. "Education Act," *Public General Acts of 1944*, chap. 41, p. 227. See Wallas, "Let Youth but Know," *Speaker* (January 20, 1906); "Oxford and the Nation," *Westminster Gazette* (April 28, 1908); "The Future of English Education in Light of the Past," appendix to H. B. Binn's *A Century of Education* (London, 1908); and *Reports of the Royal Commission on the Civil Service, 1912-1914*.

56. Wallas, *The Great Society*, p. 146.

57. Wallas believed that sensitiveness or love toward others, imagination, knowledge, curiosity, craftsmanship, and aesthetics were satisfied only through altruistic activity. Ibid., pp. 148-155.

58. Wallas, *Human Nature in Politics,* pp. 280-281. As a young man, Wallas saw the parish as a participatory civil institution for checking political manipulation. Lecture at Union Hall, Gordon Square, December 28, 1892, *W.P.*

59. Wallas, *Human Nature in Politics,* p. 191.

60. Hobhouse, *Democracy and Reaction,* pp. 230-231.

61. In the spring of 1907, for example, Sidney Webb proposed to Asquith that the powers and duties of Poor Law Guardians be transferred to County and County Borough Councils where an expert stipendiary officer would judge cases. Webb, "Notes on the Proposed Transfer of the Poor Law to the County and County Borough Councils," *W.P.,* Box 76.

62. Wallas, "Speech at Shoreditch" (January 27, 1904), *W.P.*

63. Wallas, "The Economics of Human Welfare," p. 495.

64. Hobhouse, *Mind in Evolution* (London, 1901), pp. 387-388; Wallas, *Human Nature in Politics,* p. 304.

65. Norway was Wallas's modern model, *The Great Society,* p. 368. Hobson, who had visited Denmark and Switzerland in 1906, also saw the advantages "a small nation, living upon an equalitarian level in its business and social relations, enjoyed in the working of democracy." *Confessions of an Economic Heretic* (London, 1938), p. 70.

66. Wallas, "Remember 1880," *Speaker* (January 20, 1906), p. 409.

67. In 1881, the census of England and Wales showed a total population of 25,974,439. There were 25,568 officers and clerks in the national and local civil service, the national government employed an additional 25, 182, and local government, 53,493 more. By 1891 the population had increased 11.65% to 29,002,525; the national and local civil service to 40,106, the additional central government employees to 31,560, and the local to 59,686. In 1901 there was a further population growth of 12.17% to 32,527,843; civil service figures jumped to 198,187, national employees to 57,864, and local to 83,536. *Accounts and Papers. Population. Census of England and Wales. Summary Tables. Occupation of Males Ten Years and Upwards and Females Ten Years and Upwards. Table 6.* Population figures, p. 1; Civil service analyses by year 1881, pp. xviii, x; 1891, pp. xxvi, x; 1901, pp. 186-187.

68. Baron Macdonnell, *Appendix to the First Report of the Royal Commission on the Civil Service* (April 1912).

69. The Playfair Commission of 1874-1875 had divided the Civil Service into a higher grade (1) with policy and administrative functions and a lower (11) with clerical, routine duties. Oxford Literae Humaniores graduates consistently scored the highest points in I. For the contents of the Civil Service exams see the testimony of Professor C. F. Vaughan, Representative of the University of Leeds, an examiner for the Service. *Appendix to the First Report.*

70. Ibid., *Fourth Report of the Royal Commission* (1914), pp. 109-111, 113-115; *Fifth Report* (1914), p. 45.

71. Wallas, "The Universities and the Nation in America and England," *Contemporary Review* CV (June 1914), in *Men and Ideas,* p. 175.

72. Weiner, *Between Two Worlds,* pp. 203-216.

73. H. G. Wells, *Experiment in Autobiography* (New York, 1934), p. 511. Cf. M. Cole, *The Story of Fabian Socialism* (New York, 1964), p. 55.

74. Alfred Zimmern, G. Salwyn Shapiro, and Walter Lippmann, at Harvard, were among Wallas's most dedicated students.

75. Joseph King, "Democracy and our Old Universities," *Contemporary Review* 62 (November 1892) 707-708. From the early 1890s the *Oxford Magazine* was filled with pleas for practical curriculum reform that would include the new disciplines. The Literae Humaniores school was the principal target: at the Shaftesbury Club meeting on June 5, 1904, G. M. Young expressed a strong feeling among younger men at Oxford when he moved: "That the School of Literae Humaniores is useless, antiquated and ineffectual." *Shaftesbury Club Papers,* the Bodleian Library. Founded in November 1892, the club's members included H. B. Butter, G. K. Chesterton, H. Belloc, A. Zimmern, C. S. Buxton, and W. G. C. Gladstone.

76. Wallas, *Physical and Social Science,* Huxley Memorial Lecture, 1930, at the Imperial College of Science and Technology (London, 1930).

77. *Human Nature in Politics* had been accepted as a sign of the transformation of political science from dogmatic metaphysics to the correlation of facts. It was that. But it was definitely not part of an effort no longer "so prone as heretofore to provide us with ideals of life." W. H. Winch, "Review of Human Nature in Politics," *Mind* (January 1909). J. A. Hobson was more accurate in indicating that what really concerned Wallas was "a standard of the humanly desirable." Hobson, "The Great Society." *Manchester Guardian,* July 10, 1914.

78. Wallas, "The Money-Power at War" (December 11, 1909), *W.P.*

10. *Fear of the New Democracy: The Setting for Social Psychology*

1. In 1913 Beatrice Webb observed astutely: "The whole of the thinking British public, is today the arena of a battle of words, of thought and of temperaments. The issue is two-fold: are men to be governed by emotion or by reason? ...in harmony with the desires of the bulk of the citizens or according to the fervent aspirations of a militant minority in defiance of the will of the majority? Two quite separate questions but each of them raising the same issue: the validity of democratic government." Margaret I. Cole, ed., *Beatrice Webb's Diaries, 1912-1924* (London, 1952), p. 15, December 8, 1913.

2. See John Alfred Spender, "Past and Future of the Liberal party," *Contemporary Review* LXXXII (August 1902), 157; T. R. Tholfsen, "The Transition to Democracy in Victorian England," *International Review of Social History* VI (1961), 246; J. Roach, "Liberalism and the Victorian Intelligentsia," *Cambridge Historical Journal* XIII (1957), 80. This "new liberal" philosophy was embodied in the legislative program enacted by the Liberal government in

office in 1906. See Winston Churchill's speeches to 1909, collected as *Liberalism and the Social Problem* (London, 1909); and the official Liberal Party white paper, *The Government's Record, 1906-1913: Seven Years of Liberal Legislation* (London, 1913).

3. Rivers came to Cambridge in 1893 from University College, London, as a lecturer in the physiology of the special senses. McDougall worked in Sherrington's laboratories in 1894.

4. *Reports of the Cambridge Anthropological Expedition to the Torres Straits* (Cambridge, 1903), pp. 192, 200, 201. From January to April 1899, McDougall, Myers, and several other members of the expedition accepted Charles Hose's invitation to make a supplementary expedition to Sarawak. Hose was an ethnologist and naturalist who made a prominent career in the Sarawak civil service from 1884 until his death in 1929. As a result of this second expedition, Hose asked McDougall to join him in writing *The Pagan Tribes of Borneo* (London, 1912).

5. A laboratory had begun at University College in October 1897, under Sully's initiative, with part of the apparatus Hugo Münsterberg collected before he accepted James's invitation to take over his psychological laboratory at Harvard. For prewar psychologists, the world was very small. Rivers began the actual work of the University College lab before accepting charge of the Cambridge University laboratory founded in the same year.

6. Robert Thompson, *Pelican History of Psychology* (London, 1968), p. 114.

7. F. C. S. Schiller to William James, November 25, 1903, *J.P.*

8. See *Journal of Anatomy and Physiology* XXXII (1848), 187-210. McDougall had published a *Physiological Psychology* (London, 1905) to supplement James's *Principles* by explaining the "structure and function of the nervous system." Preface.

9. For McDougall's other work see A. L. Robinson, *Introduction to William McDougall: A Bibliography* (Durham, N.C., 1943).

10. Ernest Jones, *Free Associations* (London, 1958), pp. 100-129. Trotter's papers were in *Lancet, Clinical Journal, Review of Neurological Psychiatry*, and *The British Medical Journal*, and his research on the sensory nerves was in Wilfred Trotter and H. M. Davies, "Experimental Studies in the Innervation of the Skin," *Journal of Physiology* XXXVIII (1909), 134-246. His first two essays were: "Herd Instinct and Its Bearing on the Psychology of Civilised Man," *Sociological Review* I (1908), 227-248; "Sociological Application of the Psychology of Herd Instinct," ibid., II (1909), 36-57.

11. Ernest Jones, *Life and Work of Sigmund Freud* (New York, 1955), II, 28.

12. See chap. 6.

13. Quoted in L. S. Hearnshaw, *A Short History of British Psychology, 1840-1940* (New York, 1964), p. 187.

14. Ibid., pp. 191-192, 195.

15. Trotter, "Herd Instinct," *Sociological Review*, I, 229.

16. Trotter, "Sociological Application," ibid., II, 36.

17. Arnold White, *The English Democracy. Its Promises and Perils* (London, 1895), pp. 123-124, 127, 251.

18. Marcus R. P. Dorman, *Ignorance. A study of the Causes and Effects of Popular thought with some Educational Suggestions* (London, 1898), pp. 85, 166, 271.

19. Dorman, *The Mind of the Nation. A Study of Political thought in the Nineteenth Century* (London, 1900), p. 451.

20. According to Joan Evans, Conway asked the Liberal Whip for a nomination in 1919 even though he had resigned from the Eighty Club and stopped his subscription to the Liberal Central Association by 1904. Instead, he was invited by the Conservatives to run for the University seat together with H. A. L. Fisher. Joan Evans, *The Conways. A History of Three Generations* (London, 1966), pp. 234-235, 238. Evans treats Conway as an unprincipled and irresponsible adventurer, but she does not provide convincing evidence in support of her judgment.

21. Martin Conway, "Is Parliament a Mere Crowd?" *Nineteenth Century* LVII (1905), 898. Cf. Conway, *The Crowd in Peace and War* (London, 1915), p. 26.

22. Conway, *The Crowd in Peace and War,* pp. 16, 19.

23. Conway, "The Individual vs. the Crowd," *Nineteenth Century* LIX (1906), 864.

24. Conway, *The Crowd in Peace and War,* p. 54.

25. Ibid., p. 134.

26. Ibid., pp. 97, 101, 103, 107, 113.

27. Ibid., pp. 63, 313, 316.

28. Ibid., p. 45.

29. Conway, "Is Parliament a Mere Crowd?" p. 911.

30. Conway, *The Crowd in Peace and War,* p. 163.

31. T. H. Huxley, *Evolution and Ethics,* Romanes Lectures, 1893 (New York, 1899).

32. By 1914 eight editions of McDougall's *Social Psychology* had appeared and the title had changed to *An Introduction to Social Psychology.* His reputation was so well established within a few years after the initial publication of *Social Psychology* that the new Home University Library of Modern Knowledge asked him to write the volume on psychology, which contained a chapter on social psychology: *Psychology: The Study of Behavior* (London, 1912). In recognition of his work McDougall was made a Fellow of the Royal Society and Fellow of Corpus Christi College, Oxford in 1912. At Oxford, McDougall's psychology became an elective subject in the Final Honours School of Litterae Humaniores. Hearnshaw, *A Short History of British Psychology,* p. 181. Wilfred Trotter's influence, while less conspicuous, was equally important. His essays were read before the Sociological Society, a diverse group drawn from every prominent area in contemporary British life. The members were either of great influence

or on their way to influential roles. Founded by Victor Branford and Patrick Geddes in 1904, with financial support from Martin White, a wealthy Scotsman who endowed sociology at the University of London, the council members before 1914 included Graham Wallas, Ramsay MacDonald, G. P. Gooch, E. Westermarck, H. A. L. Fisher, S. K. Ratcliffe, W. H. Beveridge, G. L. Dickinson, R. H. Tawney, L. S. Stebling, B. Bosanquet, J. Gorst, Gilbert Murray, Sidney Webb, Havelock Ellis, R. C. K. Ensor, Morris Ginsberg, V. Branford, and R. M. MacIver.

33. Brian Gardner, *Mafeking* (London, 1966), p. 10.

34. C. F. G. Masterman, *The Condition of England* (London, 1909), p. 125; and *From the Abyss* (London, 1911), p. 4.

35. William McDougall, *Introduction to Social Psychology*, 23d ed. (London, 1960), pp. 8-9 (all future references are to this edition).

36. Ibid., pp. 146-172.

37. Trotter, "Herd Instinct," *Sociological Review*, I, 233.

38. Trotter, "Sociological Application," ibid., II, 40.

39. Karl Pearson, *National Life from the Standpoint of Science* (London, 1900); E. A. Westermarck, *The Origin and Development of the Moral Ideas* (London, 1906), II, 197; J. A. Hobson, *The Crisis of Liberalism: New Issues of Democracy* (London, 1909), pp. 173-174.

40. McDougall, *Introduction to Social Psychology*, pp. 255-259; McDougall, *Psychology*, pp. 229, 238-241; McDougall, "Will of the People," *Sociological Review*, V, 99; Trotter, "Herd Instinct," ibid., I, 240-248.

41. Herbert Spencer, *Principles of Sociology* (London, 1876), I, 15-16.

42. McDougall, "Cutaneous Sensations," *Reports of the Cambridge Anthropological Expedition to the Torres Straits* (Cambridge, 1903), II, 2, 192.

43. McDougall, *Introduction to Social Psychology*, pp. 82-87; Trotter, "Herd Instinct," pp. 238-239, 242-248; Trotter, "Sociological Application."

44. McDougall, *Psychology*, pp. 242-245; Trotter, "Sociological Application," pp. 53-54.

45. McDougall, *Introduction to Social Psychology*, p. 25; Trotter, "Herd Instinct," p. 232.

11. *Social Psychology as a Solution: McDougall, Trotter, and the Elitist Refuge*

1. William McDougall, *Introduction to Social Psychology* (London, 1960), p. 13; Wilfred Trotter, "Herd Instinct and its Bearing on the Psychology of Civilised Man," *Sociological Review*, I, 227.

2. In his attempt to prove the practical value of sociology, or social science, Spencer had written in 1873 that "there can be prevision of social phenomena, and, therefore, Social Science." Herbert Spencer, *Study of Sociology* (Ann Arbor, 1961), p. 41. Both Trotter and McDougall accepted this.

3. By the 1920s the social sciences, based upon statistical research and comparative case studies, were directed toward the clarification and control of social and political institutions. For an Australian economist's summary of the comparative state of the social sciences in universities in Britain, the United States, and the Continent, see D. B. Copland, *Studies in Economics and Social Science* (Melbourne, 1927).

4. See John A. Hobson, "The Qualitative Method," *Sociological Review* II (1909), 293-294; review of Wallas, *Human Nature in Politics*, in *T. L. S.,* December 10, 1908. From the periphery of romantic anarchism, Stephen Reynolds, hardly in the mainstream of Edwardian thought, protested against the "psychological superficiality of the deductive method." Stephen Reynolds, *A Poor Man's House* (London, 1909), p. ix.

5. Spencer's synthetic philosophy was based upon this concept, developed from Karl Ernst von Baer's studies of embryonic development. For Spencer's equation of more evolved and "better," see especially Herbert Spencer, *Data of Ethics* (New York, 1879), p. 27. Biologists qua social theorists continued to use this equation after the war. See Joseph Needham, *Integrative Levels: A Revaluation of the Idea of Progress*, Herbert Spencer Lecture of 1937 (London, 1937), p. 27. Needham finds that the society most in accord with the biological basis of life is "a democracy that produces experts."

6. See the view of history as emancipation from irrational and primitive "survivals" from the past, in E. B. Tylor, *Primitive Culture*, 3d ed. (London, 1891), Vol. I, especially chap. 3.

7. When individualistic psychoanalysis came to London from Vienna on October 30, 1913, with Ernest Jones's founding of the first British branch of the International Association of Psychoanalysts, McDougall was invited to join. It is not surprising that he declined. Jones, *Freud*, II, 102.

8. L. T. Hobhouse, *Morals in Evolution* (New York, 1906), I, 365, 391.

9. The tradition of sociological individualism (see especially "Growth of Social Responsibility") is continued in Morris Ginsberg, ed., *Law and Opinion in England in the Twentieth Century* (Berkeley, 1959), p. 4. Talcott Parsons had continued the collectivist tradition, attempting to give it new standing by identifying it with a "theory of action." See introduction by Talcott Parsons and E. A. Shils, eds., *Toward a General Theory of Action: Theoretical Foundations for the Social Sciences* (New York, 1962), p. 7.

10. McDougall, *Psychology: The Study of Behavior* (London, 1912), p. 243.

11. McDougall, *Introduction to Social Psychology*, p. 179.

12. Ibid.; McDougall, *Psychology*, pp. 229, 242-243, 245, 248; McDougall, "Will of the People," *Sociological Review*, V (1912), 104.

13. McDougall, *Psychology*, p. 248.

14. Ibid., p. 19.

15. See Charles A. Beard's optimistic conclusion to his introduction of John B. Bury, *The Idea of Progress* (New York, 1955), p. xi.

16. Trotter, "Sociological Application," *Sociological Review* II (1909), 42.

17. Ibid., II, 54.

18. Ibid., II, 53.

19. Ibid., II, 43-44. At the first international meeting of psychoanalysts in Salzburg, April 26, 1908, Jones gave a paper on "Rationalisation in Everyday Life." See Jones, *Freud,* II, 41. This was published in the *Journal of Abnormal Psychology* III (1908), and reprinted in Ernest Jones, *Papers on Psycho-Analysis* (London, 1912), pp. 1-9. Trotter was the only other Englishman to attend that historic convention.

20. Trotter, "Sociological Application," p. 52.

21. This was true of J. S. Mill, Matthew Arnold, T. H. Green, and H. Sidgwick. See Melvin Richter, *The Politics of Conscience: T. H. Green and His Age* (London, 1964), p. 168.

22. A. J. Ayer, "Science and Philosophy," *Ideas and Beliefs of the Victorians* (London, 1949), p. 213.

23. A. J. Balfour, *Theism and Humanism,* Gifford Lectures of 1914 (London, 1915), p. 94.

24. Huxley separated the "cosmic" from the "ethical process" in "Evolution and Ethics" (1893) in *Evolution and Ethics and Other Essays* (New York, 1899), p. 81.

25. For a discussion of nineteenth-century paternal elitism, see R. N. Soffer, "Attitudes and Allegiances in the Unskilled North, 1830-1850," *International Review of Social History* X (1965), 429-454.

26. See Hobhouse, *Morals in Evolution,* II, 280, for a similar, although liberal-democratic, statement of the role of social science.

27. McDougall, *Introduction to Social Psychology,* pp. 9, 16; McDougall, *Psychology,* p. 145; Trotter, "Sociological Application," p. 51.

28. McDougall, *Introduction to Social Psychology,* pp. 38, 194-195, 226. See the similar, but entirely rationalist, explanation of moral consciousness from the "unreflecting" to the "reflecting" in Westermarck, *Origin and Development of the Moral Ideas,* II, 739-745.

29. McDougall, *Psychology,* p. 105.

30. McDougall, "Will of the People," pp. 99, 101; McDougall, *Psychology,* pp. 242-243.

31. McDougall, "Will of the People," p. 103.

32. Jones recalled in his memoirs that he and Trotter started from the same sociological motives and "cherished the same biological goal . . . of comprehending psychology in terms of biology." Jones, *Free Associations,* p. 157. Trotter's son, W. R. Trotter, believed that the problem occupying Trotter's mind in his last years was how to make the individual's mind into an instrument of greater practical use. *The Collected Papers of Wilfred Trotter* (London, 1941), Vol. V.

33. Trotter, "Sociological Application," p. 52 f.

34. Trotter's widow told this writer in 1960 that her husband wrote his essays on the herd late at night after exhausting days in surgery, as a social responsibility. Jones recalled that Trotter was "endowed with . . . a strong Savior com-

plex. . . . He yearned to do great things, and felt he was destined to redeem mankind from at least some of its follies and stupidities. . . . In later years this love for mankind changed to a considerable scepticism." Jones, *Free Associations*, p. 127. Jones and Trotter planned a book analyzing and denouncing contemporary problems, and Trotter wrote the final sentence first: "False hopes may be cheating us; the courage that used to resist illusion may be breaking; but surely in the long-watched east the darkness is no longer impenetrably black." Ten years later, when Trotter was a famous surgeon and teacher, he denied any memory of such a book. Ibid., pp. 128-129.

35. Trotter, "Sociological Application," pp. 42-49.

36. Trotter, "Herd Instinct," ibid., I, 228. See McDougall, *Introduction to Social Psychology*, p. 15.

37. See Carl Becker, *Progress and Power* (New York, 1936), p. 105.

38. Wallas, *Human Nature in Politics*, pp. 187, 191; Wallas, *The Great Society*, p. 302.

39. McDougall, *Introduction to Social Psychology*, p. 283. Trotter characterized imitation by pointing out that when people said, "be reasonable," they meant, "be like me." Quoted in Jones, *Free Association*, p. 103.

Postscript. *How Successful Was the Revolution?*

1. Paul Vinogradoff, *The Teaching of Sir Henry Maine* (London, 1904), pp. 10-11.

2. Charles Kingsley, "Science," in *Scientific Lectures and Essays* (London, 1885), p. 257.

3. John A. Hobson, *Free-Thought in the Social Sciences* (New York, 1926), p. 265. This book consists essentially of lectures delivered at one of the most influential voluntary organizations, the Brookings Institution, Washington.

4. Hobson, "Economics and Ethics," in William Ogburn and Alexander Goldenweisser, eds., *The Social Sciences and Their Interrelations* (Boston, c. 1927), p. 128. See Hobson, "Sociology Today," *The Social Sciences: Their Relations in Theory and in Teaching*. Being the Report of a Conference held under the joint auspices of the Institute of Sociology and the International Student Service (British Committee) at King's College of Household and Social Science, London, from the 27th to the 29th of September, 1935 (London, 1936).

5. Charles A. Ellwood, "Recent Developments in Sociology," in Edward Cary Hayes, ed., *Recent Developments in the Social Sciences* (Philadelphia, 1927), pp. 1, 47. Edward Cary Hayes, *Introduction to the Study of Society* (New York, 1916), p. 4; *Sociology and Ethics* (New York, 1921), and, *Recent Developments in the Social Sciences*, p. vii. See Robert Ezra Park, "Sociology," in William Gee, ed., *Research in the Social Sciences: Its Fundamental Methods and Objectives* (New York, 1929), p. 36.

6. Carl Murchison, ed., *Psychologies of 1925* (London, 1926) and *Psychologies of 1930* (Worcester, 1930).

7. See Kimball Young, "Social Psychology," in Harry Elmer Barnes, ed., *History and Prospects of the Social Sciences* (New York, 1925), p. 166.

8. McDougall abandoned his instinctualism and his general will theories first in "Mechanical or Purposive Striving," *The Psychological Review* (1922). His new position was developed in a Presidential Address to the Psychology Section of the British Association in 1924, "Purposive Striving as the Fundamental Category in Psychology," *Scientific Monthly* XIX (1924), 304-312; and in "Men or Robots?" I and IV, in *Psychologies of 1925;* and, in *Outline of Abnormal Psychology* (New York, 1923). The McDougall-Watson debates before the Washington Psychology Club in 1924 were published, together with McDougall's postscript in 1927, as *The Battle of Behaviorism* (London, 1928).

9. Young, "Social Psychology," pp. 165-166; Harry Elmer Barnes, "Some Contributions of American Psychology to Modern Social and Political Theory," *Sociological Review* (1921), XII, 160.

10. See *The Social Sciences: Their Relation in Theory and Teaching.* At this conference, papers were given by a galaxy of British and foreign academics: Ernest Barker, Hobson, M. M. Postan, Michael Oakeshott, G. N. Clark, D. W. Brogan, Harold Laski, J. R. Hicks, P. Sargent Florence, G. F. Shove, Karl Mannheim, Morris Ginsberg, and A. M. Carr-Saunders. R. H. Tawney and Lionel Robbins were among the chairmen and Hugh Gaitskell was one of the discussants. T. H. Marshall presented a report on "The Teaching of the Social Sciences in British Universities," endorsing the separate training of higher theory and lower practice, p. 40. So did Brogan's talk on political theory and social science, pp. 106-114. There were dissenters like Lancelot Hogben who warned, in the *Retreat from Reason* (London, 1936) that the "pitiable predilection" of the young "for action without thought is the legitimate offspring of thought divorced from action," p. 9.

11. As late as 1971, English political scientists were still complaining about the reluctance of their colleagues to take advantage of the pioneering work done in America. See Morton R. Davies and Vaughan Lewis, *Models of Political Systems* (London, 1971). Two of the most important leaders of the resistance were Michael Oakeshott, sitting in Wallas's chair at L.S.E., and Maurice Cowling at Cambridge. See esp. Oakeshott, *Political Education.* Inaugural Lecture at L.S.E. (Cambridge, 1951) and Cowling, *The Nature and Limits of Political Science* (Cambridge, 1963).

12. A generation passed before the social sciences began to develop again in England. See esp. [Privy Council Office of the Treasury] *Report of the Committee on the Provision for Social and Economic Research* (London, 1946). The chairman of this committee was Sir John Clapham (who died before the *Report* was issued), and the members included the sociologists Alexander Carr-Saunders, T. S. Simey and T. H. Marshall; the economists, Lionel Robbins, and Sar-

gent Florence, and J. R. N. Stone; the political scientist, D. W. Brogan; the historians R. H. Tawney and W. K. Hancock; the anthropologist Raymond Firth; and, the zoologist and social critic Lancelot Hogben. The Representatives from the various professional and voluntary societies testified, as did John Maynard Keynes. The *Report* concluded that in social and economic research, the universities were understaffed and underendowed, p. 3. They recommended the formation of a Social Science Research Council in the distant future when there would be a sufficient number of collaborators for systematic collaboration, p. 12. Financial support of the S.S.R.C. administration, its seventeen fellows, and its programs in 1926-1927, required a budget of $532,000. Charles Merriam, *Second Annual Report of the Chairman* (New York, 1926), pp. 9-11.

13. This is how Wesley Mitchell described the S.S.R.C. in 1927 in the *Third Annual Report of the Chairman*, p. 16.

14. See William F. Ogburn and Alexander Goldenweisser, "The Field of the Social Sciences," *The Social Sciences and their Interrelations*, pp. 5, 9. Goldenweisser was a cultural anthropologist at the New School for Social Research, and Ogburn, a sociologist at the University of Chicago.

15. Charles Merriam, "Recent Developments in Political Science," in *Recent Developments in the Social Sciences*, p. 320.

16. George R. Sabine, "Political Science and Philosophy," *The Social Sciences and their Interrelations*, p. 250; Z. Clark Dickinson, "Economics and Psychology," ibid., pp. 152-158; Charles A. Ellwood, "Recent Developments in Sociology," *Recent Developments in the Social Sciences*, pp. 19-24; Charles A. Beard, "Political Science," *Research in the Social Sciences*, p. 281. Further attempts at finding instinct and reason complementary but unequal appeared in R. H. Gault's *Social Psychology* (1923); and J. M. Williams's *Principles of Social Psychology* (1922).

17. The Social Science Research Council, Report of the Committee on Problems and Policy, in *Third Annual Report of the Chairman* (New York, 1927), p. 24. Charles Merriam was the committee's chairman and Wesley Mitchell its vice-chairman from 1923, the date of the founding of the SSRC, to 1927.

18. See *Essays on Research in the Social Sciences. Papers Presented in a General Seminar Conducted by the Committee on Training of the Brookings Institution, 1930-1931* (Washington, 1931). The participants were the once optimistic writers of the preceding decade: Charles Beard, J. M. Clark, William F. Ogburn, and Arthur M. Schlesinger. See Stuart A. Rice, ed., *Methods in Social Science: A Case Book* (Chicago, 1931). Compiled under the direction of the Committee on Scientific Method in the Social Sciences of the S.S.R.C. For more recent analyses of the state of the social sciences in the first quarter of the twentieth century see: Mary O. Furner, *Advocacy and Objectivity. A Crisis in the Professionalization of American Social Science, 1865-1905.* (Lexington, Ky., 1975), and Edward A. Purcell, *The Crisis of Democratic Theory. Scientific Naturalism and the problem of Value* (Lexington, Ky., 1973).

Index

315